THE PROBLEM OF TRUST

THE PROBLEM OF TRUST

Adam B. Seligman

PRINCETON UNIVERSITY PRESS   PRINCETON, NEW JERSEY

Second printing, and first paperback printing, 2000
Paperback ISBN 0-691-05020-1

The Library of Congress has cataloged the cloth edition of this book as follows

Seligman, A.
The problem of trust / Adam B. Seligman
p.   cm.
Includes bibliographical references and index.
ISBN 0-691-01242-3 (cl : alk. paper)
1. Social interaction.   2. Trust (Psychology)   3. Social role.   I. Title.
HM291.S3952   1997   96-51589
302'.17—dc21   CIP

This book has been composed in Times Roman

The paper used in this publication meets the minimum requirements of
ANSI/NISO Z39.48-1992 (R 1997) (*Permanence of Paper*)

http://pup.princeton.edu

Printed in the United States of America

10 9 8 7 6 5 4 3 2

Contents _____

Acknowledgments _____

I AM GRATEFUL to a number of people for their help in sorting out my ideas on trust and presenting them here in a coherent form. My greatest debt is perhaps to my students in the Sociology of Ideas seminar at the University of Colorado, Boulder, especially to Jay Watterworth, Taunya McGlochlin, and Carrie Foote-Ardah. All engaged me in a debate with these issues over a number of very fruitful years. In addition, John Holmwood read the entire manuscript (more than once) and provided extensive suggestions, comments, and encouragement. Robert Wuthnow and Dennis Wrong also provided helpful comments and saved me from making a number of embarrassing mistakes of fact and interpretation. A continuing, four-year debate with Mark Lichbach on the relative merits of rational choice theories as adequate explanations of social reality has provided a necessary background without which this book would probably not have been written.

The book draws on older discussions as well, and the analysis of otherhood and its transformation found in chapter two is drawn from material first prepared a decade ago in Jerusalem with Zali Gurevitz. Much of the argument presented in chapter four was first published as "Animadversions upon Civil Society and Civic Virtue in the last Decade of the Twentieth Century" in *Civic Society: Theory, History, Comparison* (Oxford: Polity Press, 1995), edited by John Hall, who pushed me, over the last few years, to think through these and other issues related to the problem of trust. More recent discussions and the opportunity to present some of the ideas developed here were offered by the Fundacion Manuel Garcia-Pelayo in Caracas and by the Institute for the Study of Economic Culture of Boston University and its "Working Group on Civil Society and Civic Virtue," all of whose participants offered helpful comments on work then in progress. I also owe a special debt of gratitude to the Institute for the Study of Economic Culture for a generous research grant which supported work on this book during the 1995–96 academic year. That the Institute has subsequently offered itself to me as an intellectual home is itself an instructive example of the interweaving of system confidence and individual trust in the modern world. Finally, very special thanks to Carrie Foote-Ardah must again be recorded for her selfless help in the preparation of this manuscript for publication. For all errors, I alone must assume responsibility.

THE PROBLEM OF TRUST

Introduction

SOME TIME ago Sir Ralf Dahrendorf published a trenchant and rather depressing essay on the growing uncoupling of economic well-being, social cohesion, and political freedom in Europe. It was a sobering study in the transformation of contemporary politics where in one form or another the interrelated nature of all three has been considered a Public Good of vital importance.[1] After all, the particular ideologies of political liberty characteristic of Western democracies—and however mediated in practice—have tended to encompass certain ideas of social cohesion and of economic well-being. So much is clear in T. H. Marshall's famous conception of citizenship where the parsing out of citizen rights into their civic, political, and social components well illustrates both this status (as Public Goods) and their inherently interrelated nature. It may be recalled that more than forty years ago, Marshall distinguished between the political, civil, and social aspects of citizenship which he defined as follows: "The civil element is composed of the rights necessary for individual freedom—liberty of person, freedom of speech, thought and faith, the right to own property and to conclude valid contracts, and the right to justice [that is] the right to defend and assert all one's rights on term of equality with others and by due process of law." The political element comprises "the right to participate in the exercise of political power as a member of the body invested with political authority or as an elector of the members of such body." And the social component includes "the right to a modicum of economic welfare and security [and the] right to share to the full in the social heritage, and to live the life of a civilized being according to the standards prevailing in society."[2] The very articulation of these goods as "rights," we might add, imbues them with the stature of Public Goods.

As Public Goods all are, moreover, derivative of a particular concept of the individual as standing at the core of the moral and political orders. This concept of the individual as, *pace* Emile Durkheim, something "sacred and inviolable to others" has served—within the modern West—as that principle of generalized exchange which structures the exchange of resources in society (mediating as it were the "free" flow of pure market exchange) in such ways as to create and provide for these very Public Goods.

The current crisis in which, as Dahrendorf suggests, more and more political actors are willing to sacrifice political freedom and/or social cohesion for the development of economic well-being is, essentially, a crisis in those principles of the Public Good which inform both the structuring of our economic life and the articulation of our politics, i.e., a crisis in the idea of the individual. Indeed, we need only to refer to the continuing debates between liberals and communitarians, between advocates of rights versus responsibilities, proponents of the radically situated as against the socially encumbered self to see how contested this idea of the individual is in our contemporary world. What we learn from Dahrendorf's essay as well as from all structurally orientated sociological inquiry is that these debates are, to great extent, misplaced. For the issue is not ideological in nature, not tied to a principled advocacy of this or that idea of the individual however rooted in one's moral epistemology. Rather, the issue is structural, that is to say, sociological in nature.

For the idea of the individual, if it is to serve as a principle of Public Good must, as Emile Durkheim noted long ago, structure our shared orientations to the phenomena of social life. Establishment of such a principle rests on the ability of social actors to impute, in Charles Taylor's term, "strong evaluations" to one another (that is evaluations predicated on shared moral ideas). It is this mutual "imputation" that forms of the conscience collective of any society, thus permitting the establishment of that confidence among social actors which is necessary for the orderly progress of social, political, and even economic life. This ability to assume a shared set of moral evaluations, a familiarity not based on kinship, territorial proximity, or dense social networks, but rather a familiarity of strong evaluations was, for Durkheim, Marx, and other thinkers of the nineteenth century, predicated on the shared conditions of the division of labor. Hence the formation of a class *für sich* in the Marxian reading or the unique nature of modern organic solidarity with its "sacred" reading of the individual in Durkheimian sociology.

What Ralf Dahrendorf and other scholars are increasingly pointing to is the perceived and growing difficulty in maintaining the very principle of Public Goods in contemporary politics and the sense of commitment and responsibility to the Public Good that must, of necessity, go with it. We are increasingly, in Dahrendorf's terminology, but shareholders rather than stakeholders in the myriad ventures of our life-world.[3] Our commitments and responsibilities are short-term, market orientated, and private rather then long-term, generalized, and public.

Under such conditions it is well to query if either political liberty or social cohesion can indeed be maintained. As Dahrendorf notes, freedom and confidence go well together. In fact, I would argue that the existence of the latter is an indispensable condition for the former. Without confidence all contracts, promises, and obligations—whether economic, social, or political, public or private—can only be maintained by third-party enforcers. Without confidence all human relations are reduced to Prisoner Dilemma games (and even that iteration upon which confidence in PD games rests, is lacking). Without confidence the ability to articulate and maintain the very idea of a Public Good (let alone one defined in terms of the intercon-nection of political liberty and social cohesion) becomes highly suspect.

It is in this context that we must understand the recent resurgence of such concepts as civil society, associational life, and, most especially, trust, in recent years. The rise of these concepts in both the scholarly and more partisan literature can be attributed to an awareness (if still somewhat unfo-cused and not fully articulated) of the above-noted shifts in our social and moral consciousness and of a search to find a new way of expressing the very idea of the Public Good. All three concepts have after all reappeared with a daunting saliency as presumed conceptual solutions to some of the most pressing of social ills. These terms, in their very indeterminacy, have moreover been adopted by different political groups and by individuals with strikingly different political agendas who make of them what they will. The resultant wear and tear on the concepts is now being felt, perhaps most clearly in the case of civil society where its value as analytic concept or political slogan has declined in the countries of East Central Europe only to be picked up in the West and used to legitimize very different social programs and agendas; and it has entered academic discourse with a vengeance.

Interestingly, the idea of civil society is used by political groups and thinkers on both the right and the left, and though in Europe in general it is most often the province of the left, in the United States it has been appropri-ated by both groups to advance their political agendas. Thus, for right of center thinkers as well as for libertarian followers of Friedrich Hayek, the quest for civil society is taken to mean a mandate to deconstruct many of the powers of the State and replace them with intermediary institutions based on social voluntarism. For many liberals, civil society is identified with social movements, also existing beyond the State. And while many of the former refuse to recognize that voluntary organizations can be of a particularly nasty nature and based on primordial or ascriptive principles of membership and participation that put to shame the very foundations of any idea of civil society; the latter are blind to the fact that the Achilles heel of any social movement is its institutionalization, which—one way or the other—must be through the State and its legal (and coercive) apparatus. In the meantime both communitarians and liberals continue to assimilate the idea of civil society to their own terms, invest it with their own meanings, and make of it what they will. Right, Left, and Center; North, South, East, and West; civil society is identified with everything from multiparty sys-tems and the rights of citizenship to individual voluntarism and the spirit of community.[4] Indeed, it may not be too far from the truth to see the ever so much more recent resurgence of interest in trust and associational life as coming in the wake of a disillusionment with the term civil society. As more and more people came to use the self-same term to mean very different things, the concept lost its integrity and ultimately its scholarly "use value," only to be replaced with a new set of terms whose fate may, ultimately, prove similar.

One possible way to avoid such confusion is to eschew all normative discussion of the above terms and approach them more analytically, to try then, in the case of civil society, to ascertain just what makes society civil, or even possible. And it is in this context that an understanding of the operation of trust in society is vital. For not only is trust necessary for the workings of society, but a specific form of generalized trust—rooted in modern individualist norms—is necessary for the workings of civil society. To call for the establishment of civil society without taking into consideration the fundamental terms of trust in society is but an empty exercise.

The very meaning of the term trust is itself problematic and often unscrutinzed. The "trust" existent between members of a relatively undifferentiated, tribal society would, one intuitively feels, be of a very different order than that bestowed (or withheld) among modern, contracting, market-oriented individuals, citizens of nation-states. Among these latter, the obligation to be trustworthy, and so to fulfill promises, arises from the moral agency and autonomy, from the freedom and responsibility, of the participants to the interaction. Moreover, without the prior existence of these conditions, rights really—to freedom, autonomy, and responsibility, the moral dimension of promise-keeping, and hence of trustworthiness—cannot be adequately explained. It is, in A. I. Meldon's terms, the conferring of these prior rights that "provides the warrant for the promise-keeping act."[5] Here then we may see how the moral obligation to maintain trustworthiness is predicated on those social conditions—or rights—that make such promise-keeping possible.

If this is indeed the case then "trust," at least as we know it, would in some sense be a modern phenomenon and not generalizable to all forms of social organization. Or perhaps it is only a particular form of trust that is modern. And if this is true, how are we to understand that "freedom of the will" and action which would seem both to necessitate some measure of trust in all social conditions and to define the "human condition" for time out of mind?

The seemingly (and I stress seemingly) philosophical nature of this problem should not be surprising since trust has traditionally been dealt with more by philosophers than social scientists. Among the latter, moreover, trust has tended to be explored mostly by social choice theorists (through the development of Prisoner Dilemma games) and large-scale survey literature (on "trust" in local and national governments, NATO, the UN, etc.) True, some earlier work by Niklas Luhmann and Diego Gambetta served to broaden our analytic understanding of the phenomenon (as did a host of anthropological literature on friendship).[6] Yet it is only most recently in the writings of such scholars as Francis Fukuyama and Robert Putnam (and in a somewhat different vein, Anthony Giddens) that trust and its corollary, associational life, have reentered the field of analytic inquiry.[7]

As noted above, the use of the term trust, like the idea of civil society, tends to be loose and imprecise as it ranges from micro to macro encounters and is used to express ideas akin to Durkheim's solidarity on the one hand and simple confidence in the iteration of interaction on the other. It is the combination of this imprecision in the scholarly use of the term together with an increased appreciation of just how central an understanding of trust must be to our analysis of different social formations and the changes they are undergoing at the close of the twentieth century (and as some would say the close of the modern era) that I have been led to the following inquiry. Thus, what this essay attempts is an understanding of trust as a discrete form of human interaction and an ideal model of communal life. In so doing it seeks to distinguish trust from such similar concepts as confidence, faith, and familiarity, and to attain some precision as to the social and historical conditions in which this form of interaction may emerge. Similarly, it explores the issues of public and private since it is within the perceived contradiction between them that the problem of trust is most often seen to reside.

In attempting to understand just what trust as a "social fact" may mean as well as its historical significance to modern forms of social life, especially in terms of its role in differentiating public from private spheres, I have had to return to the old and less than currently fashionable sociological concepts of role and role expectations. For those who view the structurally orientated nature of sociological analysis with a jaundiced, postmodern eye this mode of inquiry may well find little favor. Yet if we wish to avoid either the abstract moralizing of philosophy on the one hand or the rather simplistic psychological determinism of social choice theory on the other, we have little choice but to return to that structural view of society worked out in mid-century American sociology. The fundamental unit of that theoretical edifice was, as some of us may recall, the idea of social role as the position held by the social actor within the social division of labor. The nature of these roles, both analytically and empirically, have been debated and argued over by sociologists for decades. Indeed, as our own argument progresses, some of these different perceptions of role will play an important part in clarifying the social nature of trust. (An interested reader may already perceive that the concept of role gives us a terminology within which to discuss the fore-noted problem of the freedom of the will without recourse to either Augustinian theology or Kantian philosophy.)

In brief, the following argues that while some form of trust—or more properly confidence—among social actors is necessary for the continued operation of any social order (at any and all levels of differentiation), the issue of trust as a solution to a particular type of risk is a decidedly modern phenomenon, linked to the nature of the division of labor in modern, market economies. Thus, while the connection noted by Niklas Luhmann between trust and risk is accepted, I do not accept it as an ontological aspect of social existence.[8] Eschewing any "essentialist" argument about trust (which has indeed characterized much of the relevant literature), I maintain that trust, as both a solution to and an articulation of a specific interactional problem, is tied to a particular idea of the self that we identify, most broadly, with modern social formations. I further argue that any attempt to generalize the problem of trust to human history *tout court* looses that specificity that alone explains its centrality in the construction of modern forms of social life.

To grasp the structural nature of trust as a phenomenon tied to modern forms of the division of labor, much use is made, as noted above, of the sociological category of role. Roles here are used as a heuristic device, as a type of analytical shorthand the better to grasp the structurally conditioned nature of trust and remove it from all philosophical abstraction or theological justification. This is, admittedly, a dangerous enterprise as, within the sociological tradition, roles carry their own essentialist and very dour view of the human person (a point addressed, if perhaps not adequately, in the following). Throughout the following analysis the concept of role will be used as no more than a convenient manner of expressing the fundamental unit within the division of labor. This is a minimalist reading which, it is hoped, will avoid some of the more outrageous uses of the concept within sociology. The idea of social roles has, after all, become infamous for the ahistorical nature of its employment and the rather truncated vision of human agency that it contains. However, rather than discard the idea entirely, I have felt it useful to try and keep the concept but to make use of it in an historical and relational mode without dragging in the metatheoretical presuppositions that so often adhere to the social-scientific use of the term. The extent of my success in this is ultimately for the reader to judge.

As opposed to other attempts in political theory, philosophy, and sociology to deal with the phenomenon of trust, this study approaches the concept both relationally, by setting it in the context of other cognate categories (confidence, faith, familiarity), and historically, by viewing it as an emergent property of human interaction, tied to a very specific form of social organization. In this, the current analysis attempts to move the study of trust to a wholly new and sounder ground. Avoiding the Scylla of rational-choice perspectives on trust (which are often but extended studies on the conditions of confidence in any interaction) and the Charybdis of a normative perspective (which would apotheosize trust as the conscience collective of society, i.e., some aspect of a "collective mind"), it attempts a structurally informed understanding of the historical conditions that saw the emergence of trust as a type (and model) of personal and social relations. To do this, argument moves to and from different levels: from the definitional to what may be termed the phenomenological, from micro to macro, and from economic principles of exchange to philosophies of self and society. My hope, however, is that precisely this weaving of different perspectives will allow us to grasp what has proved a most elusive and hitherto poorly treated concept.

Perhaps if we could grasp that which continually seems to elude us in this concept we could buttress our current vocabulary of membership and participation in the social realm, a vocabulary that seems increasingly inadequate as the century draws to a close. If indeed, as Dahrendorf has warned, we are approaching a growing dissociation of our ideas of social citizenship, individual freedom, and economic well-being, then too those conditions for modern forms of trust (rooted as we have noted in the rights, obligations, and liberties of citizenship) are also changing. In slightly different terms, with these changes we also stand to lose those very strong evaluations, those shared orientations to the phenomena of collective life that make the mutual bestowal of trust possible in the modern world. Perhaps the framing of these issues in terms of trust and the conditions (or better, preconditions) of its existence, rather than in terms of the more accepted vocabulary of political economy or public policy analysis, will alert us to just how much we stand to lose when those shared, strong evaluations of society are disregarded or ignored. In such circumstances the problems of risk, for which trust is a solution, can ever so quickly be transformed into problems of danger—for which trust, alas, can provide little assuagement.

The following is offered as a preliminary reflection on these concerns.

Part One

THE PROBLEM OF TRUST

One

Trust, Role Segmentation, and Modernity

Introducing a Modern Problem

The existence of trust is an essential component of all enduring social relationships. As Talleyrand is reported to have said: "You can do anything with bayonets except sit on them."

Power, dominance, and coercion can, in this reading, be a temporary solution to the problem of social order and the organization of the division of labor therein, but they will not in themselves provide the basis for the maintenance of said order over time. Such aspects of social organization as the structuring of the major markets in society (of power, prestige, and wealth), the construction and definition of the Public Good (and the myriad public goods of which it is constructed), and the rules and regulations for the public distribution of private goods rest, in all societies—from the premodern to the most postmodern—on some interplay of coercion and consent, of market and community, of instrumental and affective commitments and so also of the reigning definitions, boundaries, and extent of trust in society.[1]

This insight has found its place as one of the fundamental concepts of sociology and sociological analysis. Indeed, from the nineteenth century and the theoretical insights of Emile Durkheim on the existence of a "pre-contractual" element in all social arrangements, the importance of trust to the existence of society has been recognized by many students of social life.

On the most general and abstract level it can be stated that the need for perduring, stable, and universally recognized structures of trust is rooted in the fundamental indeterminacy of social interaction. This indeterminacy, between social actors, between social actors and their goals, and between social actors and resources results in a basic unpredictability in social life notwithstanding the universality of human interdependence.[2] Consequently, any long-range attempt at constructing a social order and continuity of social frameworks of interaction must be predicated on the development of stable relations of mutual trust between social actors. Clearly, however, different forms of organizing society (on the macrosociological level) will bring in their wake different forms of establishing trust in society.

In this context one of the major arenas where the study of trust—on the interpersonal as well as the institutional level—has been central, has been in the study of modernization.[3] Here, studies in the 1950s and 1960s

concentrated on the establishment of new bases of trust in society cen-
tering on new terms of solidarity, of citizenship, and what were, in fact,
new parameters defining the boundaries of trust in modernizing social
structures.

This focus on the changing nature of trust in modernizing societies is
indeed not surprising given the extraordinary importance of a universal
basis of trust in modern, democratic societies. The emphasis in modern
societies on consensus, the ideology of pragmatism, problem-solving, and
technocratic expertise, as well as conflict management (as opposed to ideological fission), are all founded on an image of society based on intercon-
nected networks of trust—among citizens, families, voluntary organizations, religious denominations, civic associations, and the like.[4] Similarly
the very "legitimation" of modern societies is founded on the "trust" of
authority and of governments as generalizations of trust on the primary,
interpersonal level. In fact, the primary venues of socialization, whether
they be the educational system or the mass media, are oriented to the continuing inculcation of this value and what is in fact an "ideology" of trust
in society. Finally, and perhaps most importantly, the definitions of trust in
Western industrialized and "modern" societies are rooted in the idea of the
individual as final repository of rights and values. In these societies, it is the
individual social actor, the citizen of the nation-state and not any collec-
tively defined, primordial or corporate entity who is seen as at the foundation of the social order and around whom the terms of social trust are
oriented.

The current concern with and revival of the idea of civil society, as essentially a clarion call to defining new terms of generalized trust in modern
democratic societies, points to crises in those bases of trust that have
defined the modern nation-state for the past two hundred years.[5] Similarly,
the continuing debates between communitarians and liberals over the terms
of citizenship and the definition of the Public Good, as well as the seemingly irreparable chasm between normative and rational-choice theorists
over their respective visions of the social order, all point to what seem to be
fundamental problems (in theory as in practice) in the terms of generalized
trust and the modes of its operation. Any solution to these problems must
begin, however, with a clarification of terms, and the obvious place to begin is with an attempt to understand just what is meant by the term trust.
This chapter is dedicated to an explication of that problem.

While there will be occasion to return again and again to the problematic
connection between trust and modes of social organization, it may be wise,
here at the outset, to note that an awareness of the problems of establishing
generalized modes of social trust is as old as modernity itself. From the
writings of Puffendorf and Grotius to those of John Locke, David Hume,
and Immanuel Kant, the duty of "promise-keeping," of honoring one's declaration of will (*decleratio*, or *signum voluntatis*), becomes a central com-

ponent of political theory.[6] And, whereas for Grotius the obligation to fulfill promises was an element of natural law, for Kant the "perfect duty" of promise-keeping is what unites us in a moral community, is itself the woof and weave of those "bonds of mutual respect between members of a moral community."[7] Promise-keeping then is what allows the constitution of a moral community, in fact of society *tout court*. This attitude toward promise-keeping was as true for Locke as for Hume. And if for Locke "grants, promises and oaths are bonds that hold the Almighty," for Hume they were but one of the three "artifices of society," necessary for its constitution: no longer divine dictates, but nonetheless "a rule-dependent or convention-dependent road to commitments beyond family and friends to those whom we bear no 'real kindness.'"[8]

What, however, is the early modern concern with promise-keeping if not a concern with establishing social bonds of trust in a society increasingly being defined by individual agents with interests and commitments of an increasingly personal nature? The breakup of local, territorial, and, crucially, primordial ties that accompanied Europe's entry into the modern era engendered, as is well known, a new concern with redefining the nature of society.[9] With the destruction of these bonds of primordial attachment to kith and kin, to territorial and local habitus, which had defined Western European societies until the Reformation, new forms of generalized trust had to be established. The early modern concern with promise-keeping must, I submit, be viewed in this light, as essentially an attempt to posit new bonds of generalized trust in societies where primordial attachments were no longer "good to think with" (to borrow a phrase from Claude Lévi-Strauss). The promise then is an act of will that invites trust among strangers, that is, among those who share no ties of affinity, kinship, or even shared belief. It is, as has been attested by many, "a speech act whereby one alters the moral situation" by incurring new obligations.[10] The social ties predicated on these obligations and the moral force of one's commitment to them thus serve (or at least were seen to serve by early modern political theorists) as forging a new model of (and as Clifford Geertz would remind us, "for" as well) the political community—one based on a shared belief in the very act of promise-keeping.

It may even be said that the attempt to found a political community on the basis of mutual promise-keeping was essentially an attempt to construct a new community of belief predicated not on blood, but on belief itself. It may not even be too exaggerated a claim to state that the maintenance of such a community—one predicated solely on mutual promise-keeping— and so also of trust defined in generalized (and hence always potentially universal) terms has been the enduring challenge of modern societies during the past two centuries. What is certain is its centrality to social thought and political theory throughout the whole of this period. The interest in establishing nonascriptive bases for trust has been a constant theme from

John Locke's concern with "trustworthiness, fidelity, the keeping of agreements and promises and respect for oaths" as a precondition for the existence of society, through the writings of the Scottish moralists on "natural sympathy," Edmund Burke's writings on the "little platoons" of society, and down to the later, nineteenth-century theorists of society such as Tönnies, Maine, and Durkheim. Indeed, Durkheim produced what was perhaps the boldest of solutions, in essence defining the problem away by positing the basis of modern solidarity (i.e., of a moral community of belief, and so of shared trust) as resting on our shared belief in the integrity of the individual conscience: "Since each of us incarnates something of humanity, each individual consciousness contains something divine and thus finds itself marked with a character which renders it sacred and inviolable to others. Therein lies all individualism; and that is what makes it a necessary doctrine."[11] Here the necessary (and modern) doctrine of (true) individualism (as opposed to its utilitarian or Spencerian variety) rests on the collective cognizance of the sacred individuality of each member. That this "solution" to the modern problem of trust was no solution (despite the heroic attempts of Talcott Parsons and others who attempted to systematize and generalize its implications) is by now more than clear.[12]

A political or intellectual history of these debates, while certainly called for, is not our concern here. Our purpose in the above discussion is simply to establish the centrality of the issue of trust to modern social and political thought and in so doing, point out how inexorably woven together are the problems of trust and the construction of modern social and political orders: how the problem of establishing trust—or more specifically generalized trust—defines as it does the specificity of modernity. Again, this is not to say that the problem of trust is not the problem of all social order; only that the breakdown of primordial and other ascriptive identities which has (to different degrees and at different times) accompanied the "great transformation" of modernity in the West has made of this an enduring and seemingly intractable problem and one that is again of major concern to students of social life.[13]

The Problem Explained

But what is trust and how are we to understand the specific forms of social relations predicated on its existence? More especially, how are we to distinguish it from such seemingly similar terms as *faith* and *confidence*—terms which are often used synonymously but which may well carry different valences and refer to arguably different types of social phenomena? A useful point of departure may then be to try and isolate the distinction between trust and confidence. True, most social scientists tend to conflate both terms in myriad studies of the degree of trust (or, as I would argue, confidence) in social and government institutions.[14] However, we have only to recall the old German proverb *Vertrauen ist gut, Sicherheit noch besser* (trust is good, confidence better) to realize that social scientists notwithstanding, ordinary people have long distinguished between these two modes of interaction or rather the cognitive and emotional states that accompany such interaction.[15] This distinction, by the way, is preserved in some of the more recent philosophical literature on trust that distinguishes between trust and reliance.[16]

Among sociologists, some recent work has touched on this distinction between trust and confidence in ways that are not fully adequate. Thus, for example, Lewis and Weigert's statement that "trust begins where prediction ends" would seem to indicate a recognition of this distinction.[17] For these researchers as for others, such as Rotter, however, trust—as distinct from confidence—is often reduced to an individual psychological state, a generalized expectation that alter will fulfill promises or obligations, and such expectation is tied to the experiences of early socialization.[18] Similar reduction of the meaning of trust to an individual psychological (or emotional) state can be found in the work of Lars Hertzberg, T. Govier, Richard Holton, and even in the more rational account of Russell Hardin.[19] Hardin, in fact, presents a rationalized account of trust as a learned capacity that serves on the individual level to permit the extension of confidence on the general level toward the institutions of society. Thus while he does distinguish trust from confidence and attempts a rational account of the former's emergence, this account ends up being tied to the early socialization experiences of the individual (affluent middle-class white, as opposed to inner-city black children, for example), which then go on to allow one rather than the other that necessary confidence in the system to take risks. In the end, for him too, trust is tied to some psychological orientation.

A more sociological attitude can be found in the writings of Anthony Giddens, who distinguishes between trust in people and trust in "abstract systems." Trust in persons "is built upon mutuality of response and involvement: faith in the integrity of another is a prime source of feeling of integrity and authenticity of the self. Trust in abstract systems provides for the security of day-to-day reliability, but by its very nature cannot supply either the mutuality or intimacy which personal trust relations offer."[20] Giddens goes further and relates this distinction in types of trust to the old sociological chestnut of the difference between traditional and modern societies, between, in Ferdinand Tönnies's terms, *Gemeinschaft* and *Gesellschaft*. Thus he notes:

> In pre-modern settings basic trust is slotted into personalized trust relations
> in the community, kinship ties, and friendships. Although any of these social

connections can involve emotional intimacy, this is not a condition of the maintaining of personal trust. Institutionalized personal ties and informal or informalized codes of sincerity and honor provide (potential, by no means always actual) frameworks of trust.[21]

This situation he contrasts with contemporary life where, "with the development of abstract systems, trust in impersonal principles, as well as in anonymous others, becomes indispensable to social existence."[22] Here then is what in essence amounts to a threefold classification: trust in persons, trust in institutionalized personal ties, and trust in abstract systems.

Aside from the confusion involved in using the same term—trust—to describe all three forms of social relations, there is a further and more critical problem with the above scheme. For Giddens does not really define analytically the difference between institutionalized personal ties and the abstract systems of contemporary life. Institutionalized personal ties are by their nature abstract, as any cursory inquiry into medieval lineages or tribal systems of kinship affinity will prove. And while we no doubt do exist in a world of abstract systems, we also exist in a world where the bonds of friendship tie us to special places and people as well as in a world regulated by more institutionalized personal ties.[23] Moreover, and equally telling, abstract systems themselves (whether of money or, "expert knowledge") are, in essence, no more than general modes of exchange and, as such, a form (albeit highly differentiated) of institutionalized personal relations.[24] Thus, while Giddens's approach to trust leaves much obscure, it does edge us toward an appreciation of the need to distinguish between trust and confidence, despite his own, quite purposeful conflation of the two terms.

For a greater sociological appreciation of the difference between *trust* and *confidence* it is best then to turn back from Giddens to the writings of Niklas Luhmann who has provided us with what is no doubt the richest set of insights and understandings of trust currently available. Although we will have occasion to refer again and again to his writings on trust in the course of this work, here we will note only the very helpful distinction he draws between trust and confidence. For Luhmann the distinction between the two turns on the distinction between risk and danger, between the framing of life's contingencies as being of an internal or external nature. And while for Luhmann this distinction is tied up with the progress of system differentiation (which makes of risk—as opposed to danger—a particular modern, or even early modern phenomenon, and so also of trust, or rather the need for it), he does posit the crucial distinction between *trust* in persons and *confidence* in institutions.[25] In his own words: "Trust remains vital in interpersonal relations, but participation in functional systems like the economy or politics is no longer a matter of personal relations. It requires confidence, but not trust."[26] Both are modes of reducing complexity, of keeping chaos at bay—though posited to be sure at very different levels of system differentiation. In the first instance trust is necessitated by the ontological freedom of the other. It is then "the generalized expectation that the other will handle his freedom, his disturbing potential for diverse action, in keeping with his personality—or, rather, in keeping with the personality which he has presented and made socially visible."[27]

Distinct from this, however, is confidence in the proper operation of a system which is, in essence, reliance on the proper workings of general media of communication (trust, love, power, money).[28] The proliferation of these general media with the heightened differentiation of systems in modernity makes of trust something "privatized and psychologized."[29] In modern societies, these forms of relations are replaced on the general societal level with "system trust," i.e., predictions based on expert knowledge. (If I am not mistaken, what Luhmann in his earlier work terms "system trust" becomes in his later work "confidence."[30])

The distinction between trust in people and confidence in system is, I maintain, a useful if problematic one in our quest to understand the meaning of trust. It is a good starting point, but starting point only. For system trust or confidence is, if we remain in the nomenclature of traditional sociological categories, really nothing more than confidence in a set of institutions. The distinction drawn between trust and confidence then becomes a distinction drawn between trust in people and confidence in institutions. What, however, are institutions? They are, as all graduates of Sociology 101 (or at least all graduates over the age of forty) know, nothing but patterned, internalized, normative role expectations. An indication of this problem can be seen in the Luhmann quote above, where trust is placed in the *socially visible* attributes of the other's personality—what really comes down to role performance.[31] It now seems that we have opened a Pandora's box and the distinction so arduously attained between trust and confidence threatens to fall apart. Again then, the attempt to give a separate set of meanings to the idea of trust seems to have failed.

Yet that conclusion is clearly unsatisfactory: the analysis of trust cannot be collapsed into that of confidence for at least two reasons, one historical and one analytical. On the historical level we have already noted how the idea of trust emerged in the modern era as a distinct concern—at least in the form of a concern with finding a new basis of the social and political order. The importance of trust and promise-keeping in the writings of Locke, Hume, and Kant seems at all events to be a search for rooting social order (what today we would term its institutional or systemic component) and its constitutive acts of exchange in new foundations. Whether framed normatively as godly dictates (with Locke) or as artifices of society (with Hume), there was a clearly felt need to ground the ordering of social life in some external absolute, a need that arose with the dissolution of the existing bases of trust rooted in shared religious beliefs, kinship consanguinity, or territorial proximity: in our terms, a need to root institutions (system) in something beyond themselves.

On the analytic level the problem is even more pressing. For the whole of the sociological tradition stemming from Emile Durkheim's idea of the precontractual (i.e., the necessity of rules regulating markets and governing the workings of contract that are themselves not subject to contract) is in fact an argument on the way the terms of trust in society mediate the free exchange of resources in society. Thus, as has been convincingly argued by S. N. Eisenstadt in his many writings, the workings of trust in society serve as a limitation on the free exchange of resources through such mechanisms as the above-noted construction of Public Goods or public distribution of private goods—mechanisms that exist in all societies. These mechanisms are themselves structured in part by the definitions, boundaries, and concrete content of trust and solidarity in society. This structuring is achieved through the establishment of certain "unconditionalities" that specify the "limitations on institutional interaction or exchange and on access to positions." These include:

> the normative specification of the range of goals or desiderata available or permitted to the members of a certain group or socio-cultural category, . . . the basic attributes of social and cultural similarity which constitute the criteria of being a member . . . entitled to claim such rights unconditionally as well as participation in the rules of distributive justice, while being subject to certain rules of exchange. In addition, such structuring defines the duties which are interlinked with these rights in the process of interaction, clearly distinguishing between members' rights to participation as against non-members' [as well as] the general principles of distribution of power among them.[32]

If we accept these strictures (and in one form or another all social scientists do—even social-choice theorists, witness the recent attempt to "endogenize norms"), a serious problem emerges with the above-noted collapse of trust into confidence. For confidence in a system, i.e., in its institutions—in the continued functioning of patterned, normative role expectations—could not in itself mediate or limit the flow of resources in the system (in society). Rather, confidence is itself the flow of resources, is the system itself (its operating code, as it were). For precisely what defines the system, what makes system x different from system y, what distinguishes the patterns of generalized exchange in the Kula Ring, say, from those in ancient Israel are the different sets of institutions and roles defining system goals, desiderata, terms of participation, distributive justice, and so on. All these are themselves *the system* as it structures and mediates the flow of resources; and as Luhmann has noted, when confidence is withdrawn from said system, it collapses as seems to have happened in the Soviet Union and its satellites in 1989.

This is still a long way from isolating that component of trust upon which such limitation on the free flow of resources (however defined, differently in different social settings) is based. Confidence in the workings of a given system cannot then be analogous to that trust upon which the system (defined as the flow of resources in society including the limitations thereon) is based. The problem of trust remains, as does the need to distinguish it from confidence or any other term for trusting in the proper functioning of any institutionalized order. And while it is doubtless true that the precontractual forms of solidarity noted by Durkheim serve as the basis for a particularly critical type of generalized trust (here again, confidence being reliance on this generalized trust, "trusting trust" in Diego Gambetta's telling phrase), it still does not tell us what trust per se, what S. N. Eisenstadt terms "pure" or "pristine" trust, is.[33]

It is surely not surprising that when attempting to define trust in its "pure" form, philosophers and even social scientists tend to fall into a "theological" mode and end up discussing faith (i.e., trust in God). S. N. Eisenstadt quotes Buber's *I and Thou* to give a sense of this pristine trust, and Annette Baier and others tend to use examples of that relational couplet (man and God) to exemplify this phenomenon.[34] This retreat into theological speculation is, in some sense, understandable given the reigning definitions of trust and confidence currently abroad in the scholarly community. For central to the definition of trust (as opposed to confidence) is that it involves one in a relation where the acts, character, or intentions of the other cannot be confirmed. In this reading one trusts or is forced to trust— perhaps led to trust would be better—when one cannot know, when one has not the capabilities to apprehend or check on the other and so has no choice but to *trust*. This then is seen to stand in contrast to that form of *reliance*, analogous to what we, following Luhmann above, termed as confidence: when, based on one's past knowledge (or sometimes one's ability to impose future sanctions in case of "betrayal") or future possibilities to "check up on" (similar, in a sense, to sanctions), one can *rely* or place confidence in the other's words or commitments or acts. Trust then involves a vulnerability occasioned by some form of ignorance or basic uncertainty as to the other's motives. As Virginia Held points out:

> We speak of trusting a person's *opinion* (which may be uncertain), not of trusting his *knowledge* (which can only be what it is); we claim to trust a person's *choice* (which may go either way), not to trust such fully determined behavior (in principle thoroughly predictable) as his reflexes or heartbeat. In short it seems to be that trust is most required exactly when we least know whether a person will or will not do an action.[35]

Before the advent of Internet or America Online the paradigm case of this fundamental opaqueness toward the will of another (indeed of the fundamental otherness of the other) was in the relation of humankind to God, *die ganz Anderen* (the totally other): the other whose will, motives, intentions, commitments, and so on could never be known (by definition) either by past knowledge or future action—*ein begriffener Gott ist kein Gott* (a known God is no God). In some religious traditions godly attributes could neither be known nor expressed, and many religious civilizations have based their codes of ethics and behavior precisely on an attitude of trust in the dictates of the unknowable God (the *deus abscondidus* of Calvinist belief, for instance, but others as well). Indeed, it is this act of ontological trust (which in fact bypasses all epistemological procedures of verification) that is at the heart of the Jewish tradition, represented at the revelation on Mount Sinai when the Israelites are reported to have accepted godly commandments with the phrase נעשה ונשמע (*n'aseh v'nishmah*, we will do and we will listen). This act of trust—of faith—has been, in one form or another, central to all religious thought, and the curious modern, or rather secular (for they are no longer analogous), reader may be referred to Kierkegaard's retelling of the story of Abraham in *Fear and Trembling* to appreciate the profundity of this moment.

However, collapsing trust into faith does not take us any further toward an understanding of trust than does conflating it with confidence. The first takes us too far in one direction, the second too far in another. In the first instance it becomes a theological concept, in the second a functionalist one. Moreover, by identifying "pure" or "pristine" trust with faith (or trust in God), we have in essence taken the concept beyond the world of social action and projected it into the heavenly realms where it really is of no great use to us—as either scholars or citizens. Thus, in an attempt to save the concept and probe its usefulness to the understanding of social relations, I suggest that we eschew either extreme and view trust as Hume viewed promises, as no more than an artifice of society, but one of a very peculiar nature, tied as it is to a fundamental ambiguity of the human condition. To understand this ambiguity let us turn to the "artifices" of the social scientist and take another look at that concept which has been fundamental to modern sociological analysis (and one which served in our prior analysis to invalidate the correlations of trust with confidence): the concept of role. We saw above how any idea of distinguishing trust in people (or personal relations) from confidence in institutions (at whatever level of differentiation) was in effect untenable as institutions are in fact nothing but patterned, mutually enforcing role expectations.

In this understanding of role, however, we followed only one particular sociological tradition, that of Parsons, Merton, and the functionalist (or structural-functionalist) school which sees social role and normative role expectations as a function of the social system. They are defined by the mutual expectations of role incumbents and are, most generally, institutionalized within a framework of interlocking, systemic activities. The degree of negotiability is minimal because role incumbents define their activities and indeed themselves ("internalization of role expectations") in terms of those sets of mutual and patterned expectations which within the structural-functionalist perspective, are seen as "given" by the functional imperatives of the system.[36]

There is, however, within the sociological tradition a very different understanding of social role that was developed by Ralph Turner and the symbolic-interactive school whose roots are in the traditions of George Herbert Mead and Charles Cooley.[37] In this tradition, social role is defined in much less structuralist terms. Here, role-taking is described in terms of process, as emerging out of interaction, as less determined by systemic constraints, as essentially more negotiable, more a function of reciprocity between role incumbents. This process and perspective has been defined, most aptly by Turner, as the move from "role-taking to role-making." In this perspective, social actors bring different definitions of role behavior to their incumbency, and the process of role-taking is defined in terms of a "greater degree of selective emphasis" oriented less toward already established and systemically defined norms and more toward the simple requirement of consistency in role performance.[38] Roles consequently are seen to exist in "very different degrees of concreteness and consistency" and, in most, the definition of role expectation is viewed as a process of interactive, inherently tentative behavior that is not prescribed by systemic constraints and considered rather as part of a continually unfolding configuration of cultural construction.[39]

To be sure, these two versions of social role contain in them not only two different sociologies, but two different readings of human existence. In one "man is indivisible and free" and in the other "man is an aggregate of roles and conditioned."[40] This contradiction exists on both the transcendental and sociological levels. At their extremes the two positions are incompatible. For if roles are labile and negotiable, it becomes impossible to talk of social systems or even of social institutions as existing over time. If, on the other hand, roles are only normatively prescribed by system needs, it becomes difficult to explain the differences existent between roles and the actual behavior of role incumbents as well as the frequent inconsistencies between normatively defined role behavior and the opinions of reference group members toward these norms.[41] Clearly then, as we all have come to know, norms exist at various degrees of institutionalization (in different institutional settings or in the same setting at different times), and roles are concomitantly embedded to different degrees in different sets of mutual expectations. Similarly, we have come to learn that the negotiability of roles is not an open-ended process: as one of my students once told me, "You can't show up in class wearing Speedos." Rather, it is one carried out within system limits, though sometimes it redefines system in the process;

a prime example of this would be how the broadly defined "Women's Movement" has redefined gender roles in the contemporary United States. We have learned too just how important was Turner's original caveat that role behavior be consistent over time, which opens a back door into the establishment of system constraints or institutionalized patterns of action through the very idea of patterned behavior.[42]

A rather large library could be accumulated of the different sociological studies aimed at describing and analyzing these different aspects of roles and those institutional and organizational settings where one or the other of their characteristics (as closed or open, patterned or labile, etc.) tend to predominate.[43] This is not our concern at present, but the fact that social roles do partake of both sets of characteristics, being systemically defined as well as containing some degree of openness, does have terribly important significance to our study of trust. That role behavior and the mutual exchange of resources (material as well as symbolic) predicated on such behavior are open to negotiation makes possible an understanding of trust apart from and independent of confidence (or the simple reliance on the ordered workings of existing institutional arrangements). We can perhaps for the first time since we began our inquiry begin to isolate trust from confidence and appreciate the fundamental factors involved in particularized trust—in its "pristine" form—without having recourse to the idea of faith or other forms of theological speculation.

In his own analysis of the concept of role the eminent sociologist Sir Ralf Dahrendorf could do no better than quote Robert Musil on the nature of men's existence in society, and there is much in the following quote that illuminates our purposes as well:

> The inhabitant of a country has at least nine characters: an occupations character, a national character, a civic character, a class character, a geographic character, a sex character, a conscious character and an unconscious character and perhaps a private character as well. He combines them all in himself but they dissolve him and he is nothing but a small channel washed out by these trickling streams. . . . This is why every inhabitant of the earth has a tenth character as well, which is nothing more nor less than the passive fantasy of unfilled space. It permits man everything except one thing: to take seriously what his nine or more other characters do and what happens to them. In other words, then, it forbids him precisely that which would fulfill him.[44]

It is in this tenth character and its contradictory relations to the myriad roles that we assume in society that trust—its necessity as well as its potentiality—is to be sought.

Thus I propose that without knowing exactly what trust is we have, tentatively, found a new way to understand and approach it. Trust is something that enters into social relations when there is role negotiability, in what may be termed the "open spaces" of roles and role expectations. Another way of saying this is that trust enters into social interaction in the interstices of system, or at system limit, when for one reason or another systemically defined role expectations are no longer viable. By defining trust in this way we manage to "save" the phenomenon sociologically from either a reduction to faith or belief on the one hand or to confidence in the fulfillment of role expectations on the other. We also cut through many of the current philosophical debates on trust which in the main, turn on either the viability (or rationality) of belief or the existence of sufficient (verifiable or not) bases for confidence.[45] Thus, for example, the very important work of Annette Baier on "Trust and Anti-Trust," on trust in the "discretionary power of the other," of the plumber, for example, "to do a nonsubversive job of plumbing" is really reliance on role performance.[46] The same may be said for Susan Shapiro's work on social control, which deals with trust in the discretionary powers of the myriad "agents" (similar to those who according to Giddens or Luhmann may be said to possess expert knowledge) upon whom society relies for its functioning. Here too the trust discussed is really confidence in the fulfillment of role expectations and the various forms of social control and sanctioning mechanisms that ensure such performance. This indeed seems to be its usual connotation in the sociological literature from Parsons through Peter Blau and other exchange theorists and, indeed, down to the most important recent work by Bernard Barber on the fiduciary responsibility inherent in trusting relations.[47] As Barber is one of the most frequently quoted of contemporary writers on the problem of trust, it may be worthwhile to cite him at some length, the better to establish this inherent connection of trust with what I am defining as confidence in systemically defined role expectations:

> Whether we have in mind expectations of the persistence of the moral social order, expectations of technically competent performance, or expectations of fiduciary responsibility, we must always specify the social relationship or social system of reference. What is regarded as competence or fiduciary responsibility among friends may be different from the trust within a family group, and both kinds probably differ from that in a work organization or in the society as a whole. Confusion may occur if this point is not heeded, especially with regard to conflicting expectations from different social systems, at the same level of generality or from systems at different levels of generality . . . Moreover, expectations of trust within one relationship, group or system may explicitly exclude competent performance or fiduciary obligation elsewhere.[48]

Here we see how Barber both relates trust to what is in essence role performance and, interestingly enough, sees the possibility of conflict between the performance of different roles in one's status set. But he fails to see trust as something that may emerge in such interstitial spaces as indeed he cannot, given his reigning definition of trust as (what we here term) confidence. In itself, then, this points to the real problems involved in any theoretical attempt to define trust solely by the terms of confidence.

Finally, we should note that most current studies of trust revolve around rational-actor analyses of iterated Prisoner Dilemma games.[49] Here too, the very iteration of the interaction points to an evolving structuring of preferences based on an evolving attribution of expectations (even when the valuation of these preferences is in purely rational-choice, profit-maximizing terms). Thus Partha Dasgupta notes: "For trust to be developed between individuals they must have repeated encounters, and they must have some memory of previous encounters. Moreover, for honesty to have potency [what we would term the fulfillment of normatively defined role expectations] as a concept there must be some cost in honest behavior. And finally, trust is linked with reputation, and reputation has to be acquired."[50] The very process of iteration, the memory of previous encounters, and the construction of a reputation are all functional equivalents of what we are calling confidence in system (as is the iteration of the interaction).[51]

In our own reading, however, not only is trust not analogous to either faith or confidence, but mistrust is defined as something very different from lack of confidence. By this I wish to draw a distinction between lack of confidence in (a) any particular system or set of institutional arrangements or (b) the capabilities of a given role incumbent to fulfill his or her role in a manner meeting the accepted standards of role expectation (and I realize with Dahrendorf that there may be very different interpretations of accepted standards), and (c) the phenomenon of mistrust directed at an individual irrespective of his or her role performance. I, for example, may have confidence in the general pragmatic of American medicine or I may lack confidence in it (i.e., feel that its epistemological premises are flawed and therefore go to a faith healer or to Lourdes or "confide" the treatment of my ailments to the care of homeopathic medicine). Similarly, I may have confidence in the overall assumptions of American medicine (and it is to this that I believe Giddens refers when he discusses abstract systems) but lack confidence in the treatment I am receiving in a particular hospital or at the hands of a particular physician. In both cases we are dealing with forms of confidence in "expert systems" per se and/or with their particular institutional manifestation. In neither case are we facing the phenomenon of mistrust, though we will often say that we "mistrust" such and such a doctor, dentist, or university administrator. If the foregoing analysis is correct, we must admit that this is a misuse of the term. For if trust is to be distinguished from confidence, then mistrust must also refer to something other than lack of confidence. Admittedly we do not know as yet what trust is and have but a tentative understanding of those situations where its emergence may be assessed, but let us proceed slowly, thus ensuring that every step of the way we are on solid ground.

Trust then may come to exist at system's limit, at the interstices of system, in that metaphorical space between roles, that area where roles are open to negotiation and interpretation. Some interesting light can be shed on this proposition through a brief review of the work carried out by the anthropologist Keith Hart on the Frafas in Ghana. The different tribes comprising this group of migrants were caught, as Hart so brilliantly explains, between two different types of system: the traditional form of social organization predicated on ties of kinship and a more modern one based on the workings of the market, of contract. Faced as they were with the task of "build[ing] economic relations [read: exchange relations] from scratch in a world lacking both orderly state regulations and the segmentary political structure of their customary society," the Frafas were literally coerced into finding a third mode of establishing social relations, one determined by what Hart terms trust—though for him that term is close to synonymous with friendship (a connection that we will have occasion to discuss below when viewing the thought of the eighteenth-century Scottish Moralists).[52] "Trust," Hart tells us "is located in the no-mans land between status and contract."[53] It was a "last resort" when recourse to confidence in either long-standing (but now eroded) ties of kinship or nascent (but not yet institutionalized) bonds of contract could not be had.[54] These migrants in Ghana in the late 1960s thus faced a social situation where "system" in fact did not exist and so there could be no basis for reliance on (or confidence in) system constraints, no basis for any role expectations or performance thereof. They could not but "trust' in the tenth character of their fellows.

In line with this and before we turn to a more analytic characterization of the relations between system and its limits (in order to get that much closer to an understanding of trust), it may be interesting to note the correspondence of this idea of trust as emerging at system limits with the historical emergence of transcendental or "Axial" religions, those great world-historical religions which reorganized the course of civilizations. If we follow Eric Voegelin's understanding of the rise of monotheism we see that the new "faith" emerged during what he terms "the times of troubles," of "cosmological disintegration."[55] This was true not only of Israelite monotheism, but of other varieties of "Axial" religions as well: Islam, for example, which emerged and took root in Mecca and Medina in the seventh century, during that period of transition between a pastoral and semi-nomadic mode of social organization and the growth of mercantile centers that saw the emergence of new forms of social organization, of new roles and the redefinition of existing ones at the partial expense of existing tribal solidarities.[56] The emergence of these "Axial" civilizations has indeed been linked to a heightened degree of differentiation among societal units occasioned by the "breakdown of tribal communities and their restructuring into broader units often connected to the establishment of the early states in pre-literate societies."[57]

There is, as we can see, an analogy here to Hart's study of Ghana. Just as trust, as a new form of association, emerged among the Frafas in a situation marked by the disintegration of social systems, so too Voegelin shows us how faith—which is in fact also a new form of social organization—emerged in periods of cosmological disintegration. The different forms of system that have reached their limits bring in their wake different forms of social organization and association. This insight into different types of system limits must be explicated and their relation to roles and role behavior clarified. For if we remain solely with the works of Hart (or Voegelin, for that matter), trust becomes an exceedingly rare phenomenon, whose emergence can only be explained in periods of transition, of system breakdown, or of institutional failure. There is something profoundly counterintuitive about this suggestion because we think (or perhaps would like to think) of trust as an essential component of our daily life and social relations. (I will in fact be arguing that trust—or even mistrust—is something liminal and far less pervasive than we would like to think, but for somewhat different reasons.)

If indeed trust is something (remember that we do not as yet know precisely what) that emerges at the limits of system—beyond the mutual frame of expectations of role behavior—a number of further distinctions and specifications must follow. Most importantly, the nature of these limits must be specified.

This can be broken down into a number of further issues: (a) The connection between different types of system coexisting in one territory and the limits on each such duality imposes (and hence the nature of trust that may emerge). Here the focus would be on the concrete content of the different systems. An example of this would be the coexistence of Christianity, animism, and (to a much lesser extent) Islam in southern Sudan, of Christianity and Buddhism in parts of southeast Asia, or even of life in American prisons where the formal definitions of roles and nature of exchange exist side-by-side with less formal rules of exchange (and so of trust—in the exchange of cigarettes among inmates, for instance). (b) The nature of system limits as structured by the different types of roles existent within any particular system. Thus for example, the status set of the late-twentieth-century university professor is constructed of very different types of role complements than that of a nineteenth-century Irish priest. Hence the type of limits on each set of interaction out of which trust may emerge will be very different. In slightly different terms, because the "system" of role expectations (its normative expectations, goals, nature of integration, coordination mechanisms, and so on through the Parsonian paradigm) is different in each case, so also the nature of the confidence in the fulfillment of role expectations will be different. Hence too, the existence of any terms of mutuality and association beyond the framework of these expectations, beyond simple reliance on the proper working of expectation by role incumbents, will also be different.

Finally, however, we come to the most important aspect of these limits: (c) The emergence and the type of structural conditions that engender limits to role fulfillment and so confidence therein. Here we would do best to return to Robert Merton's famous discussion of reference groups and analysis of the mechanisms for the articulation of roles in a role set. It is, I maintain, precisely in these mechanisms that we can find the relevant structural variables that lead to the type of "limits" I have been discussing. These include differing intensity of role involvement among those in a role set, differences in power of those in a role set, and the possibility of insulating certain role activities (or aspects thereof) from observability by different members of the role set.[58]

In all these cases, different structurally determined expectations of different members of a role set and/or the ability (sometimes need) to play off one from the other lead to what can, I believe best be described as a structurally determined limit on the ability to have confidence in or rely on the normative fulfillment of role expectations. Crucial among these variables are the (again structurally determined) differentials in power among status-set members who, in their different and contradictory demands, will lead a role incumbent to make certain behavior more or less visible to different status-set members. In all cases we can see how any system imposes structural limits on the normatively prescribed fulfillment of role behavior, irrespective of the concrete content of the roles involved. Moreover, these limits would exist in any system, regardless of its level of differentiation. Indeed, there exists a substantial body of literature in anthropology on roles and role conflict in tribal societies.[59] We have only to recall the tragedy of Antigone or of Orestes, indeed the very definition of tragedy in ancient Greek society, to appreciate the existence of role conflict and of conflicting demands on role incumbents in such societies. The level of social differentiation and diversification will itself effect the extent and frequency of such role conflicts and hence the potential for trust to emerge (a point to which we shall return).

In line with this more structural consideration of limits to system confidence, there is yet another avenue that could be explored: how the very unintended consequences of meeting and fulfilling role expectations may well lead to types of behavior that are no longer encompassed (or sanctioned—and I use sanctioned here in its traditional sense and without the negative contemporary associations) by existing role expectations. To clarify this we may imagine a number of role relations taken from the canvas of our daily life. We may think, for example, of parent-child roles, or doctor-patient, or teacher-student. In all cases the proper (or successful) fulfillment of these role expectations will lead to a transformation (and in some cases, ending) of the mutual relations. Now though you can well say that at this point a new role relationship is engendered, between doctor and patient (they may become friends or lovers), or between teacher and student (they become colleagues), and parent-child roles are continually being redefined, there is a time (space) between the one role relationship and the other (this is what adolescence is all about) when expectations must be renegotiated, where past expectations no longer hold and new ones are not yet institutionalized.[60] For this renegotiation to succeed, some element of trust (in the unknown and in the what-can-be) must be forthcoming for interaction to continue.

Beyond these more micro, or interactionist, perspectives stand the more macro level and comparative considerations into different types of social organizations where such "limits" exist in greater or lesser frequency. For, as noted above, different types of system—existing at different levels of differentiation—will thus engender different frequencies of the type of "Mertonian" variables discussed above. The more role-sets one is enmeshed in, the greater potential for structurally determined dissonances and conflicts between, as well as differentials in power among, different status members.

Trust, Friendship, and the Specificity of Modern Role Formation

Given our own concern with understanding the contemporary problems of establishing structures of generalized trust in Western democratic societies (and the debate around civil society that this has occasioned), it is on this last set of problems that we must focus our attention. An inquiry into the meaning of trust in contemporary societies, a questioning of its specificity both in terms of early modern (and what may be termed classical modern, or classical liberal) social forms of organization as well as in pre-modern social formation would thus be a plausible way to explore the usefulness of our own foregoing definitions of trust and to provide us with an understanding of what is increasingly being seen as a major problem in contemporary life.

To begin such inquiry we must ask if there really are differences between premodern and modern social formations in the nature of their social trust. After all, if trust is that which exists at the limit of system, there are, as we know, limits in all systems and thus the potential for the emergence of trust, of some form or another, in all systems. If we were satisfied with this, our task would be more or less complete. We would sit down and work through the potentialities of those structurally conditioned limits noted above as they become manifest in different social settings and orient our inquiry around a topology of different types of limits in different systems and the different forms of trust they may engender (comparing university professors and Irish priests, for example). However, the sense remains that trust, or at least its perception, is indeed very modern. It is articulated in early modern political theory, both by proponents of modern natural law (Grotius, Puffendorf, Locke) and by its detractors (Hume, Smith). It emerges linguistically, in French, for example (in the difference between *confiance* and *confidence*), in the sixteenth century. By contrast, certain late-coming societies to the modern world still preserve the element of faith in the linguistic designation of trust (for example, the hebrew word אמונה *emunah*).

Even more crucially the language of the eighteenth-century Scottish moralists, of Shaftesbury, Millar, Ferguson, Blair, and even Smith, that same language of civil society so often cited in contemporary debates, is really a language of trust, of a quest for and establishment of new bonds of community and association based on an idea of trust posited as one of the conditions of civilized society. Trust was, for these thinkers, defined as "natural sympathy" or as "natural benevolence"—an almost protopsychological datum that stood at the core of social life (in fact of civil society) and made social life possible. Held together by the force of these "moral sentiments," the Scottish thinkers of the eighteenth century predicated the very existence of society on something very close to what we have been defining as trust (though to be sure in Samuel Johnson's dictionary of the eighteenth century there is no clear distinction between trust and confidence, which are treated as virtual synonyms).[61] As Adam Ferguson reminds us:

> What comes from our fellow-creature is received with peculiar emotion; and every language abounds with terms that express somewhat in the transactions of men, different from success and disappointment. The bosom kindles in company, while the point of interest in view has nothing to inflame; and a matter frivolous in itself, becomes important, when it serves to bring to light the intentions and character of men . . . The value of a favor is not measured when sentiments of kindness are perceived; and the term misfortune has but a feeble meaning, when compared to that of insult and wrong.[62]

Insult and wrong, dissociated here from the workings of interest, point to a model of society, of human association based on trust (in, as seen above, "the intentions and character of men").

In line with this new appreciation of (or, if you wish, search for) new models of human association we should note the emergence in this period of friendship as a peculiarly modern form of social relations. More than anyone else, perhaps, the work of Alan Silver has stressed just how central the idea of friendship was to the social thought of the Scottish Enlightenment and how, counterintuitive though it may be, the very proliferation of market relations in the capitalist society of the eighteenth century engendered a realm of social interaction existing apart from and independent of the calculations of interest and the laws of the market. Thus he notes that while "it is not peculiar to modern society that ideals of friendship express some of the 'noblest' potentials of human association . . . an idea of friendship so contrary to the forms of association that dominate the larger society is distinctive to our times."[63] Friendship, Silver goes on to explain, emerged in the early modern era as a realm of interaction distinct from the motives of self-interest and rational calculation. More specifically, it emerged in contrast and explicit rejection of those types of behavior identified with aristocratic court society, where the calculation of every word and gesture was necessary to achieve success (and thus we may note to meet the highest standards of role fulfillment). In the following quote, Norbert Elias gives us perhaps the best of feelings for precisely this type of behavior which was, in the thought of the Scottish Moralists, replaced by their ideas of trust and mutuality:

> The court is a kind of stock exchange; as in every good society, an estimate of the "value" of each individual is continually being formed. But here his value has its real foundation not in the wealth or even the achievements of ability of the individual, but in the favor he enjoys with the king, the influence he has with other mighty ones, his importance in the play of courtly cliques. All this, favor, influence, importance, this whole complex and dangerous game in which physical force and direct affective outbursts are prohibited and a threat to existence, demands of each participant a constant foresight and an exact knowledge of every other, of his position and value in the network of courtly opinion; it exacts precise atonement of his own behavior to this value. Every mistake, every careless step depresses the value of its perpetrator in courtly opinion; it may threaten his whole position at court.[64]

In distinction to this type of behavior the new idea of friendship was posited as one whose attributes infused all existence with a new ethical valuation. As Adam Ferguson notes:

> The disposition on which friendship is grafted glows with satisfaction in the hours of tranquility, and is pleasant, not only in its triumphs, but even in its sorrows. It throws a grace on the external air and, by its expression on the countenance, compensates for the want of beauty, or gives a charm which no complexion or features can equal. For this course the scenes of human life derive their principal felicity; and their intimations in poetry, their principal ornament. De-

scriptions of nature, even representations of a vigorous conduct, and a manly courage, do not engage the heart, if they be not mixed with the exhibition of generous sentiments, and the pathetic, which is found to arise in the struggles, the triumphs, or misfortunes of a tender affection.[65]

Similarly and perhaps even more importantly, we should note that such a valuation of friendship was shared even by such "fathers" of current profit-maximizing theories of human nature as Adam Smith and David Hume. Indeed, and as Silver points out, the very place of "natural sympathy" in Smith's sociology was as a moral foundation for the organization of society. As Silver makes clear,

> Smith establishes the moral basis of commercial society in the associations of private individuals meeting in a social space not shaped by institutional constraints. The mutual control of behavior that results, though a complex play of interacting and reflexive mechanisms, is both source and prototype of moral conduct. Sympathy moderates ideas and conduct and distributes fellow-feeling in an essentially democratic spirit. The exclusive bonds defined by custom, corporate group, state and estate are dissolved. Sympathy generates a kind of social lubrication throughout civil society, and is key to a deinstitutionalized moral order no longer authoritatively sustained by religious, economic or political institutions.[66]

Clearly this stress on friendship in the writings of the eighteenth century moral philosophers carries with it important implications for our understanding of the emergence of the private realm and of that distinction between public and private spheres so central to modern life (and upon whose synthesis many prescriptive statements on the value of civil society are seen currently to reside). As such it will emerge again later in our study, when we take up the problem of public and private in modern life (and, perhaps getting ahead of our argument, when we shall explore the correlations between our account of trust and the developing idea of the private realm as existing beyond the purview of systemic role definitions). Here, however, we note its emergence for another reason: to again stress the growing awareness of trust (which, as we saw above, took the form of friendship) as a distinct form of social relations in the modern era. We cannot but assume that thinkers as diverse as Ferguson and Hume, Shaftesbury and Smith, were all responding to an awareness of the changed nature of social relations in their lives and, at the same time, seeking to posit one aspect of these changed relations—that existent beyond the formal and explicit rules of "contract, market exchange, . . . division of labor and impersonal institutions" as constitutive of the social order.[67]

If Silver's analysis of friendship is correct—as I believe it is—and in light of our broader understanding of trust as somehow specific to modern social formations, we seem to be facing a contradiction between, on the one hand, the idea of trust as existing (or as a potential that could emerge—and this distinction will prove important in the following) in the interstices of all systems, premodern as well as modern; and, on the other hand, the idea of trust as a particularly modern phenomenon tied in some way to modern forms of social organization.

In fact, what I would like to maintain is that both propositions are to some extent true but at very different levels of realization and institutionalization. That is to say, the potential for relations of trust may indeed exist in many social formations. Yet its place within modern societies is still unique—in the moral value we assign to it, the frequency of its occurrence, and the institutionalized arenas where it can be manifest. Notice, moreover, that the potential for trust is not the same as an instance of its occurrence. And the fact that such potential may have (theoretically) existed in archaic, tribal, or other, premodern social formations does not in itself indicate its existence. Indeed, I would maintain that the existence of role conflicts or system limits is a necessary but not sufficient condition for the existence of trust. They provide the opportunity for trusting relations to emerge but cannot in themselves provide the basis for its emergence. For that, a number of additional variables are necessary. In this context and given our foregoing discussion of friendship as an instantiation of trust with the emergence of modernity in the eighteenth century, it would be useful to review, however briefly, some of the existing anthropological perspectives on friendship in tribal and other non-Western societies.

One fact that emerges when comparing modern and premodern social formations is that while role conflict and hence system limits (occasioned by conflicting formal obligations) do exist even in archaic societies— and we may recall here the example of Antigone—they do not, in themselves, lead to the establishment of either friendship relations or those of mutual trust. At most they lead to the privileging of some set of role identities and obligations over another. This was the point made by Gabriel Herman in his study of how the obligations of "guest-friendship" in classical Greece came to conflict with those obligations of civic community.[68] These came to exist as "two competing moral systems . . . one archaic and pre-political and the other stemming from the political structure."[69] Less important for us here are their inherently contradictory sets of obligations and more the simple fact that his analysis shows how ritual friendship serves to root personal relations (among certain groups of social elites) within a cross-cutting set of kinship obligations often going back many generations.

A similar point was made some forty years ago in S. N. Eisenstadt's seminal paper on ritualized personal relations in which he discussed "friendship" in particularistic societies where roles are defined according to familial, kinship, lineage, and ethnic properties.[70] In these societies, blood brotherhood and other forms of ritualized friendship serve to define or include the exogamous other within prescribed role expectations. Far from being a phenomenon connected to trust, friendship in these societies is used to draw a relationship that cannot be encompassed in the logic of the existing system (i.e., one based on primordial categories) into the system.[71] Rather than being a recognition of the limits of the system (its incapacity to provide definitions for relations based on universalistic rather than particularistic ties), ritual friendship served to obfuscate or negate the very existence of such interstitial points within the system. Thus, if we can say that modern societies do in some way institutionalize the existence of system limits (the outmost boundaries of role expectations) in the moral weight we place on the idea of trust and in the interpersonal space of friendship (that relationship based on something other than reliance on the fulfillment of role expectations), premodern society denies the very existence of such limits, which is what is at the core of the rather widespread phenomenon of ritual friendship. And while it is true that the establishment of fictitious blood relations often sets up a competing and conflicting system to that of existing kinship relations (thus engendering new types of role conflicts and of system limits), it remains the case that "the claims of institutionalized friendship are exercised in a functional relationship to existing kinship rights."[72] Thus, and as was noted by Evans-Pritchard in his classical study of Zande blood brotherhood, "a man could not enter into a pact solely on his own initiative, since its clauses bound also his kin, who became subject to its sanctions. He would therefore first consult his father and uncles and would only carry out the rite of blood brotherhood after he had obtained their consent."[73] As summed up by Robert Paine, studies of "institutionalized friendship suggest that the particularistic, solidary group is likely to manipulate, according to its own will, the persona of the individual member. Where this is so, his friendships are not only institutionalized ... they are also approved, occasionally even prescribed, by the group."[74]

In this sense and as S. N. Eisenstadt notes, "friendships are firmly set within the basic structural principles of these societies. They do not go beyond the basic orientation of the society and the consequent expectations of their members."[75] Such a statement, however, is as true for modern as for premodern societies, the difference being in the orientations of the society and the expectations of its members—which are different in each. In the premodern they are almost totally constrained by formal, well-defined expectations of ascriptively prescribed role behavior; in the modern something else that is not predicated on such prescriptions comes to play and this something has to do with the idea of trust. As such it sets up a very different dynamic of friendship than can be seen in either archaic Greek or tribal society.[76]

The position we have been arguing is that in these later social formations friendship is really a phenomenon based on confidence, one deeply rooted in system constraints rather than a trust of something beyond institutionalized role expectations (of what precisely we are, admittedly, still ignorant).[77] Indeed, so much is this the case that following Eisenstadt and others we see that ritualized friendship is itself nothing but a "fictive" attempt to incorporate into the system of existing categories types of social relations that the system cannot adequately represent.[78] This is accomplished not by a recognition of the anomalous nature of these relations, existing as they do beyond the ties of ascription, but precisely by their translation (or fictitious transformation) into blood ties, i.e., into the only grammar that the system has to recognize their existence.[79] Here the existence of those limits that any system contains in its ability to represent social reality does not lead to the type of social phenomenon that we identify with trust, but essentially to the rearticulation of these relations in terms more amenable to the existing categories of classification. We may in this context recall Radcliff-Brown's quote from one of his respondents to the effect that "I can tease my mother's brother and I can take something away from him which belongs to him because we are great friends; I am the son of his sister."[80] Friendship and family, trust and confidence have not been dissociated in the manner we have grown accustomed to, and what "permits" the "trust" necessary to the joking relations, to the teasing and to the ludic theft is not trust at all, but a confidence in the existence of well-represented (and sanctioned) role relations of an ascriptive nature.

Thus the potential for trust is not the same as its existence, and the meanings of friendship are very different in different social contexts. Limits to systemically defined role behavior do certainly exist in all social formations, but that does not guarantee the emergence of trusting relations. The rational calculation of exchange involved in certain "trusting" relations, such as those explored by Malinowski in the Kula Ring or by modern anthropologists in contemporary tribal and even peasant societies, are as different from the trust idealized as "natural sympathy" by Shaftesbury, Ferguson, and the other moral philosophers of the eighteenth century as the ritualized friendships of archaic societies are from their idea of friendship.[81]

Friendship and the trust upon which it is based is thus a modern phenomenon, and decidedly not an aspect of premodern social formations. The rather simplistic way we usually envision modernity as a society of "strangers," as one without trust is, therefore, at least in some respects, incorrect. True, there is often (perhaps most of the time) mistrust or lack of trust, but it is also only within these social formations that the potential for trust and hence the possibility for its realization may exist. What is naively seen as the trusting nature of premodern societies, is, in fact, nothing but confidence in well-regulated and heavily sanctioned role expectations (of an ascriptive nature). Systemically defined role expectations may be either ascribed or achieved, they may be based on either kinship relations (real or "fictitious") or on contractual obligations (such as between Annette Baier and her plumber). In both cases, the continued operation of the given system of social relations depends not on "trust" but on "confidence" in (what can ultimately only be termed the legitimacy of) the given forms of social relations. This is a point well worth noting. For we tend to think of modernity as a very different type of civilization than other types of social organization. So much of the social-scientific literature, from Tönnies to Parsons, has stressed this difference in the dichotomous categories of status and contract, *Gemeinschaft* and *Gesellschaft*, ascribed and achieved, mechanical and organic. I am far from maintaining that these distinctions do not hold or that they are irrelevant for an understanding of modern social formations. What I am stressing is that these are differences in the nature of system classification—thus relevant for studying the difference in the basis of *confidence* in the different systems. In themselves, they do not bear on the difference between confidence and trust, which is a different matter entirely. All systems, tribal or contractual, those based on status and those based on contract, need confidence in their classificatory scheme to exist and maintain themselves. The "trust" that is so often seen to bind members of tribal, peasant or other types of premodern societies is not trust at all but confidence in a very particular mode of social organization based on ascriptive categories (the same would hold for contemporary Japan).[82]

Having stressed this point, we must not neglect the fact that it is only in the later societies—those based on achieved role expectations, united by organic forms of solidarity where the obligations of mutual reciprocity are based on contractual relations rather than status attributes—that trust can emerge. Confidence either exists in all forms of social organization or does not, in which case societies undergo periods of change and transformation. Confidence may also exist in very different degrees, as anthropological studies have shown in the case of Western impingement on tribal societies which brought in their wake a process of social disruption and loss of confidence in tribal forms of social organization. This was the point made by Hart in his study of the Frafas noted above and was made most saliently by Evans-Pritchard in his study of the Zande, where he noted that "since European occupation of their country . . . people no longer regard their obligations seriously . . . custom has crumbled . . . losing its moral force."[83] (This knowledge is by now a staple of anthropological literature.) Trust, however, is an attribute of modern societies. How then are we to understand this difference and the unique emergence of trusting relations (or rather the possibility of their emergence) in modern social formations?

Given the nature of our analysis thus far, it would seem plausible to look first at the variable of system differentiation to explain the emergence of trust as a modern phenomenon. This is not to say that system is either more or less salient in modern or premodern societies, but there is, undoubtedly, greater differentiation. Greater differentiation means that there are more roles. With the proliferation of roles in modern, highly differentiated societies, there is also a fundamental transformation in the nature of the status positions existent in society.[84] For concomitant with the increase in roles, each role also circumscribes fewer types of behavior. Each role contains fewer distinct types of status members in its role-sets. And though all together there are most probably more relevant others in ego's system of reference—through the very multiplicity of roles as well as of role-sets—each role in itself encompasses fewer distinct statuses and hence defines a more limited range of behavior patterns. Thus, for example, the nature of relations one enters into on assuming a modern occupational status (and its concomitant role-sets) tend to be defined solely by that particular status (though of course one can marry one's teacher, client, doctor, and so on). It is certainly the case that in many modern status positions the relevant others (role-set members) may well be more numerous than in traditional occupational statuses. (It can be argued that the modern corporate lawyer has more members in her different role-sets than a Bedouin cattle raider. It is also the case that some modern statuses bring with them fewer role-sets than in traditional societies—such as in spousal relations.) However, there is much less overlap between different statuses within the particular role-sets of any modern role. That, in fact, is the true significance of system differentiation.[85] Not only are there more roles, but through the multiplication of roles, each role is more discretely defined in terms of one type or set of relations (of reciprocity, obligations, commitments). In premodern societies there were fewer statuses and most probably fewer role-sets within each status, but each role defined multiple types of status. It is this type of social organization that Ernest Gellner has termed "multistranded" wherein, for example, "a man buying something from a village neighbor in a tribal community is dealing not only with a seller, but also with a kinsman, collaborator, ally or rival, potential supplier of a bride for his son, fellow juryman, ritual participant, fellow defender of the village, fellow council member."[86] This is very different from the "single-stranded" relations we enter into when purchasing a commodity, wherein our calculations are, on the whole, orientated around purchasing the best possible commodity for the least price.

Let us clarify this point with only one further example. As a member of American society in the late twentieth century, I undoubtedly fulfill more roles than a contemporary Bedouin or a twelfth-century peasant in Languedoc. Moreover, my status as a university professor probably contains a greater number of role-sets than would most occupational positions in nonmodern societies. Together these factors would account for giving me a broader set of (potentially conflicting) reference groups (both between my different roles and between members of the different role-sets within any one role). However, within any particular status (however multitudinous its role-sets) my relations with role-set members will be defined solely by expectations defined by that status and not by others that I may hold. Thus my filial obligations to my sick mother will be only marginally relevant to the different members of my professional role-set. Though, to be sure, within one status my different obligations to different role-set members will maintain a certain relevance. Thus I could discuss my obligations to my students with colleagues (let us say to explain my research unproductivity) in a way that will (perhaps) carry a certain legitimacy that reasons based on family obligations will not carry. In sum, modern social relations may be characterized by:

  a. fewer status positions encompassed by any one role,
  b. more roles,
  c. more complex and differentiated role-sets within any one status position,
  d. greater numbers of reference group members.

Graphically this distinction between modern and premodern societies may be portrayed as in the figure on page 40.

This much is standard knowledge, but what is its relation to our study of trust? The hypothesis I wish to put forward is simply that the greater the number of roles or statuses (and the concomitant increase in the complexity of role-sets within any one status position), the greater the potential for those types of conflict and contradictions between roles and between the (sanctioning) power of different members of the role-set discussed by Robert Merton. The more roles, the more room or space for precisely those types of "Mertonian" dissonances noted above and hence the greater potential for negotiation in the fulfillment of role expectations. The more roles, the greater the possibility of differentials in role involvement in any one role (or role-set) and the greater the potential for insulating certain role activities from observation by other members of the role-set (within any particular role) or between different roles. In short, the greater the differentiation of system and concomitant proliferation of roles, the more it becomes possible to assign a degree of lability to any particular role (or role-set) and hence the more a certain degree of negotiability of role expectations becomes possible—perhaps even necessary. The greater indeterminacy and the greater negotiability of role expectations lead to the greater possibility for the development of trust as a form of social relations. (The corollary also holds: the more potential for the development of mistrust as well.) Broadly speaking, the more confidence

Premodern

Ego   Relational Matrix Role A

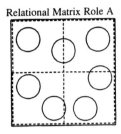

Modern

Ego   Relational Matrix Role A

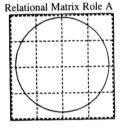

A - P   Social Roles   ◯   Status Positions
☐   Roles in System   ⊡   Role-sets

in a system of role expectations cannot be taken for granted (because of the systemically "mandated" possibility of dissonance in role fulfillment and expectations), the more difficult it becomes to establish role reciprocity which can only be met by the establishment of trust.[87] By a somewhat circuitous route we seem to have returned in a way to the idea proposed by both Luhmann and Harding that confidence in the modern system of role expectations can be maintained only through trust on the personal level. In our reading, however, trust is to be understood as something emerging in the interstices of systemically defined role expectations—that very lability that is built into modern systems of confidence and which allows the emergence of trust in a manner that was not possible in other forms of social organization.

To get a better grip on this aspect of trust as role negotiability, it may be helpful to recall Mary Douglas's discussion of restricted and elaborated codes of social classification and control. Drawing on the linguistic analysis of Basil Bernstein, Douglas develops a topology of two different modes of social communication and classification—in essence, of systemic organization.[88] The first is defined by what she, following Bernstein, terms "restrictive rules" that emphasize unambiguous relations, privileging solidarity over difference (of members) and appealing to codes of impersonal status behavior as well as to the basic similarity of the referenced (in our discussion, of the role incumbent) with others in their group. As opposed to this system, the "elaborate code" of communication (and of control and sanctioning) is based on personal relations and an appeal to reason and abstract principles. Its sanctioning and regulations (what for us would be the maintenance of role expectations) are imposed through appeals to the thoughts and feelings of the incumbent.

Basil Bernstein developed his work on restricted and elaborate codes of speech in his research on control mechanisms among different types of families in London. Mary Douglas expanded it to a mode of classification of broader social systems. Its application to the age-old distinction between traditional and modern societies is immediately clear. And while on some level it is but a reformulation of well-known distinctions, it does help us clarify the analytic point in question here; for it emphasizes that aspect of modern role definitions that are open to negotiation. If role expectations are oriented to persons and to principles rather than to solidary groups, there is, as noted above, a built-in aspect of lability and negotiability in their fulfillment that cannot exist when role performance is strictly defined in terms of its correspondence with the performance of other group members. Moreover, if a system is orientated toward a greater degree of negotiability in role performance, it must correspondingly be orientated to a greater degree of trust (or at least a potential for such).

The more the negotiation, the more the need for trust because the less the boundaries and content of specific role expectations can be explained according to rigid or formalized codes. And here is the relevance of the different types of roles in the different social formations: the very fact that traditional roles encompassed different status positions made for regulation of role performance by formalized and restricted codes of conduct. Negotiation would have been inimical to the very existence of such an overlapping system. In modern social formations, the increased distinctions between status and roles both allow for and in fact necessitate such negotiation: allow for, in the dissociation of roles from status and definitions of role in terms of one discrete status (in ideal typical terms, of course); necessitate, in the existence of role conflict both within and between roles that ensues from such dissociation.

Still, we have not defined trust. We do not yet really know what it is. We know that it is something different from both faith and confidence and that its emergence is concomitant to, indeed predicated on, the existence of role negotiability—or more generally, dissonance or "open spaces" within the definitions of role behavior. These dissonances may exist on different levels and may be caused by different factors. In the case study by Hart they were occasioned by the transformation of one set of role expectations to another. However, as we have tried to argue, the dissonances may also be constitutive of a social system itself and not be just a transitional phenomenon. Indeed, the point we have been arguing is that one of the specific aspects of modern social formations and of their highly developed division of labor is precisely that the very nature (or rather extent) of role differentiation leads to such a potential for the emergence of trust—again, through the lability and negotiation inherent in role performance in modern social structures. That in itself is still not an explication of what trust is but simply an understanding of why its existence (or perhaps its felt need) is greater in modern social formations. The systemically structured limits on confidence in modern highly differentiated systems are therefore what engenders the need for trust.

With this insight we are now in a better position to understand the emergent idea of friendship as moral value in the eighteenth century and beyond. We can, as it were, theoretically grasp Alan Silver's historical argument. For the transformation of social relations which engendered the rise of friendship was precisely the increase in social differentiation, that very "distinction of callings" and increased division of labor that so caught the attention of the eighteenth-century moral philosophers as perhaps the defining aspect of civilized or "polished" society.[89] This "separation of arts and professions" upon which the wealth and prosperity of nations were based was inimicable to existing types of association based on solidary group identities. As Adam Ferguson noted:

> Under the distinction of callings by which the members of polished society are separated from each other, every individual is supposed to possess his species of talent, or his peculiar skill, in which the others are confessedly ignorant; and society is made to consist of parts, of which none is animated with the spirit that ought to prevail in the conduct of nations.[90]

This loss of collective unity, of a sense of the collective whole, was replaced by a new mode of individual association, of more privatized union, predicated on the idea of friendship. What was lost on the societal level was gained on the individual one as the possibilities for a qualitatively new type of tie between individuals emerged, a tie based on trust and articulated as the bonds of friendship.[91]

Both developments, the waning of one type of relationship and the waxing of another, occurred concomitantly and were both tied to the increased progress of the division of labor. And what this increase in the division of labor implied was a greater differentiation of roles within the social system. The greater differentiation of roles brought, in turn, a greater possibility of dissonance between roles, of role conflict and indeterminacy that could, in turn, be met only by a heightened degree of negotiation and of trust as an aspect of human relations existing somehow beyond the purview of mutual role expectations and, for that matter, of reciprocity in role relations. This took the form, as Alan Silver has shown, of a new valuation of friendship as a moral ideal, an ideal wherein, as the following quote by Hume demonstrates, the workings of a new form of sociability or sympathy are at play.

> It is remarkable that nothing touches a man of humanity more than any instance of extraordinary delicacy in love or friendship, where a person is attentive to the smallest concerns of his friend, and is willing to sacrifice to them the most considerable interest of his own. Such delicacies have little influence on society because they make us regard the realest trifles, but they are the more engaging, the more minute the concern is, and are a proof of the highest merit in any one who is capable of them. The passions are so contagious that they pass with the greatest facility from one person to another and produce correspondent movements in all human breasts. Where friendship appears in very signal [sic] instances, my heart catches the same passion and is warmed by those warm sentiments that display themselves before me. Such agreeable movements must give me an affection to every one that excites them.[92]

We see here all the social attributes attendant on this new form of social relations that we have identified with the workings of trust:

  a. its emotional value to the individual concerned,
  b. its existence beyond the realm of reciprocity, exchange, and instrumental calculation,
  c. its individual rather than social scope,
  d. its moral valuation as the height of individual virtue,
  e. its role as a new form of social solidarity (that very "lubrication" that Silver notes in reference to Adam Smith).

Having established the connection between trust as friendship and the proliferation of roles with the increased division of labor, we must now embark on the most difficult part of our enterprise: to understand just what trust is. Having isolated the conditions of its emergence, both analytically and to some extent historically, we must proceed with the labor of definition. We may now assume that trust is some sort of belief in the goodwill of the other, given the opaqueness of other's intentions and calculations. The opaqueness, we recall, rests precisely on that aspect of alter's behavior that is beyond the calculable attributes of role fulfillment; if it were otherwise, alter's actions would not be unknown but assessable within the framework of the defining system of role expectations and hence reflect confidence and not trust. What then is the nature of this belief? For while we have come to understand trust as something that exists beyond system, existing in its interstices, in the undefined "spaces" between its role definitions, we have not yet defined its content. To this task we must now turn.

Two

Agency, Civility, and the Paradox of Solidarity

Unconditionalities and Individual Agency

Trust as we have come to see in the preceding chapter is a form of belief that carries within it something unconditional and irreducible to the fulfillment of systemically mandated role expectations. This is perhaps one of its most central attributes. In contrast to the Latin meaning of *fides*, which implies the certainty of remuneration, a certainty based most often on ascriptively defined loyalties, the unconditionality of trust is first and foremost an unconditionality in respect to alter's response.[1] As Max Weber, among others, has noted, "what one owed to another according to *fides* depended on the peculiar nature of the concrete relations."[2] This must be contrasted to our emerging definition of trust, for were the trusting act to be dependent (i.e., conditional) upon the play of reciprocity (or rational expectation of such), it would not be an act of trust at all but an act predicated on confidence (in the existence of systemically defined modes of exchange and reciprocity in society). It is this very connection to unconditionality that explains why so many attempts to explain trust led to a "theological" mode of explanation, for the defining characteristic of faith is precisely its unconditionality and the same is true of trust—with important differences between them.

Thus, while both faith and trust share the attribute of unconditionality, the object of this unconditional belief is very different in each case: in the one, God; in the other, man. This is perhaps too the greatest paradox in the idea of trust: the forging of unconditional bonds with entities that are by their very nature highly conditioned. It was, in a sense, an awareness of this paradox that led John Locke to his particular vision of political order. For what, in the final analysis, "conditions" human agents is no more nor less than the pursuit of their own interests. This pursuit, the free agency it involves and the ensuing problems of collective action, was in fact at the heart of Locke's political philosophy.[3] So much was Locke aware of the collective action problem (in essence the problem of trust), which for him was the problem of maintaining moral obligations among autonomous human beings, that he looked to the fear of other-worldly recriminations as third-party enforcer of contracts. Hence too his profound skepticism about the trustworthiness of atheists: in John Dunn's terms his "logical presumption about the necessary absence for them of any good reason, in the last instance, for curbing their own selfish and socially destructive desires."[4] Indeed, it may be said that for Locke the iterated PD game continued into the other-world in such a way that "neither faith (*fides*) nor agreements, nor oaths, the bonds (*vincula*) of human society can be stable and sacred for an atheist: so that, if God is once taken away, even simply in opinion, all these collapse without him."[5] For Locke it was ultimately fear of God's wrath—as third-party enforcer in the future life—that kept people's passions, interests and temptations in line and guaranteed the fulfillment of promises.[6]

However, given the fact that we are all now a society of atheists, we have no choice but to understand the unconditional nature of trust as something existing beyond the frame of mutual role expectations in society. And given the contemporaneously mundane dimensions of the problem we should note the connection between trust and what anthropologist Victor Turner has defined as "liminal" phenomena, existing "betwixt and between" the given categories of gender, occupation, hierarchy, subordination, and age—in short, beyond the categories (or roles) of any systemically defined division of labor.[7]

One important aspect of the liminal for Turner is its existence as an interstitial moment when social hierarchies and differences collapse, allowing the (always ritually circumscribed) emergence of "communitas," defined as the realization of that "generalized social bond" existing beyond (or at the base of) all human interaction and society.[8] The total laying aside of social difference and distinction as expressed in such ritualized activities as nakedness, foolishness, role reversal, silence, etc. is here what permits the reaffirmation of unconditional mutual recognition (unconditioned by the different roles and statuses the participants hold within the social system). Sameness then is the precondition for mutuality and collective self-affirmation. The liminal moment of "communitas" existing beyond system differentiation is a moment of sameness.[9] Contrast this with what we have learned in regard to the liminal aspect of trust and we begin to approach the heart of the modern dilemma; for in contrast to the tribal societies studied by Turner, the liminal moment of unconditioned belief is predicated not on the sameness or identity of the participants but on their very difference or otherness. What one trusts is some unknown, unverifiable aspect of alter's behavior (or response) which, while existing beyond system classification (as does ritualized communitas), makes no claim to the essential identity of the participants in the interaction. It is in the very otherness of the alter that one puts one's "faith" and not in any communality of traits shared.

It is precisely in relation to this "otherness" of the human other rather than a transcendent entity that trust differentiates itself from faith. In fact, it is in the increasing move of otherness inward to the world of man and human concerns that the problem of trust emerges (as we have seen in our brief discussion of friendship). It may therefore be useful at this juncture to review this particular aspect of the secularization process because it provides us with the proper backdrop to appreciate the growth or felt need for trust in a world increasingly divested of faith.

To emphasize once again the uniqueness of trust as an attribute existing in contrast to faith, but one nevertheless predicated on the opaqueness, the fundamental otherness, of alter's intentions, it may be useful to recall some of the well-known definitions of religion such as those by G. van der Leeuw, Rudolf Otto, or Emile Durkheim.[10] Durkheim has emphasized the absolutely distinct and separate character of the sacred.[11] The otherness of the sacred, or, in Rudolf Otto's terms, the numinous, is manifest in its inexpressibility.[12] The very characteristic of the numinous, existing as objective and outside the self, is what makes it ineffable. A feeling of "indefinite and general remoteness" has, from its inception, characterized man's attitude toward the supernatural, however perceived.[13] As such thinkers as Durkheim and van der Leeuw have emphasized, the fundamental basis of all religious belief is a "highly exceptional and extremely impressive 'Other.'"[14] The sense of amazement and awe evoked in the presence of this otherhood is precisely what is meant by the idea of the sacred. "The awe and fascination of the totally other," the *totaliter aliter*, constituted, for Rudolf Otto, as for Peter Berger, the "leitmotif of the encounter with the sacred."[15]

However, while the representation of otherness in and as sacrality characterized religious thought *tout court*, Western religious tradition developed the notion of the numinous other in a very particular way. For the sacred "otherness" that Durkheim found in totemic belief was articulated within the great historic religions in transcendent terms. Simply put, the notion of the totally other is the notion of God. Or, contrariwise, and as noted earlier, *Ein begriffener Gott ist kein Gott*. It is, moreover, precisely vis-a-vis this otherness that self and the relation between selves were defined in the Judeo-Christian tradition. God is conceived of as an "object" existing "over against the Self." As such, as the totally other, God can never be known. In contrast, the Self "is in no sense an Other . . . it is . . . what we already and fundamentally *are*."[16] The self and the knowledge of self stand in opposition to the otherhood of God which can never be known. This transcendent otherhood, precisely in our ignorance of it, stands as the root of all knowledge of self and, as we shall see, as a referent to all attempts to *know*, in fact to place confidence in, the more terrestrial others of our life.

The core moment in this process is the original differentiation in the orders of existence; the very positing of a transcendent beyond in opposition to the exigencies of mundane existence. This chasm between mundane and transcendent orders has been seen by Karl Jaspers, Max Weber and others as the root of all the world-historical religions, of all theodicies.[17] Its importance lies in breaking down the original monism of the magic world view, the view of the world as an enchanted garden. By breaking down the mutual embedment of transcendent and mundane orders, world-historical or ethical religions posited a new conception of the social order as autonomous from, but in constant tension with, the cosmic (henceforth conceived of as the transcendent) order.[18] The tension between these orders and the attempt to overcome what has been termed the Axial chasm lay, according to Max Weber, at the core of all theodicies, and thus of all attempts of world-rationalization, and hence of verifiable, confidence-induced knowledge.[19]

The attempt to bridge this chasm, to achieve, in Weberian terms, salvation, had, moreover, profound implications for the representation of otherness within religious thought. Otherness was no longer represented as the otherness of demons, diverse deities, or wandering souls. That *Hinterwelt*, the "world behind the world" formerly given to magical coercion, was thenceforth projected outward beyond the world of daily affairs and events.[20] In this move, the otherness of enchanted nature took on transcendent properties. Within Western religious tradition, otherness was apotheosized in the logos of a personal creator-God. This was achieved primarily in the radical transcendence of the Jewish Yahweh.[21] Totally beyond and outside the cosmos, it was only over and against this transcendent being that the very historicity of human existence was defined.

As already noted and of crucial import is that the absolute, transcendent otherness of God became the primary referent for the sense of self. The individual exists primarily as an individual-in-relation-to God. Each individual is a unique entity "immediately responsible to God for the welfare of his soul and the well-being of his brother."[22] The valorization of the individual is through his "consecration to God."[23] It is, in Troeltsch's words, "only fellowship with God which gives value to the individual." As pointed out by Marcell Mauss, the notion of the person as a rational substance, individual and indivisible, owed its metaphysical foundation to Christianity.[24]

Equally significant is the fact that in Christian thought, the relations between individuals were based on a common fellowship in God. Union in the totally other defined not only the individual self, but also the community of fellows in God. As Troeltsch specifies: "individualism only becomes absolute through the ethical surrender of the individual to God, and being filled with God; on the other hand, in possession of the Absolute, individual differences merge into an unlimited love whose prototype is the Father-God Himself to whom souls are drawn and in whom they are united."[25] We may almost represent this new understanding of relations graphically as in the accompanying figure. What we witness then is a

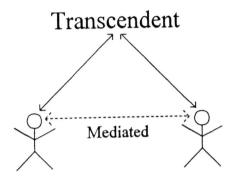

relationship whose very bonds were rooted in a set of meanings beyond the bonds themselves, no longer those of Aristotle's virtue but of the new terms of faith expressed by Augustine as: "*Amicitia numquam nisi in Christi Fidelis est.*"[26]

Thus, in the transcendent otherness of God and of *amore Dei*, people found not only their own individuality, but the very model for relations with the mundane other. Hellenistic Eros was remodeled along the lines of Christian Agape.[27] The love of God, *caritas*, defined the love of man, *cupidas*. Erotic love, as expressed and experienced in the mundane sphere, was reevaluated in terms of the transcendent, all-encompassing love of God—Agape.[28] Although different scholars posit alternative interpretations of the relation of Agape and Eros in Christian thought, all agree that with the emergence of the Christian notion of Agape, love's source was posited in the transcendent other.[29]

The great paradox of Western thought is, however, that the positing of an ineffable and unknowable other in transcendent and other-worldly terms eventually led to its very negation. This reached its apogee in the attempt of ascetic Protestantism to unite nature and grace, the world and the Church, and led to a radical reformulation of the dynamics of self and otherhood. The relative dissociation of this-worldly from other-worldly spheres that had characterized medieval Christendom was refuted. The attempt to remake nature in terms of grace and to restructure the world according to other-worldly postulates resulted in the eventual loss of transcendent otherhood. Whereas medieval Catholicism had mediated the tension between other-worldly and this-worldly spheres through the sacraments, the doctrine of works, and the mediatory figures of the Virgin Mary and the saints, the Reformation reinstated the tension between these orders in a radical manner.[30] The very saliency with which the tension between nature and grace, or this-worldly and other-worldly orders, was reinstated led to the equally forceful attempt to resolve or overcome this tension. One of the solutions adopted in this attempt was that uniquely inner-worldly asceticism characteristic of ascetic Protestant sects. Bringing the Church into the world, or rather, remaking the world in the image of the Church, took the form of a particular type of world mastery or rationalization: that is, of restructuring this-worldly mundane nature in terms of other-worldly and transcendent grace.[31] The dynamics of world rationalization through world mastery led not only to an ever-increasing differentiation in the orders of existence. It also eventually led to the loss of the transcendent referent itself.[32]

Ultimately, the introjection of grace within the individual believer and within the orders of mundane existence led to the loss of its transcendent locus. The *deus absconditus* of Calvinist religiosity increasingly lost all relevance to the world of man. As grace became secularized into such ideals as the romantic imagination and national virtue, otherness lost its transcendent properties.[33] Faith could no longer be supported by the armature of a transcendent God nor could it provide the nexus for interpersonal relations. What took its place was, in the broadest of terms, a search for trust. In fact, what I would like to claim is that the process of secularization and the replacement of godly by human attributes also implied the replacement of faith by trust (or rather, the search for faith with the search for trust). This process has become a central component of what we have come to call modernity. To return to our graphic metaphor, we may say that when the apex of the triangle is truncated, a new form of relations between selves must emerge, involving a direct relation between the individuals unmediated by the third relation common to both.

To some extent, the history of modern consciousness can thus be viewed as a continuing attempt to construct an alternative to that ultimate locus of faith once posited in the transcendent realm. In terms of the model we have been using, this constituted a search for some ideational nexus beyond the realm of (systemically defined) social relations which could, despite its mundane and hence socially circumscribed nature (circumscribed precisely by what we have been defining as role expectations), represent the totality of human experience, or what Turner has termed the "generic human bond."

One interesting example of this was during the age of exploration and discovery which brought with it not only an awareness of other lands, but also, more fundamentally, of other people. The debate in Valladolid, in 1550, between Las Casas and Sepulvida on the Indians of South America was precisely over the nature and extent of their otherness; or counterwise of their humanity and so compatibility with existing systems of social classification—in this case those of the Christian religion.[34] In a different vein, the "otherness" *Of Cannibals* provided Montaigne with the opportunity to evaluate his own society, torn by religious wars.[35] Indeed, as Edmund Leach has acutely argued, the positing of other peoples as apart (sometimes monstrously so) has consistently served as a mode of constituting and representing ourselves (as human beings).[36] However, notwithstanding the moral evaluation of the other—from Columbus's fantasies of tailed men to Clyde Kluckhohn's *Mirror for Man*—the selfhood of Western men and women has itself been constituted more often than not by its referent to the "savage" or oriental other.[37]

More to the point, the search for an alternative to faith which would represent and validate individual identity, and with it the play of social relations, took the form of a search within the individual for the locus of meaning-giving order. The introjection of this representative function to within the individual took many forms. In the psychological tradition, it is most accessible in Freud's very conception of the "timeless" unconscious, independent of reality and consciousness. In a similar manner, Jung posited the archetypes of the collective unconscious as a "collective, universal [system] identical in all individuals," independent of their existence yet constitutive of their being.[38] What unites these psychologies (and indeed sociologies) of modern consciousness is precisely the positing of a wholly (if not holy) other within the human psyche. Man's own psyche becomes the locus of the *Other*. This would seem to be the reality underlying Foucault's quip that "man is an invention of recent date."[39] Man became a problem for human knowledge only when, with the death of God, man became his own matrix.

The otherness of the soul and therefore of men and women to themselves was evinced in many literary pieces, such as Mary Shelley's *Frankenstein*, for example, in which internal otherness took the form of the *Doppelgänger*. In fact, the theme of the *Doppelgänger*, the double, was a favorite of nineteenth-century writers. E. T. A. Hoffman, Jean Paul, Oscar Wilde, Maupassant, Musset, Edgar Allen Poe, and Dostoyevsky all made use of it in a number of their works.[40] The double was often posited as a rival of the self. Sometimes, for example, as in James Hogg's *The Private Memoirs and Confessions of a Justified Sinner*, it was portrayed as the satanic epitome of evil. Most importantly, though, for our concern here, the double was an image of self—competing with it, but also, through articulating its darker side, constituting it in its entirety. In the words Poe put in the mouth of William Wilson's double: "In me didst thou exist—and in my death, see by this image, which is thine own, how utterly thou hast murdered thyself."[41] In the absence of God, man becomes his own double, constitutive (and sometimes, as was often the case in the *Doppelgänger* motif, destructive) of self. This was then the mirror image of that idea of friendship and of the valorization of self in the eyes of the other that defined the Scottish Enlightenment tradition (but then we are a good three generations later).

In his analysis of the *Doppelgänger* motif in literature, Otto Rank relates it to two themes: the fear of death and narcissistic self-love.[42] In terms of the first, it is thus part of our eternal (or rather modern) search for an entity that can replace the transcendent sphere through which the fear of death was resolved in traditional religious theodicies. In this sense, as an attempt to deal with and conquer the void left by the disappearance of God, it is one of the dominant themes of nineteenth-century literature.[43] In a world collapsing in on itself, men and women turned inward for structure. In Richard Wagner's words: "*Selbst dann / bin ich die Welt.*"[44] But as writers such as Baudelaire, Flaubert, and Mallarmé realized, this, ultimately, was insufficient; for in a void, "the shell of personal identity collapses, the yolk of individuality is split."[45] This immediately bears on the second theme: the difficulties of establishing human relations in a world devoid of a transcendent referent for otherness and so one that relies on what we have termed the replacement of faith by trust.

Both themes are essentially contained in the knowledge that grew in the eighteenth and nineteenth centuries, that the individual creates himself, that man was a "self creator."[46] Within the literary tradition, this was articulated as the individual's positing of himself as creator of otherhood. In the creator myths of Blake, Byron, Keats, and the Shelleys, a new cosmography was proffered. This cosmos was a human construct. In the words of Herder, "the artist is become a creator God."[47] The Romantics transposed the creative act from God to the human self. In their theories of Art, mimesis was rejected for the idea of art as imitative not of nature but of God, and thus as an expression of humanity's creative capacity. In the words of Novalis: "artistic creation is thus as much an end in itself as the divine creation of the universe, and one is as original and grounded on itself as the other."[48] Founded on the autonomy of the individual (which is another way of stating his lack of transcendent representation), the Romantic vision amply expressed the type of "immanent otherhood" analyzed above.

This selfsame dynamic was manifest in the existence of a type of human relationship which, together with the differentiation of roles—indeed, with the Romantics in protest to such differentiation—sought another form of association or relation, more "pure," more "pristine," more "whole." Again, in fact we are at the valorization of friendship which, as some have claimed, could reach its full potential only in light of the transformation (loss of transcendence and faith) we have been tracing. As M. J. Khan suggests:

> Through the presence of God man found for some three thousand years a unique instrument both of relating to himself and objectifying his own nature . . . crucial friendship with the other became exigent only when there was a gap left by the

absence of God's presence; and the first example is Montaigne's relation with La Boétie in the sixteenth century. It was not necessary for St. Augustine to involve himself in human relationship in order to write his *Confessions*. God was sufficient witness and object for him to achieve that end.[49]

Friendship then emerges as a realm where trust comes to replace faith as the new terms of unconditionality in modern societies at the same time as the search to represent the generic human bond of communitas is manifest not in the celebration of human sameness or identity, but in individual difference or otherness—with the individual here replacing the transcendent as the definitional matrix of what is other and unknowable. From this perspective we can now put in place another crucial building block of our understanding of trust, one that has been implicit all along but only now emerges in all its salience: the role of the individual or, rather, the very idea of the individual as a central focus of any understanding of trust as opposed to either faith (in the divine) or confidence (in system attributes). Without the idea of the individual as an entity—or even as a potentiality—existing outside or beyond role expectations, there can be no idea of a relationship between individuals that is not conditioned by the mutuality of systemically reinforcing role expectations.

We have seen this earlier when we contrasted the idea of trust to that of *fides*, and it is also immediately apparent when we contrast ideas of honor to those of conscience. The former rests on the reciprocity of a system of interlocking solidarities, the latter on the autonomy and moral agency of the individual. Honor is an attribute of personality contingent on external circumstances. This is as true for the contemporary Bedouin notion of 'ird, the traditional Arab idea of *nasab*, as for the European idea of *êre* (though the circumstances surrounding the loss or attainment of the one or the other are very different).[50] In each case one's own honor and so the nature of relations with one's fellows were defined by externally imputed role attributes (wife's fidelity, daughter's virginity, father's status position, and so forth). Not surprisingly, the European idea of honor underwent a transformation—to refer to internal aspects of the individual's character and personal qualities—in roughly the same period (though accounts are conflicting) and as part of the same dynamic of system differentiation and role proliferation that we have been analyzing.[51] In the words of Frank Stewart, one of the foremost contemporary students of the idea of honor:

> The pace at which the internal aspect of honor came to be emphasized no doubt varied considerably from one Western European country to another. When the process started in English is unclear; all we know for certain is that it was already underway in the sixteenth century. . . . [B]y the nineteenth century the internal

aspect of honor was prominent among speakers of all the major European lan-
guages. The change is probably just one small aspect of a great shift in sensibility
that took place after the Renaissance.[52]

Stewart quotes one scholar as saying that "the sense of personal integrity or
inner voice did not become widespread before the middle of the eighteenth
century."[53]

This "internalization" of honor as referring to individual attributes rather
than social status progressed together with the well-known development of
conscience as the internal focus of individual agency and consciousness.[54]
As scholars such as Weber, Groethuysen, Nelson, Dumont, and others have
shown, the Reformation of the sixteenth century played a crucial role in the
nascent idea of the individual as possessing conscience (and also agency
and intentionality)—a point with significant derivatives on the changing
ideas of law, morality, politics, and economic organization.[55] One scholar
has even shown just how the progress of the Reformation in England led to
the "moralization of politics" which undermined traditional ideas of the
role of honor in structuring political action.[56]

In extremely schematic form we may note that the ascetic Protestant
"obsession" with grace took, by the end of the seventeenth century, a very
particular form, best described as the "internalization of grace." In this "internalization" grace came gradually to be identified as conscience; while as
an idea this was perhaps inherent to early Christianity, it was only fully
developed throughout the seventeenth century in the soteriological doctrines of the different ascetic Protestant sects. It continued in the devotional
movements of the late seventeenth and early eighteenth centuries and in the
privatization of grace beyond the boundaries of any given community of
saints. Examples of this can be found in the "ethical inwardness" of the
Cambridge Platonists as well as in developments in late-seventeenth-
century New England, or among the French Jansenists or the Dutch Collegians.[57] The stress of the Cambridge Platonists on moral activity as partak-
ing of a "Universal Righteousness" and on the bifurcation of individual
identity by a reasoned virtue (which is "natural") and the vice of excessive
appetites marks just such a move toward the interiorization of Puritan beliefs among English Protestants of the Restoration period. Benjamin
Whichote's dictum that "Hell arises out of a Man's self: and Hell's Fewel
is the Guilt of a Man's Conscience" and that Heaven "lies in a refin'd
Temper, in an internal reconciliation to the Nature of God, and to the Rule
of Righteousness. So that both Hell and Heaven have their foundation
within Men" was a fundamental tenet in the thought of this circle.[58] It reso-
nates beyond the boundaries of England in a new appreciation of the internalization of grace, now transformed into conscience that points forward to

the ideas of those such as Lord Shaftesbury (who in fact published Whichote's sermons) and the moral basis of the civil society idea in the Scottish Enlightenment.[59] Ultimately these sets of ideas led to our more contemporary notions of the individual as possessing metaphysical and moral value.[60] As pointed out by Marcell Mauss:

> It is the Christians who have made a metaphysical entity of the "moral person" (personne morale), after they became aware of its religious power. Our own notion of the human person is still basically the Christian one . . . From a simple masquerade to the mask, from a "role" (personage) to a "person" (personne), to a name, to an individual; from the latter to a being possessing metaphysical and moral value; from a moral consciousness to a sacred being: from the latter to a fundamental form of thought and action—the course is accomplished.[61]

While one could debate with Mauss just how accomplished this course of development is, even (or especially) at the end of the twentieth century, it does serve to highlight the intimate connection between our ideas of the person and the attribution of conscience to such persons. As conscience comes to replace honor (and for that matter, as guilt comes to take the place of shame), the focus of moral agency is relocated to the individual and separated from the externalities of role and status.[62] To restate this point in Peter Berger's terms:

> The concept of honor implies that identity is essentially, or at least importantly, linked to institutional roles. The modern concept of dignity, by contrast, implies that identity is essentially independent of institutional roles. [Thus] in a world of honor, the individual discovers his true identity in his roles, and to turn away from the roles is to turn away from himself. . . . In a world of dignity, the individual can only discover his true identity by emancipating himself from his socially imposed roles—the latter are only masks, entangling him in illusion, "alienation," and "bad faith."[63]

It is precisely this move which makes of trust an issue in human relations with modern (or even early modern) societies. That is to say, the transformation of the terms of confidence from those based on group affiliations (and so encompassed by some ideology of honor) to contracts between individual selves—as the self becomes the locus of moral order—engenders both the possibility of trust and perhaps also its growing necessity as whole arenas of human interaction can no longer be encompassed by externally attributable patterns of behavior (i.e., by role expectations).

When presented as an ideal form of human interaction this type of relationship went under the rubric of friendship. Yet, as we have argued, it also emerged, *in minora*, as a potential, in myriad other forms of relations due to such purely structural aspects of role behavior as the increasing contradictions between roles and role-sets held by individual incumbents. The greater the number of roles, the greater the potential conflicts and inconsistencies between them, hence the greater degree of negotiability necessary to their fulfillment. And hence too the greater the necessity of partners in an interaction to "trust" in something beyond systemically standardized definitions of role behavior for the interaction to continue and develop—a trust that had to be based on some idea of conscience and no longer on behavior tied to status attributes (of honor, loyalty, and so on). This trust (as a form of "faith") is thus placed in something beyond the role, something irreducible to the role's fulfillment. It is moreover placed in something unconditional (not that the trust is unconditional, but that in which one places one's trust is unconditioned by normative role expectations). Not only is this object of trust placed beyond the conditionalities of role performance, it is also unconditioned by any idea of a generic identity between the interlocutors (as was the case, as we saw above, with communitas). It is, in fact, predicated on their fundamental difference, a difference that makes the will, intentions, and calculations of the one opaque to the other (if not, we would be dealing not with trust but with some form of confidence in mutually reinforcing expectations). Crucially, and as we have seen, this fundamental imperviousness of one to the will of the other becomes, with the breakdown of traditional categories, a relation between individuals in society and not (or not only) between man and God. It becomes, in Buber's nomenclature, constitutive of the I-Thou relationship (which for him is seen to mirror the relationship between man and God) and rests, as we have seen, on the emergent idea of the individual as imbued with moral agency and value.

Trust, then, which emerges as a function of negotiation (between and within social roles), is also predicated on human agency. Without the idea of agency, any notion of negotiation would itself be severely limited. Role complexity, which brings in its wake negotiation of role behavior, also extends the workings of agency into qualitatively new domains. For trust to emerge as a potential form of human interaction, it is thus not sufficient to posit solely the existence of system limits (limits of existing role definitions of whatever nature, some of which have been discussed above). We must add to this the idea of the individual as a source of agency who, in fact, emerges as a locus of moral value in the same period that the idea of trust begins to take on its very modern characteristics. As an example of this we may think of presacramental marriage. Prior to the Fourth Lateran Council, marriage roles were poorly defined with great room for "negotiation." Yet this "negotiation" of spousal relations tended, often, to be a rather violent business and not one lightly to be identified with the workings of trust.[64] Indeed, the "informal" (i.e., extra-systemic) nature of marital behavior continued well into the late medieval period.[65] This in itself did not make for trusting relations between the parties concerned. The myriad studies of marriage patterns in Western Europe have left historians with the rather strong argument that companion marriage, or marriage based on love relations (which we can assume for our purposes to include a strong element of trust), was a product of a much later time, in fact of societies and cultures privileging individuals and the valuation of individual selves. Romantic love as the basis for marriage developed together with the growth of individualism, market mentalities, and high social mobility (thus too with role differentiation). And while there continues a great debate among historians as to the periodization of these changes—with historians such as Shorter, Stone, Aries, and Flandrin placing these developments in the eighteenth century and more contemporary historians placing these developments a good two to three centuries earlier—any understanding of the development of love relations in marriage remains, as Alan Macfarlane has argued, inherently bound up with the development of a culture of individualism and of societies in which formal kinship networks are relatively weak.[66] Here too we see the two elements of trust working in tandem: the possibility of negotiating role expectations, together with the existence of individual selves as the locus of such negotiation.

If the existence of system limits (in the relatively circumscribed definition of marriage as a set of reciprocal role relations) is a necessary condition for the emergence of trust (in this context, of love relations in marriage), it is not a sufficient condition. It must be supplemented by the additional variable of individual identities, which, as we have seen, were actually a central component in the emergent practice of marriage as a love relationship.[67] Having established this, we need to define just what type of individualism and of self we are referring to when discussing the emergence of trust; for if defined simply as agency or intentionality we would be on shaky ground indeed. Recall in this context our earlier examples of Antigone as caught between conflicting role expectations and thus as an illustration of both the existence of system limits (through the very existence of these conflictual demands) and the projection of agency and intentionality in her decision to privilege one type of decision over the other. Both conditions, of negotiation and individual agency, thus seem to have been met and yet we are still a long way from a world defined by trust—at least in the terms that we have been advancing throughout this essay. Does this then put our assumptions in doubt? As Bernard Williams has convincingly argued, the ability (agency, really) to choose between different courses of action, including between those incumbent on different role-sets (burying one's brother or remaining loyal to one's uncle the king), was already an aspect of Greek thought and praxis.[68] Our notion of agency in connection to the idea of trust must thus be honed down and specified.

What, after all, is the difference between Antigone and our modern corporate lawyer who is also a wife, mother, colleague's lover, coach of her daughter's soccer team, patient daughter herself, PTA member, and registered Republican? When placed in these terms the difference becomes clear. Antigone, by choosing one course of action over another (through the expression of agency and intentionality), becomes fully identified with one role or another. Our modern supermom by contrast, remains somehow apart from all social roles. The different commitments and responsibilities to her different role-sets which pull her in different directions and force her to prioritize her time and commitments do not thereby encompass her self (recall here Musil's tenth characteristic). She is reducible to none of her roles—spousal, political, occupational, erotic, or recreational. If she is reducible to anything it is to the bundle of options, the choices that she continually makes, the actions of will rather than their result, the act of choosing rather than the choice. (This is precisely the difference from traditional categories of self, where even when intentionality was acknowledged, it was the choice that defined the self rather than the act of choosing and so what makes of Antigone or Orestes or Prometheus tragic heroes.) When we say that we trust her (as opposed to having confidence in her legal prowess, political astuteness, knowledge of girl's football, and so on), we are referring not to any particular aspect of her role incumbency (in which we may or may not place confidence; for instance, knowing of her extra-marital affair, I may feel more or less than confident in her fulfillment of her spousal obligations) but to the decision-making agent herself, an agent that remains irreducible to any particular decision or set of decisions. The extent to which I *cease* to trust her is the extent to which I identify her totally with one or another of her role incumbencies and see her as subsuming all other commitments to the fulfillment of that one role. This is indeed congruent with the insights of Peter Berger on modern role fulfillment and its relation to personal identity, a relation wherein the later redefines itself

> apart from and often against the institutional roles through which the individual expresses himself in society. . . . [Thus] the reciprocity between individual and society, between subjective identity and objective identification through roles, now comes to be experienced as a sort of struggle. Institutions cease to be the "home" of the self; instead they become oppressive realities that distort and estrange the self. Roles no longer actualize the self, but serve as a "veil of maya" hiding the self not only from others, but from the individual's own consciousness. Only in the interstitial areas left vacant, as it were, by the institutions (such as the so-called private sphere of social life) can the individual hope to discover or define himself."[69]

They do so, we might add, through the actualization of agency beyond the formal constraints of role fulfillment.

This aspect of agency as locus of self not only differentiates our modern lives from those of classical Greece, but also defines the emergence of modernity as a civilizational project:[70] when it is less the social role that individuals conform to and more the simple ability (in fact, necessity) to move between them and to negotiate their boundaries that defines our sense of selves—and so also the necessity to build trust into the relations between role incumbents. This very movement was in fact at the heart of that "sociability" which defined eighteenth-century public culture and played such a great role in the analysis of Habermas and his imitators on the development of a "public realm" (*qua* realm of sociability and, *pace* the Scottish moralists, of trust) in eighteenth-century culture. It was this that was represented in the new bonds of civil society. The rise of new forms of mediating institutions—neighborhood associations, guild and craft confraternities, vocational, kinship, and youth organizations, clubs of every size and devoted to every purpose (and in which, according to one contemporary observer, more than 20,000 Londoners met every night)—was predicated on the ability to move between, to negotiate and identify with more than one set of role identities and status positions.[71] This proclivity was deemed by Diderot to be a uniquely French attribute, and while we would do well to temper the comparative aspect of the following quote, it does go a long way to ward describing the newly emerging types of social interaction that characterized this century's vaunted sociability.

> A Frenchman swarms about in his own town more than ten Englishmen, fifty Dutchmen, or a hundred Moslems do in theirs. The same man in the same day will be at court, in the center of town, in the countryside, at an academy, a salon, a banker's, a notary's, a barrister's, a solicitor's, a great seigneur's, a merchant's, a workman's, at church, at the theater, and with the call girls. Everywhere he is equally free and familiar.[72]

In this catalogue of interactions we thus see the greater differentiation of roles and role-sets that came to characterize life in the eighteenth century as well as the growing potential for role conflict between different role-set members and such other aspects of system limit as the potential (if not the necessity) to keep certain aspects of role more or less visible to role-set members in different social contexts.

Here is not the place to make yet another argument for the sociability of eighteenth-century culture. We may assume that the basic parameters of that argument are well enough known. We wish only to stress the fact that their "sociability" rested on the process, noted above of *(a)* role differentiation (and its concomitant derivative of potential role conflict); *(b)* the consequent need to negotiate role identities; *(c)* the continual assertion of agency and intentionality in negotiating the boundaries and content of these different roles; and, hence *(d)* the development of individual identity through these continual quotidian acts of negotiation, what amounted to choosing social and, by implication, at least sometimes, moral identities.

While we have distinguished analytically between these different aspects of modern social identity, they are really of a set, all different aspects of the same process and one which provided the foundation for the developing idea of trust or even for the realization that it was in some sense a fundamental problem.

Thus we have come to see that it is not the space between roles per se which leads to either individualism or to trusting as a form of social relations (that space, as negotiability existed also in premodern social formations but did not engender either individualism or trust). Rather, the emergence of individualism in our sense of moral and agentic selves rests on the ability to move between roles and role expectations, and trust emerges precisely from such movement or rather from its very potential. (The connection of this movement between roles and the rise of individualism will be developed in the next section.) Thus, simply undefined spaces between role expectations (as, for example, in presacramental marriage) do not in themselves engender individual identities—or trust. These can emerge only with the agency and reflexivity that is incumbent on the ability to move between roles.

Some awareness of this connection between high levels of role segmentation and the development of individualism has been noted by the late Rose Laub Coser. She notes how, "as role expectations are more diffuse, and as attitudes (in contrast to behavior only) are the basis for their allocation and judgement, more decisions are left to the individual. . . . Individualism thrives under conditions of role-set complexity because such conditions make it possible for individuals to decide whether or not to involve their internal dispositions when they try to conform to the demands of some role partners."[73] An earlier and decidedly presociological appreciation of this distinction can be found in Montaigne's dictum that

[m]ost of our business is farce. . . . We must play our part properly, but withal as the part of a borrowed personage; we must not make real essence of a mask and outward appearance; nor of a strange person, our own; we cannot distinguish the skin from the shirt: 'tis enough to meal the face, without mealing the breast. I see some who transform and transubstantiate themselves into as many new shapes and new beings as they undertake new employments; and who strut and fume even to the heart and liver, and carry their stake along with them even to the close-stool: I cannot make them distinguish the salutations made to themselves from those made to their commission, their train, or their mule. . . . The mayor of Bordeaux and Montaigne have ever been two by very manifest separation.[74]

In this context and bearing in mind the importance of Montaigne in the development of the idea of friendship, the value of the private, and the idea of personhood, we may find support for the foregoing argument in the different meaning of the private in premodern and modern societies. In all societies there is an idea of the private (one that exists beyond system-defined roles), but in premodern cultures it has either a negative or neutral value while in modernity it is positively valued. As noted by Max Weber:

> Precisely the ultimate and most sublime values have retreated from public life either into the transcendental realm of mystical life or into the brotherliness of direct and personal human relations. It is not accidental that our greatest art is intimate and not monumental, nor is it accidental that today only within the smallest and intimate circles, in personal human situations, in pianissimo, that something is pulsating that corresponds to the prophetic pneuma, which in former times, swept through the great communities like a firebrand, welding them together.[75]

This form of representing social life stands in stark contrast to other forms of social organization where the private realm, when existent, was defined solely in negative terms of either that which was not public, or often, that which was secret, hidden from public view. Here the paradigmatic statement on this relation between public and private was offered by Hannah Arendt in terms of the meaning of the private (the *oikia*) in classical thought.[76] Similarly, work carried out by anthropologists in tribal and relatively undifferentiated societies points to the strong correspondence of private with that which is hidden or secret (often shameful) in those societies.[77] We will have more to say on this distinction of modern consciousness and society from premodern social forms in later chapters. Here it is sufficient to note but one point: the ingredient that moves the private realm from a negative (or neutral) to a positive valuation is the idea of the individual as source of value. It is this individual (around whom trust can be built) that lends the private realm a positive value—as the case of Montaigne and La Boétie makes clear.

The connection of trust and the value of the private realm as resting on the idea of the individual (him/herself developing out of the increased negotiation plus the workings of agency) that modern capitalist society engendered can be found in the writings of the Scottish moralists. We know from Alan Silver that for them the private realm of friendship was posited as an ideal. We also know (from Hutcheson, Shaftesbury, Ferguson, and others) that society was held together by "natural sympathy," "moral affections," innate sociability, and so on. All this "stuff," all of these moral attributes are really forms of trust which emerge only in "polished society," which for these writers is nothing but ones with increased levels of social differentiation. For the writers of the Scottish Enlightenment it is precisely this process of social differentiation (with, as we know, its exponential increase in roles and, as we have argued, potential conflicts between them) that permits the emergence of this new form of sociability. And while the Scottish moralists did not distinguish between trust and confidence, or between different aspects of role incumbency or their potential conflicts, I believe that the distinction they posited between rational calculation of interests and the needs of "sympathy and approbation" (for Adam Smith) or "vanity" (for Adam Ferguson) do point to precisely this type of distinction. In fact, moral sentiment by which "men are united by instinct, that they act in society from affections of kindness and friendship" was, for the thinkers of the Scottish Enlightenment, an axiomatic property of human mind (though our reading of such feeling is as a relatively modern phenomenon).[78] On the epistemological level it was an attempt to ground human existence in an intimately human propensity of innate mutuality. This takes the form, for example, with Adam Smith, in *The Theory of Moral Sentiments*, which argues that the moral basis of individual existence is the need for recognition and consideration on the part of others. "To be observed, to be attended to, to be taken notice of with sympathy, complacency, and approbation" are for Smith the driving force of "all the toil and bustle of the world . . . the end of avarice and ambition, of the pursuit of wealth."[79] Thus, as is tellingly pointed out by A. O. Hirschman, economic activity itself is rooted, in *The Theory of Moral Sentiments*, in the noneconomic needs for sympathy and appreciation.[80] Human interest in "being the object of attention and approbation" is for Smith what leads to the complex of activity that defines economic activity (and to that type of rational calculation that I am identifying with assessable role behavior).[81]

This stress on mutuality and recognition runs through all the writings of the Scottish Enlightenment on civil society, and thoughts similar to those quoted above can be found in Adam Ferguson's assertion that

> [t]he mighty advantages of property and fortune, when stripped of the recommendations they derive from vanity, or the more serious regards to independence and power, only mean a provision that is made for animal enjoyment; and if our solicitude on this subject were removed, not only the toils of the mechanic, but the studies of the learned, would cease; every department of public business would become unnecessary, every senate-house would be shut up and every palace deserted.[82]

Vanity here is central and plays the same role as Smith's "attention and approbation." It builds on the social nature of our existence and on our very self-identity in and through the eyes of others. Both concepts posit a type of relation beyond the calculable aspects of public roles (in the market, counting-house, or government office) as the basis of both sociability and, indeed, of self.

If all this holds together, then I believe we have found a way both to explain the emergence of trusting relations as a modern ideal form of social interaction and to understand its specificity, especially when contrasted to such similar ideas as faith or confidence. While we have concentrated on but one aspect of trust's emergence, that connected to role negotiation, we have only begun to chart its connection to the second necessary idea, that of human agency upon which such negotiation rests. Since this idea of agency plays a crucial role in the new terms of sociability characterizing the modern era—and so too with the move from "pristine" to generalized trust—further development of this theme is now called for.

Civility, Strong Evaluations, and the
Problem of Familiarity

It is perhaps best to approach this developing concept of the agentic self (and its role in the constitution of trust) through what may be best termed the "interactionist" perspective of the Scottish moralists quoted above. Their ideas of "vanity," "sympathy and approbation," and so on express a model of self predicated on other's perception of us (a sort of Meadian social self *avant la lettre*). This perspective was not based on status attributes or simple role performance (of either ascribed or achieved characteristics) but on the needs for "sympathy, complacency, and approbation," that is, on a recognition of self that, whatever its communalities with that generic human bond noted by Turner in ritualized communitas, does not seem to rest on an idea of fundamental identity or sameness. (This becomes especially clear in Adam Smith's idea of the "impartial observer," which will be taken up in a later chapter.) The act of recognition, is essentially a recognition of self which exists also beyond the role (Musil's tenth character yet again) and is for the Scots not only the basis of kindness and friendship, but indeed, of an element of all social interaction—infusing public roles no less than private selves.

It is, moreover, or so I would like to argue, a fundamental component of the developing modern idea of trust. Trust that emerges with the opacity of the other's will (and so with the development of some idea of personhood that is beyond role incumbency) implies beyond anything else a fundamental recognition of that other personhood irreducible to roles. We have already established that it is precisely this idea of the person as standing somewhere beyond his or her social role that defines modern ideas of self and trust. These ideas, I venture to say, involve the recognition of this aspect of alter's existence.

Trust then is a recognition of alter's agency, an agency which, we recall, only appears when the "fit" between the person and the role is loose, when the role does not—indeed cannot—circumscribe all of alter's possible behavior. This is the meaning of that freedom of the other that Luhmann refers to in explaining the emergence of trust. The freedom involved is not an ontological condition of existence but a socially determined and structured aspect of personality which—for reasons worked out above—develops most saliently (if not uniquely) in modern social formations with their increased division of labor and system differentiation. For we do not have to "trust" in other's agency until that agency becomes a realizable potential. When most aspects of alter's behavior can be convincingly explained (and planned for) in terms of their role incumbency, trust is not called for, confidence in systemically defined normative patterns is sufficient. It is only when aspects of alter's behavior (or intentions) cannot be so accounted for that trust emerges systemically as an aspect of social organization. Thus, as noted by Peter Johnson, "To speak then of the origins of trust is to describe the variety of ways in which agents become conscious of the freedom of others."[83]

Trust and mistrust thus develop in response to agency, as different responses to aspects of behavior that can no longer be adequately encompassed within the matrix of normatively defined role expectations. As an illuminating aside we may note with Pollack and Maitland that the legal concept of agency (not as an aspect of personal intentionality but as a deputy, as in the king's agent) "is hardly to be distinguished from the germ of another institution . . . the 'use, trust or confidence.' "[84] Thus, even in the strictly circumscribed use of this term in the sense of ownership and possession of property we see how ideas of trust are inexorably bound up with the terms of agency (a point to which we shall have to return in our section on generalized exchange).

It is only when agency can come to play a major role, when it emerges as a potential for shaping the nature of interaction, that trust must also come to play a part in defining interpersonal relations. This is the connection made earlier by Luhmann between trust and risk. Trust is not only a means of negotiating risk, it implies risk (by definition, if it is a means of negotiating that which is unknown). The risk implied is precisely that which is inherent in alter's realization of agency: were all action circumscribed by role expectations and normative definitions there would be no risk, only confidence or lack thereof. Trust, by contrast, implies the risk that is incurred when we cannot expect a return or reciprocal action on alter's part (which we could, at least within certain boundaries, when interaction is defined solely by the reciprocally defined nature of role obligations and commitments). In Luhmann's terms, "trust cannot be demanded, only offered and accepted." What it is that cannot be demanded but only offered must then be something existing beyond role expectations. (The latter can be "demanded"; i.e., students may demand certain behavior—or at least a certain range of behavior—from teachers, commuters from bus drivers, storekeepers from customers, and so on. Note: behind the demand lies the possibility of sanctions, formal or informal.) It would seem that this something is connected to that aspect of personal identity not so circumscribed by roles, which is tied to a recognition of alter's agency.

To illustrate this connection between risk, agency, and trust, I suggest thinking through an example most probably familiar to many university professors and students: the use of foul language by a professor in the classroom. What is involved in such an action? For one, the professor is clearly stepping outside of role expectations and engaging in (verbal) behavior not generally thought to be part of his or her role. By doing so the professor is incurring a risk (at present that she may be charged with sexual harassment and at an earlier time, of the moral opprobrium of his colleagues if and when word of this behavior got out). In doing so, the professor sets up the possibility of interaction with students that is not (or not only) defined by system expectations. By taking the risk of stepping beyond systemically defined role expectations, the professor also opens the possibility of establishing a relation which includes some element of trust and not solely of confidence. I am far from claiming that confidence is replaced by trust (at least not in today's college environment) but only that an element of trust may enter into a relationship defined hitherto by the rules of role expectations and so of confidence. Stepping out of "role" thus involves risk-taking, which will be met by either trust or mistrust, which are indeed the only possible responses to behavior that cannot be encoded within the existing prescriptive formula of role definitions.

So much has this become an aspect of modern social life that a whole set of injunctions has arisen which formally acknowledge this agency while circumscribing its manifestations: the rules of etiquette and civility. What, after all, is the difference between asking someone to "Please pass the salt" as opposed to the demand of "Give me the salt"? When asking and prefacing our request with "please" we are, however formally, acknowledging the possibility of the other to refuse. We are, in a sense, recognizing the other's agency and in so doing recognizing the other's selfhood. Any parent who has struggled to teach her or his child manners can attest to just how important that recognition of selfhood is to their relationship (in this case the child's recognition of the parent as a distinct entity and not solely a function of its own interminable needs). Anyone who has been through that stage of child rearing knows just how important a request prefaced by a "please" (even an unmeaningful one) is. How easy it is to acquiesce to demands so phrased and how one's back goes up when demands are put in the perennial "gimme" form.

We have internalized this type of speech over such a long period of time that we have become blind to its essential meaning, which is clear as soon as we take time to think about it. Bracketing a request with the terms "please" and "thank you" is a recognition (however formal and stylized) of the contingent nature of that request's fulfillment, making of even the smallest of matters a sort of symbolic gift. In so doing, it recognizes the fact that alter could have refused our request, was not in any way mandated to carry out our request, and did so "of his own free will," as it were. Recognizing choice, we thus recognize agency and in so doing, in essence, recognize the selfhood of our interlocutor. In some sense it may be claimed that the codes of etiquette are a democratization of deference; deference once restricted to those above us in the social hierarchy is transformed into an aspect of all (or almost all) interaction as mutual recognition becomes an aspect of modern social formations: those same social formations, we recall from the beginning of this section, which place the individual at the center of the conception of moral agency and around whom the terms of trust are orientated.

The rules of etiquette and politeness are different in different cultures, reflecting the type of self and nature of social relations privileged in different contexts. Thus, for example, Arjun Appadurai has shown how, among the Tamil in South India, one should refrain from too profuse a use of "thank you" as it implies a termination of the relationship. "The reluctance of benefactors to be directly thanked for their generosity is, in part, rooted in the pervasive feeling that every act of generosity is built on some other one and that the direct expression of thanks, in suggesting a terminal source of generosity, is dangerously misleading and must therefore be carefully hedged."[85] Here the codes of politeness are such that what is expected is a recognition of ongoing networks of exchange and reciprocity rather than of individual agents and of the monadic self who remains autonomous of the interaction.[86]

This democratization of deference is a salient element of that civilizing process as analyzed by Norbert Elias, as the concept of *courtoisie* is replaced in the early eighteenth century with the term *civilité*, only to be replaced, in turn, by the end of the century with the term *politesse*.[87] Thus the embourgeoisement of courtly culture becomes the basis for modern ideas of civility and codes of mutual recognition. In Elias's terms, that inhibition of drives which stood behind the history of manners is another form of the recognition of the other through what may perhaps be termed the circumscription of self. The whole set of developing manners charted by Elias pertaining to the use of separate utensils by different people at table, prohibitions against putting food once bitten back in the common dish, against spitting on (later at) the common table, blowing one's nose in hand or sleeve, and so on, are all no more than developing forms of behavior based on the recognition of the other. The growth of inhibition parallels a growing appreciation of a distinction between behavior relegated to the private and that permitted in the public realm. Thus the growing perception of a private realm also carries with it an idea of individual selves whose mutual acts of recognition are recorded in the progress of manners and the growing culture of civility.

In the above discussion I am not arguing that civility and trust are analogous concepts, but I do wish to stress the strong connection between the growth of civility and the growing potential for trust to play a role in the formation of social relationships. Trust and civility are far from identical social phenomena. Both, however, develop in similar circumstances, sometimes in the same historical period, and share a common referent. Both recognize individuals and individual agency. While the rules of civility seek to limit this agency (if through its very recognition) and to distinguish the realms of individual (private) behavior from those of public manners, trust emerges only within and through a more positive recognition of the workings of agency. The slow progress of the rules of civility and of the civilizing process, *pace* Elias, are thus the gradual establishment of new role expectations that develop concomitantly with the development of new public roles. It is therefore not surprising that these rules were, among the bourgeois, most developed in France where the middle classes of the late eighteenth century played a much greater public role than they did in Germany (which is Elias's point of comparison). In his own words:

> whereas the middle classes already play a political role in France at this time [18th century], in Germany they did not. In Germany the intellectual stratum is confined to the realm of mind and ideas; in France, along with all the other human questions, social, economic, administrative and political issues come within the range of interests of the courtly/middle-class intelligentsia.[88]

(Hence the difference, as Elias notes, between the ideas of *Kultur* and *Zivilisation* in the German usage as opposed to the concept of *civilisation* in French.) In the merging of aristocratic and bourgeois society that characterized France in the eighteenth century new public roles were developed among the bourgeois whose codes of behavior came to be defined by the rules of *civilité*. The history of the civilizing process is in other words, the history of the development of new status attributes and role expectations together with the development of new (bourgeois) public roles. Inherent to these new roles (or more properly to the different types of behavior expectations that went with them) was a recognition of precisely that lability and negotiability in role performance that necessitated the codes of civility and manners. And if the history of manners is the growth of new role expectations, the history of trust, predicated on the selfsame recognition of agency (in the structurally determined limits on role fulfillment), is its mirror image. The same structural changes are at the root of both developments: system differentiation and development of new complex roles and role-sets, and so increased conflict between them, leading to greater instances of structurally determined limits on system confidence and hence on its insufficiency for interaction to take place. The one in essence re-corded the development of new roles and redefinition of existing ones, the other, an emergent potential for interaction that could not be defined by either. They are in a sense opposites and the relation between them does seem, intuitively, to be of a reverse nature: i.e., the less trust the more careful we are (even today) of maintaining the codes of civility and its mannerisms; the more trust, the more relaxed our observance of these ritu-alized behavior patterns. Certainly my manners at home with the family, in private, are very different from when there are guests and different once again when I dine at the Spanish Embassy in Caracas. Yet they emerge together, reflecting the same social transformation, and are rooted in the same recognition of human agency—the one as an aspect of the newly developed public roles and the other of that lability of behavior that was invested in them.

Thus far we have viewed trust as emerging with the "freedom" of the other to move between social roles or even in the more limited ability to highlight (or hide), to privilege, or to subsume some aspects of their social roles over others. We have argued that the more roles one assumes the greater the potential (indeed often the necessity) for this type of behavior as the more conflicts between expected role behavior in one's role-set become manifest. These conflicts represent a form of system limit (leading to a limit on the extent of confidence one can have in its workings). Moreover, we have sought to argue that while this type of limit on the workings of a classification system no doubt exists in all social formations, its workings are heightened with the increased division of labor (leading to growth in complex roles and the process of role segmentation) that defines modern social systems. Hence the specificity of trust to modernity, as a solution to the problem of "freedom" or, as we have termed it throughout, to the devel-oping agency of the other and the privileging of individual selves which defines the modern social order.

Through this line of reasoning we have come to recognize the inherent connection between the developing ideas of trust and those of the individ-ual which progressed together (and for much the same reasons). Hitherto we have limited our understanding of the individual to the workings of intentionality or agency in the fulfillment of social roles. By all accounts this is an insufficient view of agency (and so also of the individual). As Harry Frankfurt has noted, the simple ability to make choices (i.e., realize agency) is not the unique province of the human species.[89] Rather, as we know from the writings of Charles Taylor, it is the ability to qualitatively evaluate our desires that defines human action and agency. Our individual-ity is thus not only an aspect of the reflexivity inherent in our having what Frankfurt called *second order desires* (i.e., our ability to evaluate our de-sires and privilege one over the other). Rather, for Taylor, the fact that this evaluation can itself be divided into strong and weak evaluations is the essential component of human agency. The distinction between the two types of evaluations he describes as follows:

> In weak evaluation, for something to be judged good it is sufficient that it be desired, whereas in strong evaluation there is also a use of "good" or some other evaluative term for which being desired is not sufficient; indeed some desires or desired consummations can be judged as bad, base, ignoble, trivial, superficial, unworthy, and so on. It follows from this that when in weak evaluation one desired alternative is set aside, it is only on grounds of its contingent incompatibility with a more desired alternative. I go to lunch later, although hungry now, because then I shall be able to lunch and swim. But I should be happy to have the best of both worlds: if the pool were open now, I could assuage my immediate hunger as well as enjoying a swim at lunch time. But with strong evaluation this is not necessarily the case. Some desired consummation may be eschewed not because it is incompatible with another, or if because of incompatibility this will not be contingent. Thus I refrain from committing some cowardly act, although very tempted to do so, but this is not because this act at this moment would make any other desired act impossible, as lunching now would make swimming impossible, but rather because it is base.[90]

Strong evaluation thus takes us beyond utilitarian calculations and into a realm of "qualitative constraints." For the strong evaluator

> the desirable is not only defined for him by what he desires . . . it is also defined by a qualitative characterization of desires as higher and lower, noble and base and so on. Reflection is not just a matter . . . of registering the conclusion that alternative A is more attractive to me, or draws me more than B. Rather the higher desirability of A over B is something I can articulate if I am reflecting as a strong evaluator. I have a vocabulary of worth.[91]

As can perhaps be adduced, the plot here begins to thicken. For the immediate question must be regarding the sources of this "vocabulary of worth." From where do we, in Taylor's reading, draw our qualitative categories upon which our strong evaluations are made? The answer is always from our social milieu which provides us with standards of moral worth, with our ideas of moral revulsion and approbation—in fact with that moral grid upon which we make our strong evaluations.

This being the case we (though not Taylor) would seem to have a problem. For on the one hand, we have defined trust as a recognition of alter's freedom and agency. On the other hand, we have just defined agency as including the aspect of strong evaluation, which itself rests on one's embedment within a shared social vocabulary of moral worth. Agency itself has thus been defined as the ability to weigh alternative modes of action according to a scale of values that is always inherently social. If we hold with Taylor's definition of self—as many do—trust becomes nothing more than trusting in alter's strong evaluations: reducible perhaps to neither confidence nor faith, but quite possibly to familiarity.[92] Familiarity (what I will call stickball) can be most readily understood as shared strong evaluations: because like me, Fred played stickball on East 13th Street in Brooklyn, I may assume that we share certain moral codes—about the importance of neighborhood, fair play, male competitiveness, the joy of a good workout, or whatever. In fact, this is a "game" that we play all the time. In certain situations (deciding whom to sit next to on a train or bus) we make assessments of people based on their clothing, behavior, general demeanor, that lead us to sit by the side of one rather than the other. We do so by "telling stories" to ourselves about stickball. We build, as it were, an imaginary identity for that person based on an imputed familiarity: he is the kind of person who looks like he played stickball as a youth, as opposed to one who looks like he ran numbers for the mob; thus we probably share strong evaluations, thus it makes sense to "trust" him (at least in this relatively unthreatening situation of sharing a subway seat, or more probably, at least to trust him more than that less familiar-looking character at the other end of the car).

If this is indeed the case (and we have only developed one minor variant of the relation of trust to familiarity), then we seem to have a serious problem with our prior argument which tied trust to the freedom, agency, and hence, fundamental inscrutability of the other. For, if agency is itself predicated on a shared moral code, it can never be wholly opaque and unknowable (though of course not all moral codes are shared by all societies, but this is another matter, one that we will in fact get back to).

The dilemma is not insurmountable and its explication will lead us back (eventually) to Durkheim and the idea of the individual as standing at the foundations of modern ideas of trust (qua precontractual) that we noted at the beginning of our inquiry. Trust, we recall, is predicated on risk; with Luhmann, it is a way of negotiating risk, and the paradigm case of this risk is the unalterable freedom of the other, a freedom that if it is to have any meaning at all points to those potentialities of behavior unconditioned by the social role. This element of unconditionality is, as we have seen, at the core of trust and quite different from the actions of strong evaluation which are, by their very definition, conditioned by the social mores, norms, and meanings upon which we build our evaluations. Familiarity or the assumed communality of strong evaluations is, in this sense, analogous to Turner's communitas, to the establishment (real, or often, fictitious) of that generic human bond rooted not in difference, but in sameness or identity. Trust, by contrast, recognizes difference including the different possible bases for alter's strong evaluations and "trusts" that these will limit alter's freedom, channeling the use of other's agency in ways not inimicable to our own interests or desires.

Here we begin to see why trust is so fragile and in its fully realized state so rare a phenomenon. For most acts of exchange that we engage in (symbolic and material both) can be more than adequately accounted for or managed through a system of shared role expectations which define the nature, rule, and content of the exchange. Where these expectations (and so confidence in the shared system of role expectations) are not sufficient, we often fall back to some assumed or imputed familiarity, an assumed sharing of strong evaluations in order to maintain the interaction—to provide the basis for confidence. This insight has been validated in the empirical work of Kahneman and Tversky, who have examined the ways social actors deal with uncertainty and ambivalence in different social situations.[93] Their findings point to a "strong tendency for ambiguous or incomplete information to be interpreted in line with the individual's preconceptions."[94] These preconceptions are most often based on assumed familiarity (or lack thereof) and thus, ultimately, on ideas of shared or divergent strong evaluations. Where familiarity (real or assumed) is sufficient (and it often is), we are spared from taking the next step into trust. Rather we can make do by "translating" our idea of shared strong evaluation directly into role expectations, parsing them out, as it were, into the more precise language of roles and the reciprocity of role fulfillment: because he looks like someone who played stickball, I will assume that he did and thus that he knows the value of teamwork, and mutuality, and so I won't overly suspect him of looking out only for himself but rather of pursuing his own interests within the boundaries of the "rules of the game"—these being those role-sets we happen to be in. But trust approaches the agency of the other in a different manner and does not assume its circumscription by role fulfillment or by ideas of shared community, that is, of familiarity, or what in Taylor's terms would be a shared basis for strong evaluations.

In its pristine form such an attitude is very rare, for we are rarely in the company of others among whom no attributes of familiarity can be imputed (if not assumed). As a component of social relations—and most social interaction is most probably predicated on some combination of confidence (in roles), familiarity, and trust—the argument about second-order desires and strong evaluation lends weight to our prior claim for the very modern nature of trusting relations, and indeed of its very emergence as a problem, for with increased social differentiation and the growth of new roles and role commitments, familiarity (again, as the ability to impute shared strong evaluations) becomes more and more difficult to maintain. Different roles after all involve us in different forms of social relations, each as part of a differentiated social system and each with (to some extent) different moral commitments and evaluative criteria of action. The shared webs of significance that formed the basis for strong evaluations have become more and more difficult to assume, and trusting in the agency of the other comes to be less a trusting in the similarity of our common basis for agency (in evaluation) and more a trusting in a set of moral norms (strong evaluations) that I can no longer recognize or be sure of as my own; just as the interstices of systems of role expectations can no longer be reduced to a (however amorphously defined) shared web of moral commitments (or rather as such a reduction became more and more difficult, progressing differently in different countries with the course of modernity). In such circumstances we can only trust in alter's agency, meaning that his or her moral commitments that serve as the basis of their strong evaluations will limit alter's freedom in a manner consonant with a recognition of my own.

And here we come to the fundamental difference between the argument we have been making on the origins and meaning of "trust" and that theoretical exposition of trust provided by Emile Durkheim as the basis of modern social theory. Similarly, I believe, we have also come to understand why Durkheim's understanding no longer seems to hold, as witnessed by the continued jeremiads on the loss of trust and the attempts to resurrect its basis in modern industrial, or perhaps, postindustrial societies. Rather than an understanding of trust based on the essential difference of the other—on the free play of the other's agency—what Durkheim attempted was in fact a rearticulation of the basis of familiarity in modern societies. Recognizing the play of social differentiation which progressed together with the increased division of labor, he was more than cognizant of the inability to base trust on the old certainties of kinship or other forms of ascription. Heir to the Scottish Enlightenment tradition, he was also not willing to relegate social order to the play of the utilitarian tradition of profit-maximizing individuals engaged in contracts. His solution to the problem of the constitution of social solidarity in modern society was not the positing of new terms of trust, but of new terms of familiarity; he attempted to make of the "universal otherhood" of modern social formations a fundamental sameness based on a new form of the *conscience collective*, on a new idea of the precontractual.

The problem was simple. If the individual is perceived as sacrosanct and autonomous—a universal value in itself—what are the possible terms of solidarity existing between such individuals? If each is an autonomous legal, moral, and economic agent, what binds society together beyond the calculus of mutual self-interest? Durkheim's whole theoretical endeavor (and, in fact, the foundation of modern sociology with the idea of the precontractual basis of the social order) was an attempt to answer this question and to construct a theoretical edifice of mutual solidarity out of the idea of morally autonomous individuals. The idea of the precontractual, we recall, was the existence of rules and regulations of contract that were themselves prior to and independent of any contract. Such rules as, for example, the prohibition of selling oneself into slavery were for Durkheim socially given; they rested on a set of moral priorities that defined the basis of trust and mutuality in society and came to be defined in Durkheim's later thought as the *conscience collective.*

The positing of solidarity or mutual trust as existing (analytically) prior to the contract and as the basis for any contract was Durkheim's answer to the utilitarian and contract political theory of the nineteenth century, in effect, his attempt to square the circle of modern solidarity. For Durkheim this precontractual trust, in modern, organic (*Gesellschaftlich*) society, was based on the ethical valuation of individual personhood, that is, on a vision of the individual where the sources of moral action rested on the cognizance of the individual sanctity of each member of society. For Durkheim the solution to the problem of modern solidarity was thus to be found in a shared set of moral commitments where "the only moral ways of acting are those which can be applied to all men indiscriminately; that is, which are implied by the general notion of 'man.'"[95]

Via Kant's idea of the "transcendental self" Durkheim posits a unity of second-order desires and strong evaluations that are or should be (for the line between the descriptive and prescriptive in Durkheim is not always clear) shared by all members of modern society. In essence, then, Durkheim is attempting to explain the continued existence of solidarity in modern society by positing a new model of familiarity, predicated on a new set of what Taylor has termed strong evaluations that are grounded in the autonomy of the individual conscience. The social component of individual identity which is so central to Durkheim's theorizing is a mutual recognition, not of the fundamental alterity of the one's fellow citizens but of his or her fundamental identity based on our shared moral commitments. These commitments (strong evaluations) are no longer to such corporate identities as the Catholic Church or other particular groupings but to a shared valuation of the idea of the human person itself. For Durkheim the source of social solidarity in the wake of increased division of labor and defined by the ethic of individualism was to be found in a common orientation to the moral worth of the individual. This idea stood at the core of his concept of collective representations which he came to define in *The Elementary Forms of Religious Life* not as a common subjectivity of ideas but as a shared normative orientation to the phenomena of social life.[96] In this move the modern discipline of sociology was founded and the nature of morality defined sociologically as the domain assumptions (fundamental premises) of modernity were integrated with those of sociology, i.e., the universality of the individual ego based on the categorical *a priori* structure of knowledge.[97]

In this manner Durkheim attempted to solve the conundrum of modern social life and posit a new basis of solidarity in such societies. If our foregoing analysis is correct, we can now understand both the genius of Durkheim's solution and where he went wrong. His solution was indeed ingenious for he turned the problem of social differentiation (and hence difference) on its head and made of it the basis for identity, for sameness, that is, familiarity. Indeed, he rooted this fundamental identity of social actors in their very differentiation. The very progression of social differentiation in organic societies itself necessitated the emergence of a new mode of collective consciousness, one based on the valuation of the individual as a universal self. From differentiation itself he extrapolates familiarity (or sameness, in the crucial realm of shared moral commitments, i.e., of shared strong evaluations).

While we would agree with Durkheim that this then becomes the basis for familiarity (and through familiarity for system confidence in the type of process noted above), the problem of trust is not thereby solved. Durkheim does not provide a solution to that risk engendered by the greater freedom of the other that is itself a unique aspect of modern role fulfillment. In premodern forms of social organization the recognition of our essential identity (we are all sparrows or oak trees) may well have been sufficient for the provision of social solidarity, especially as we have noted the lesser potential for systemically structured system limits and hence the basic sufficiency for confidence to be the operating principle in social systems. In modern forms of social organization (Durkheim's organic solidarity), this type of solidarity, our recognition of our fundamental identity, Turner's "generic human bond," is insufficient. Given the differentiation of roles characteristic of these societies, solidarity cannot be predicated on familiarity, on sameness alone (however ingeniously Durkheim has formulated this sameness as emerging out of our very differentiation). It must, rather, include some element of trust as well, some recognition of our essential difference (a difference that is predicated on alter's agency and the opacity of his or her will, necessitated by role lability). This aspect of trust, of what cannot be encompassed by positing shared moral commitments (strong evaluations) is not dealt with in Durkheim's theory. The type of risk (as opposed to Luhmann's danger) that is built into the very structure of modern role-sets is not really recognized by Durkheim in his idea of the precontractual basis of modern social formations. It is, I believe, this risk and the necessity for trust to emerge in order to negotiate its shoals that is the peculiar problem of modern societies—and upon whose rocks we seem to be continually floundering.

Thus the problem for which trust is a solution only really emerges in modern societies and any reduction of its content to the terms of familiarity based on our shared moral commitments is more an elusion of the problem than a solution. When the unconditional becomes conditioned by a shared morality (Durkheim's *conscience collective*), it is no longer unconditional and the focus of our analysis is subtly changed from trust to some aspect of familiarity or confidence. Only when the will of the other can no longer be conditioned—or rather when its conditionality can no longer be imputed on the basis of either familiarity in shared strong evaluations or confidence in the fulfillment of role expectations—does the problem of trust emerge in social formations and only then does Kierkegaard's "leap of faith" become orientated toward a mundane other rather than a transcendental one. As we have tried to argue throughout, this fundamentally problematic aspect of social relations is, in the final analysis, predicated not on ideological factors or symbolic orientations, but quite simply in a structural phenomenon rooted in the nature of roles and role conflict that defined modern social formations.

It would seem imperative at this point to extend our inquiry into the development of trust beyond the more "phenomenological" aspects studied above. For if trust, as opposed to faith, confidence, or familiarity, is a unique aspect of modern social formation, evidence of its existence should appear in areas beyond the "informal" spheres of friendship, civility, or love relations. Indeed, the viability of the above analysis can only really be ascertained if trust can be seen to emerge in modernity as a specific form of generalized exchange, as a component of society's unconditionalities that regulate not only informal and private interactions, but the more formal, public, and institutionalized realms of the polity and the economy. To these aspects of trust we must therefore turn our attention.

Three _____

Trust and Generalized Exchange

GIVEN the preceding argument, which defined trust as a function of the agency of the social actor existing beyond systemically defined role expectations, and bearing in mind the growing body of work on "trust"* in economic and political theory, which views trust as a form of social capital that makes the creation of economic prosperity possible, it would seem imperative to bring our own understanding of trust to bear on more established usages and definitions, if only to test its viability and usefulness in understanding the development of modern politics and society.[1] To appreciate whether this is indeed the case, the role of trust as an "important lubricant of the social system"—to use Kenneth Arrow's expression (and recalling Alan Silver's understanding of "sociability" with Adam Smith)—must be further specified.[2] A number of recent comparative studies have stressed just how central trust is to the structure of that associational life based on cooperation that makes economic development, if not civil society, possible at all.

This was, for example, the focus of Robert Putnam's recent and influential analysis of different areas in Italy as well as of Francis Fukuyama's recent analysis of economic growth in different nation-states.[3] The results of these studies are surprisingly similar, the differences in the cases studied notwithstanding. Putnam has shown that where civil life and civic engagement are strong, citizens

> are engaged by public issues, but not by personalistic or patron-client politics. Inhabitants trust one another to act fairly and to obey the law. Leaders in these regions are relatively honest. They believe in popular government, and they are predisposed to compromise with their political adversaries. Both citizens and leaders here find equality congenial. Social and political networks are organized horizontally, not hierarchically. The community values solidarity, civic engagement, cooperation and honesty. Government works."[4]

* Quotation marks are used here to distinguish the accepted usage of trust in political economy from the definition we have been proposing. The aim of this chapter is, in fact, to bring these two usages together and to provide a specificity to the use of trust not often recognized in current writings on this subject. Within a few pages these distinctions in the usage of the term will be clarified. I have refrained, however, from cluttering all references to trust in established writings with quotation marks assuming the reader will easily distinguish between the different meanings attributed to the term.

Opposed to these are those uncivic regions characterized by *incivisme* where

> few people aspire to partake in deliberations about the commonweal, and few such opportunities present themselves. Political participation is triggered by personal dependency or private greed, not by collective purpose. Engagement in social and cultural associations is meager. Private piety stands in for public purpose. Corruption is widely regarded as the norm, even by politicians themselves, and they are cynical about democratic principles. Compromise has only negative overtones. Laws (almost everyone agrees) are made to be broken, but fearing others' lawlessness, people demand stronger discipline. Trapped in these interlocking vicious circles, nearly everyone feels powerless, exploited, and unhappy. All things considered, it is hardly surprising that representative government here is less effective than in more civic communities.[5]

The difference between these two regions, ultimately, is accounted for by the presence or absence of civic traditions of mutual association and trust—as developed after the unification of Italy and rooted in norms that go back centuries. Trust, norms of reciprocity, and networks of civic engagement and association are all presented as crucial foci of social capital; as symbolic media of exchange with real, practical value in enabling the operation and efficacy of the political (and economic) systems. In many ways Putnam's analyses presents a latter-day validation (and theoretical elucidation) of Banfield's study of amoral familism among the Montegranessi in southern Italy. In that study Banfield showed how societies so characterized were lacking in group or community interests, politicians were corrupt with few checks on their actions, the law was disregarded because there was no fear of punishment; therefore collective agreements were impossible to negotiate as was the possibility of organizing collective action.[6] There too the root of these evils was in the inability of the social actors to subject themselves to a discipline of the group, which in this case meant establishing the institutions of an extended family and networks thereof (the reasons for this failure are not our concern here).[7]

In a very different set of contexts but with strikingly similar conclusions stands Fukuyama's study of trust as the "art of association" and its role in the creation of economic prosperity. For Fukuyama trust is

> the expectation that arises within a community of regular, honest and cooperative behavior, based on commonly shared norms, on the part of other members of that community. Those norms can be about deep "value" questions like the nature of God or justice, but they also encompass secular norms like professional standards

and codes of behavior. That is, we *trust* a doctor not to do us deliberate injury because we expect him or her to live by the Hippocratic oath and the standards of the medical profession.[8]

It is this trust which creates a moral community among social actors by providing a form of social capital that can only be acquired and utilized by the group as a whole and which allows for the existence of *generalized* trust among its members (as opposed to individual capital which can be acquired by individuals and used for the pursuit of private goods, such as education, training, etc.). Fukuyama sees this form of capital as differentially distributed among countries with different capacities for association (Japan and Germany, for example, would be high and the contemporary U.S.A. low) and in different degrees within the same society (Middletown, U.S.A., i.e., Muncie, Indiana, would be high and inner-city ghettos like Harlem, low). Most of Fukuyama's analysis stresses the role of communal solidarity, as exemplified most saliently in the Japanese corporation or *kaisha*, in the engendering of economic growth and prosperity through the establishment of mutual commitments to the collective endeavor (thus allowing for the maintenance of low transaction costs and in essence doing away with Olson's "free-rider" dilemma as individual interests are reinterpreted as being "strongly identified . . . with that of the group"—recall here Taylor's strong evaluations).[9] The case of Japan is presented as the paradigm case of this type of collective organization and is then duly contrasted with other southeast Asian countries as well as with those in Europe and with the United States.

In many ways Fukuyama's analysis points to conclusions very similar to those of Putnam, but also to important divergences which will have to be dealt with. But the broader point is the same in both, i.e., the high correlation between communal ties and a well-functioning social order (for Putnam, defined more in political terms and for Fukuyama, more in economic ones). The divergences as we shall see, are tied to the different forms of community which played a role in the different societies. Here, however, I wish to focus our attention on the analytic point involved in both studies: the way trust is used as essentially a form of social solidarity. In Fukuyama's terms:

> As a general rule, trust arises when a community shares a set of moral values in such a way as to create expectations of regular and honest behavior. To some extent, the particular character of those values is less important than the fact that they are shared: both Presbyterians and Buddhists, for example, would likely find they had a great deal in common with their co-religionists and therefore form a moral basis for mutual trust. . . . In general, the more demanding the values of the community's ethical system are and the higher are the

qualifications for entry into the community, the greater is the degree of solidarity and mutual trust among those on the inside. Thus Mormons and Jehovah's Witnesses, who have relatively high standards for community membership like temperance and tithing, would feel stronger mutual bonds than, for example, contemporary Methodists or Episcopalians, who allow virtually anyone into their communities.[10]

Trust then is identified with social solidarity as well as with something that arises when expectations of regular behavior are created. In the very ambivalence of this definition we can, I believe, see the different elements of associational life, the foundations of social solidarity, that we have attempted to argue above: on the one hand, simple confidence in the system of role expectations (expectations of regular behavior) and on the other, the fact that these expectations themselves are induced by a shared or common identity (i.e., by the familiarity of strong evaluations)—in the above quote evinced by the commitment to a shared religious tradition, and, of major importance to the study as whole, to those of shared kinship, as is the case in Japan.

The sources of this social solidarity, as we know, can be very different. The civic solidarity of northern Italy is of a very different nature than the kinship-based solidarity of Japan. In both cases what trust qua social capital means is the existence of strong bonds of association. These bonds, expressed as confidence in alter's adhering to the "rules of the game" are rooted in a combination of confidence in the system together with the ability to impute strong evaluations to alter's intentions (i.e., familiarity). This familiarity of strong evaluations may, as in the case of Japan, be rooted in the continuation of a very particular type of kinship system into the modern industrial era, and this has been the exception and not the rule (witness not only the trajectory of Western European development but Fukuyama's own astute remarks on the Chinese kinship system). Such familiarity, as Putnam's study of modern Italy makes clear, may also be based on the establishment of a civic consciousness, that is, on strong evaluations based on a shared tradition of civic engagement rather than a generalized sib affinity. This point is, I believe, implicit in Fukuyama's own dictum on Mormons and Methodists. The very "demanding values" of the communal ethical system make it possible to impute shared strong evaluations to one another in a manner impossible to more open (liberal-individualist perhaps) communities. Japanese, Mormons, and the good citizens of the Emilia-Romagna region of Italy all share the capacity to impute strong evaluations to one another and through this action to overcome the process of social differentiation that defines the modern division of labor. The difference between the strong evaluations of the first and third communities is the difference between what, in the Western context, was seen as the forms of mechanical and organic solidarity respectively.

If we take the Mormons as representative of a solidarity based on adherence to strong religious codes of conduct, we may see "them" (or rather that type) as an intermediary case in the development of Western models of solidarity; this was precisely Weber's point in his study of *The Protestant Ethic and the Spirit of Capitalism*, where the trust necessary for the establishment of market relations was occasioned by shared adherence to a rather rigid code of conduct. As Ernest Gellner has noted: "Protestantism in Europe made its adherents loyal to the norms of their *calling*, irrespective of advantage. (They did not think that other-worldly advantage could be bought, and did not wish to buy advantage in this world.) This made them *individually* and *unconditionally* trustworthy and thus, according to the theory [of Max Weber] they made the modern world possible."[11]

In all cases we are essentially dealing with a form of what economists term "externality," a good or commodity that enables further production of articles of worth that cannot in itself be traded on an open market. We are positing a "self-reinforcing" mode of behavior that obviates the necessity of any third-party enforcer to contracts.[12] It is this very property of what the above-noted authors have termed "trust" that makes of it such a potent "system lubricant." And as we have noted, the more system develops and its roles differentiate, the more this lubricant must come into play for the system to continue functioning.

However, what is at work here is not trust as we have been laboriously trying to differentiate it from confidence or familiarity, but, in fact, familiarity itself (as a mode of solidarity). This becomes clear when we recall the connection of familiarity to Taylor's strong evaluations. For what made of strong evaluations *strong* evaluations is precisely that the identity of the actor is bound up with them. It is not an external preference orientation (such as eating a chocolate eclair or mowing the lawn, which can be subjected to a rational calculation of costs-benefits and returns, i.e., losing a pound versus gaining a pound and the quality of my sports life which may ensue) but one bound up with my very sense of self. Strong evaluations are such strong self-reinforcing mechanisms because the very identity of the social actor is tied to them. This too is why familiarity, based on kinship or shared circumstances or shared religious beliefs, is such a strong provider of associational life: because the collective good that is posited as of equal (or sometimes greater) worth than the individual's interests is not seen as an external preference (and so given to rational calculations) but as a constitutive part of the self.[13] This insight of how a sense of self is tied to the unconditionalities of human relationships as structured by the external conditions of social interaction has been the focus of a fascinating philosophical inquiry by Bernard Harrison who reminds us that:

> Morality is rooted more deeply in us than either social conditioning or nervous sensibility could root it, because its imperatives spring from the *formal conditions* [my emphasis] for the existence of types of relationships into which individual human beings must enter with one another, because such relationships provide an essential framework around which the personalities and goals of individuals organize themselves.[14]

Having said this, we must note that the familiarity of shared strong evaluations, whether based on the ties of kinship or shared religious belief or any shared set of strong ideological commitments, provides what is essentially a form of solidarity, that is, a form or type of unconditionality: a mode of interaction not based on the ad hoc, one-shot-only workings of market exchange; "relations between actors which are not based on the direct, conditional, but on the indirect, long-range, give-and-take of services or resources and on the setting up of "titles" or entitlement to such resources or services."[15] This *symbolic credit* is precisely what stands behind the lubricatory metaphor of Kenneth Arrow and is what is at the root of all types of social capital (recall too the workings of iterated Prisoner Dilemma games in terms of this symbolic credit).[16] Crucially, social capital (what Fukuyama and others have mostly called trust) is in essence no more than the forms of associational life based on different types of *confidence* in the workings of the system and its institutional arrangements. The social capital (i.e., confidence) itself rests on different types of unconditionalities, which is precisely what is provided for by the different terms of solidarity in its different forms. This relationship between the different terms may be represented as follows:

SOCIAL CAPITAL = Associational Life = Confidence

(rests on)

UNCONDITIONALITIES = Principles of Generalized

Exchange = Solidarity

The bases of society's unconditionalities may be very different and here is where the element of trust—at least as we have been defining it, as a rather unique type of interactional matrix—comes into play. For while the familiarity of shared strong evaluations may be based on kinship (as in premodern societies) or on shared religious belief (Weber's Protestants and Fukuyama's Jehovah's Witnesses) or on the very existence of dense social networks (what may be termed familiarity *simpliciter*), it may also be

based on that particular type of *conscience collective* that values the autonomy and integrity of the individual actor. All are different forms of generalized exchange, different bases of solidarity. The latter was of course that
basis of solidarity that Durkheim posited in modern organic society. It is
only in this latter form of solidarity, only within this latter principle of
generalized exchange, that those particular forms of risk may emerge (i.e.,
those occasioned by the agency of the other) for which trust is a solution.
Trust then emerges only in the later form of familiarity, as a necessary
component of a very particular type of solidarity that we identify with modern social formations. The emergence of trust as an aspect of modern forms
of solidarity is of a very different order than the simple existence of principles of generalized exchange upon which confidence in any social system
must be based.

Generalized exchange, we recall, is to be distinguished from "specific"
or market exchange in that, as opposed to the latter, it provides the "conditions of solidarity, the "precontractual" elements of social interaction
which include the obligation to engage in social interaction and to uphold
one's obligations; or in other words, generalized exchange, if successful,
helps to establish the conditions of basic trust and solidarity in society, to
uphold what Durkheim has called the precontractual elements of social
life"[17] (note again the habit to conflate trust with the principles of generalized exchange itself). The existence of generalized exchange was perhaps
first noted by Marcell Mauss in his famous study of *The Gift* and has been
developed in different ways within different anthropological traditions as
distinctions between "general" and "specific" exchange (in the works of
Claude Lévi-Strauss) or "generalized" and "balanced" reciprocity (in the
works of Marshall Sahlins).[18] In both these authors what is contrasted is the
direct, immediate, and balanced reciprocity of items transacted (symbolic
or material) as against a reciprocity that does not demand an immediate
return or exchange of such items. In the latter case, a form of symbolic
credit is granted to the receiver who benefits from the "trust" of the other
partner to the interaction to offer a return in goods received at a later date.
In this sense, and perhaps to stretch a point, every exchange partakes symbolically of the character of a gift in that reciprocity is not immediately
expected.[19]

A very good example of this type of unspecified reciprocity or generalized exchange can be found in the Jewish commandments to bury those
dead who have no one to bury them. This is, in Jewish law, the paradigm
case of חסד *chesed* (piety or graciousness—it does not translate well given
the heavily Christological connotations of grace in our language) beyond
measure. On the one hand, it is quite clear that the one who partakes of this
righteous deed can expect no recompense from the dead (or from relatives,

who if they existed would obviate the need for the act itself). It is thus an almost perfect gift. On the other hand, the performance of the deed is seen as ensuring the overall "store" or "capital" of trust, goodwill, and reciprocity in society (so that if the performer of the deed, or indeed anyone, should be in similar circumstance they could reasonably expect the same treatment). Of all similar deeds of piety (marrying off an orphan, visiting the sick, hospitality to guests), the burying of the dead is deemed the most important act of grace, precisely, I would maintain, because direct or immediate reciprocity is, by definition, impossible. (Anthropologists and other social scientists should beware because an awareness of the importance of both the existence and workings of such principles of generalized exchange can arguably be said to be already present in thinkers such as Moses Maimonides in the twelfth century.)[20]

As pointed out by Putnam, Fukuyama, Arrow, and others—each in their different ways—it is precisely this granting of symbolic credit that makes social and economic life possible at all. It is this symbolic credit, based as it is on a set of developing expectations, that provides the basis of cooperation in iterated PD games as well. Its implications for the development of market economies, based as they are on the activities of middlemen (positioned between the producer and consumer), have been studied by scholars such as Janet Landa and Avner Grief.[21] Both have emphasized the necessary role of "reputation" (even intergenerationally) in establishing confidence in trading activities (a point made by Coleman as well).[22] This reputation, based on the iteration of trade activities, become the basis for new role expectations and hence for confidence in the system of interacting activities.

The different terms of symbolic credit upon which such confidence is based thus make economic life possible, but they also structure social life and exchange in very specific ways. As S. N. Eisenstadt has noted, they do so by providing

limitations to the free exchange of resources in social interaction, and the concomitant structuring of the flow of resources and social relations in ways that differ from "free" (market or power) exchange. Such structuring stands in contrast to the purely conditional, instrumental or mostly adaptive, activities that characterize simple or specific exchange. But it does not deny adaptive or instrumental relations. Rather it creates a connection between instrumental and power relations on the one hand and solidarity and expressive relations on the other.[23]

These limitations take the form, most generally, of (a) the establishment of Public Goods, such that no one member or group in the collectivity has exclusive access to such goods and (b) the public distribution of private goods in which the redistributive mechanisms of the collectivity reward groups and allocate resources according to criteria other than those of pure market exchange (priestly tithes, welfare entitlement, or German tax-allotment to the Church would all be examples of the latter).

Of course, the terms of these generalized exchanges are different in different societies, tied in turn to the way the "unconditionality" (i.e., solidarity) is articulated in the different societies (the bases, if you will, of "reputation"). Most of the more penetrating work on this has been carried out by anthropologists working in smaller, relatively undifferentiated or traditional societies where these unconditionalities were formulated in terms of an ascriptive- or kinship-based solidarity. As the work of Parsons, Mayhew, and Eisenstadt himself has shown, a similar dynamic pervades more developed societies as well where the different legally defined entitlement of citizen rights play a similar role.

On the more micro and purely economic level the current work and concern with Rotating Credit Associations (RCAs) exemplifies this awareness of how symbolic credit or generalized exchange works as a form of social capital, allowing the development of economic life. The case of the RCAs is also important for our own concerns—with the terms and emergence of unconditional bases of exchange—in that it focuses attention on two important areas: first, RCAs too develop in the interstices of a system, in conditions characterized by "uncertainty of context, indeterminacy of relationships, scarcity of resources or ambiguity of statuses."[24] Indeed, for Ibanez, in his study of RCAs among Mexicans and Mexican-Americans, the elements of "indeterminacy and uncertainty" provide the "necessary and sufficient" conditions for the growth of these forms of economic association (whatever the sources of this ambiguity in the different contexts). Second, the basis for the formation and criteria for membership in these RCAs (especially those with long-range goals) rests on the density of existing relations "generated by multiple ties, such as friendship, fictive kinship and residence in the same area."[25]

RCAs have developed most often among the poor or in immigrant communities and thus among those for whom the established system of roles and role expectations is weak, among those whose economic existence is somehow liminal or interstitial or, more analytically, among those for whom the institutionalized form of society's unconditionalities only minimally structure their interaction (and so prevent them from taking part in the more generalized, society-wide process of exchange). Their members develop their own form of generalized exchange or symbolic credit. This new system or "mini-system" is predicated on a more idiosyncratic (or particularized) type of unconditionality that is defined by what we, above, have termed familiarity—that is, by the ability to impute strong evaluations to its members and on the bases of these strong evaluations to extend symbolic credit to one another (which when successful becomes its own system

of shared expectations and confidence in the fulfillment of expectations).
Note, then, not only the formation of new forms of social solidarity—
what Durkheim termed the precontractual—in the interstices of broader,
more institutionalized systems, but also the basis for this type of solidarity, which is familiarity: the type of solidarity that characterized those
social formations we term premodern, or mechanical, or with Tönnies,
Gemeinschaftlich.

Returning to our earlier point on how the terms of society's unconditionalities (its solidarity) both make society possible and structure the processes of exchange in different ways, we may contrast the establishment
of RCAs among Mexicans and Mexican-Americans with the behavior of
the Frafas in Ghana noted above at the beginning of our study. In that case
the social actors also existed in an interstitial situation, at system limits.
There, however, the inability to rely on, to have confidence in, a set of
role expectations led to the establishment of *trust* among the parties. In
the case of the Mexican RCAs the disembedment of the social actors from
system definitions was not as radical in that they maintained forms of association based on kinship, friendship, and so on, and on the basis of the
familiarity inherent to these relations they were able to establish new unconditionalities or principles of generalized exchange. This is a crucial
difference and one not always recognized (or at least not always recognized by economic theorists): the different nature of unconditionalities
upon which symbolic credit is granted to social actors in different settings. Hence the different models of sociability, of associational life, and
of principles of generalized exchange, of precisely those forms of social
capital too often lumped together as trust, that make social and economic
life possible.

The significance of our attempt to distinguish among trust, confidence,
and familiarity is to show the threefold confusion inherent in this identification of trust with *(a)* all forms of unconditionalities or principles of
generalized exchange and *(b)* with the workings of confidence, i.e., the
existence per se of social capital as an economic externality in all societies. Perhaps, indeed it is this usage that has blinded some analysts to the
very different types of externalities, or principles of generalized exchange,
at work in different societies. For, as we have argued above, while confidence may or may not exist in any system of shared strong evaluations
(i.e., confidence in the societal principles of unconditionality, its bases of
generalized exchange), trust emerges only as a component of a very particular type of unconditionality, one orientated toward the autonomous
acts of individual agents. Different types of unconditionality provide different types of confidence, for they are based on different modes of association (though in practice they exist together in different "mixes," privi-

leging one over the other as the major component of unconditionality in society).

In each case confidence remains the system of role expectations which, in their very definitions, contain the terms of unconditionality defined by their respective systems. In each institutionalized system (and systems are always, by definition, institutionalized), there is the potential for system limits, for crises of confidence (on different scales, some of the reasons for which have been adduced above), and in each case such crises lead social actors to refer back to the unconditionalities that stand behind the system and their confidence therein. (We may note in passing that what defines most of ethnomethodological inquiry is precisely the uncovering of those elements of familiarity at system crises.)

Having said this we must recall that trust only comes to play a role in structuring social relations within one form of such unconditionality. It emerges and is predicated on only one particular way of providing the unconditional bases of system confidence. It is, I wish to argue further, one that is undoubtedly connected with the "rise of the West." It is thus the unfortunate habit of taking the West in general and Britain more specifically (and more recently the U.S.A.) as models for the modernization process that has led us to confuse trust as a mode of unconditionality with the existence of unconditionalities (or forms of social solidarity) per se. For it was in the Anglo-Saxon countries most especially that some form of trust (defined as we have above, as a recognition of the agency of the other) has indeed formed a major component of that unconditionality upon which system confidence rests. And while this is not the place to enter into a history of economic liberalism or of the development of capitalism in the West as a whole (or in its different national variants), the connection between this development and the idea of the autonomous individual agent must be explicated.

This connection is best exemplified in the very development of contract law, which progressed together with the transformation of an economy based on reciprocity and redistribution to those based on self-regulating markets.[26] Not surprisingly, contract law as such did not exist in early, relatively undifferentiated societies.[27] As P. S. Atiyah has noted: "Since the law of contract is . . . primarily concerned with self-imposed obligations, its very existence naturally presupposes a society and a legal system in which people have the right to choose what obligations they wish to assume."[28] This process of change saw the gradual freeing of the contract from its symbolic encumbrances (and so the emergent idea of freedom of contract), the creation of legal equality out of the "monopolistically granted privileges of closed organizations," the transformation of the loan from an "interest-free form of emergency aid among brothers" to a form of credit, the development of tort law, and so of obligations through contract and the creation of the "juridic person."[29] At the root of these developments and as noted by Max Weber stood two crucial sets of privileges:

> The first is constituted by the so-called freedoms, i.e., situations of simple protection against certain types of interference by third parties, especially state officials, within the sphere of legally permitted conduct; instances are freedom of movement, freedom of conscience or freedom of disposition over property. The second type of privilege is that which grants an individual *autonomy* to *regulate* his *relations with others* [original emphasis] by his own transactions. Freedom of contract, for example, exists exactly to the extent to which such autonomy is recognized by the legal order. There exists, of course, an intimate connection between the expansion of the market and the expanding measure of contractual freedom or, in other words, the scope of arrangements which are guaranteed as valid by the legal order, or, in again different terms, the relative significance within the total legal order of those rules which authorize such transactional dispositions. In an economy where self-sufficiency prevails and exchange is lacking, the function of law will naturally be otherwise; it will mainly define and delimit a person's non-economic relations and privileges with regard to other persons in accordance, not with economic considerations, but with the person's origin, education and social status.[30]

If we take law—and in this case the law of contract—to represent the unconditional aspects of exchange, we see in this quote the very specific type of unconditionality that characterized capitalist expansion in the West: based on the agentic freedom of the individual.[31] Hidden within these two privileges is a recognition of the basic freedom of the individual where the "juridico-economic position of the individual . . . is determined . . . by contracts concluded by him, for him, or in his name"—a point that stood at the center of Marx's critique of capitalism.[32] (In England this principle was expressed in the singular reluctance to restrict the "freedom of contract" with any encumbrances.[33]) Simmel has in fact focused our attention on this connection of individual freedom in the very origins of market economies based on monetary transactions when he noted that "the lord of the manor who can demand a quantity of beer or poultry or honey from a serf thereby determines the activity of the latter in a certain direction. But the moment he imposes merely a money levy the peasant is free, in so far as he can decide whether to keep bees, or cattle or anything else."[34]

The growth and development of this process, of self-regarding capitalism, saw the transformation of "clan comradeship to [a] universal society" of impersonal relations where the principle of private interest rather than those of group solidarities (and hence familiarities based on strong evaluations) came to serve as the unconditional principles of generalized exchange.[35] Thus, the oft-noted "disembedment of economics from politics" is not really a disembedment or uncoupling at all. Rather, it is a transformation in the nature of politics, a transformation in the nature of those unconditional principles of market exchange, from those predicated on kinship familiarity to the recognition of the autonomy and freedom of the individual. The individual, rather than the solidary group, becomes the new locus of exchange relations, and so the strong evaluations which define market exchange are no longer those of familiarity but of the individual himself (for most of this period, decidedly himself and not herself).

It was this individual who more and more came to be conceived as the profit-maximizing individual of current exchange theory and upon whose acts of exchange or rather upon whose promises reliance or confidence (Arrow's social capital) could be seen to rest—at least according to nineteenth-century utilitarian theory (recall here Stewart's earlier-noted discussion on the internalization of honor).[36] It was this transformation that P. S. Atiyah has traced in the development of contract law within the English common law tradition. It is reflected perhaps first and foremost in the English aversion to "principle": what is often termed the pragmatism of the English legal tradition but is, to a large extent, the hesitation to impose ideas or principles of public order on contracting parties. In a sense, therefore, it is a most unqualified acceptance of the idea of the free agency of the individual as unconditional principle of market exchange.[37] This idea of the individual, as what may be termed unconditional locus of exchange, was, as Atiyah has pointed out, a development that progressed gradually from the 1600s to the 1800s. In the nineteenth century, classical liberal, laissez-faire doctrine saw that the mutual respect "for the persons, property and choices of others" was what made cooperation (social order) possible.[38]

It is this very moral idea of the individual and of the cooperation arising from individual choice which has been institutionalized in the legal rights of the individual (and in the idea of his liability) to such an extent that—and to take only the case of English common law—existing limitations on the negotiability of contracts are such as, and limited to, guaranteeing the free agency of the contracting parties. (Thus, there are rules against securing acceptance by duress, by fraud and sharp dealing, by a negligent statement, by innocent misrepresentation, and rules requiring disclosure).[39] This principle is exemplified in the legal idea of the *caveat emptor* which frees party A in a contract from informing party B about future conditions that party B may have an interest in knowing and incorporating into the contract. It stresses the free choice of the contracting parties and the responsibility each has to attend to their own interests. It is a principle whose emergence dates, not surprisingly, to the early seventeenth century.[40] Behind such forms of regulation are the development of capitalism and the transformation of economic life from "communal limited and conditional ownership to modern, individual and absolute ownership."[41] This new sense of property and its relation to the new terms of unconditionality regulating economic exchange was perhaps best expressed by Louis Dumont when he noted that "it is in the guise of possession or property that individualism raises its head, knocks down any remnant of social submission and ideal hierarchy in society, and installs itself on the throne thus made vacant. . . . [E]conomics as a "philosophical category" represents the acme of individualism and as such tends to be paramount in our universe."[42]

It is precisely in this development that England "led the way" and where, according to Macfarlane, in the thirteenth century England was already characterized by "rampant individualists, highly mobile both geographically and socially, economically "rational," market-oriented and acquisitive, ego-centered in kinship and social life."[43] There the shattering of kinship bonds (most especially in property relations as manifest in the early development of the freedom of the testator) led to a society "constituted of autonomous equal units, namely separate individuals, and . . . such individuals are more important, ultimately, than any larger constituent group. [This situation was] reflected in the concept of individual private property, in the political and legal liberty of the individual, in the idea of the individual's direct communication with God."[44] Again our interest here is not in entering into the debate over the origins or timing of such development but only in reestablishing the well-known connection between capitalism and individualism which also implies the transformation of the unconditionalities at work in society (an aspect of this development that is perhaps less remarked upon).

Within this transformation the very nature of contracts came to be regulated by new principles, principles which were at the still unarticulated heart of Maitland's own understanding of contractual law when he noted that

> [i]n the really feudal centuries men could do by a contract, by the formal contract of vassalage or commendation, many things that can not be done nowadays. They could contract to stand by each other in warfare "against all men who can live and die," they could (as Domesday Book says) "go with their land" to any lord whom they pleased; they could make the relation between king and subject look like the outcome of an agreement; the law of contract threatened to swallow up all public law. Those were the golden days of "free" if "formal" contract. The idea that men can fix their rights and duties by agreement is in its early days an unruly, anarchical idea. If there is to be any law at all, contract must be taught to know its place.[45]

That "place" established by "law" was the one of legal rights and entitlements which recognizes the legal autonomy (freedom of will) of the individual—of the moral principles of the individual as value—and makes of it a restriction on certain types of contracts.[46] We may note that the whole development of contract law saw its slow emergence as a substantive principle (from being merely "evidential" to the aspect of "considerations" which defined pre-Natural Law ideas of contract) to a principle of substantive justice itself where "the rule of the market place is equivalent with the rule of law."[47] It was this principle that served as the classic nineteenth-century laissez-faire idea of contract law; its centrality to our understanding of trust as arising from the principles of individual agency as economic unconditionality (or principle of generalized exchange) is such that it is worth quoting Atiyah at length on this theme:

> The autonomy of the free choice of private parties to make their own contracts on their own terms was the central feature of classical contract law. Its influence is to be found in every corner of contract law. . . . [T]he importance attached to free choice, and to the idea that a contract was a vehicle for giving effect to the will of the parties, had a profound effect on the very functions of contract law as it was perceived by the Courts. The primary function law came to be seen as purely facultative, and the function of the court was merely to resolve a dispute by working out the implications of what the parties had already chosen to do. The idea that the Court had an independent role to play as a forum for the adjustment of rights, or the settlement of disputes, was plainly inconsistent with this new approach.[48]

At this point I well realize that I may be accused by even the most generous of readers of having spent their time beating the proverbial dead horse. The connection between capitalism and the emergence of individualism is well known, and there would seem to be little point reiterating this argument. The point of the foregoing exercise, however, was to highlight the fact that what this correlation implies is a transformation in the terms of generalized exchange, of the unconditionalities regulating social and economic life, from those based on familiarity of group relations to those based on some form of individual agency and hence, by implication, based on the developing idea of trust between these individuals. The issue of trust emerges precisely from a morality oriented toward the self-regarding acts of this individual engaged in market exchange. In fact, the trust so necessitated is the foundation of a new morality: the basis of that revaluation of values that defines modernity. As pointed out by Dumont, this revaluation of morality recognized the "emancipation" of economic actors "from the general or common run of morality, but it is accompanied by the recognition that economic action is by itself oriented toward the good, that it has a special moral character of its own."[49] This moral character is itself constituted by the fact that:

> each subject defines his conduct by reference only to his own interest, and society is no more than the mechanism—or the Invisible Hand—by which interests harmonize . . . In other terms, the transition from traditional morality to utilitarian

ethics (when fully accomplished) represents the expulsion of the only and last form under which, in the modern world, the social whole still constrained individual conduct: the individual is free, the last chains have fallen from him.[50]

The logic of this new morality was first remarked on by Bernard Mandeville in which "Millions endeavoring to supply Each other's Lusts and Vanity" leads to a situation where "every Part was full of Vice, yet the whole Mass a Paradise."[51] Thus, in avowed contrast to the idea of sociability proposed by the Scottish moralists (who were following on the lead of the Earl of Shaftesbury, Mandeville's bête noire), Mandeville posits any "natural Propensity to Friendship and love of Company" as nothing more than occasions "to strengthen our Interest."[52] Indeed, in Mandeville, the self-regarding individual of economic theory makes his first appearance in the author's assertion that "the imaginary Notions that Men may be Virtuous without Self-denial are a vast Inlet to Hypocrisy."[53] Virtue, or Dumont's "common run of morality," is antithetical to economic interests whose realization nevertheless makes of the "whole Mass a Paradise."

Behind this "Paradise" is a vision of morality based on the self-regarding individual and no longer on familiar, shared strong evaluations. As Mandeville took pains to point out: "In the Works of Nature, Worth and Excellency are uncertain and even in Humane Creatures what is beautiful in one Country is not so in another. How whimsical is the Florist in his Choice! Sometimes the Tulip, sometimes the Auricula, and at other times the Carnation shall engross his Esteem . . . In Morals there is no greater Certainty."[54]

In such a world, where shared strong evaluations based on familiarity are increasingly difficult to assume and where "Man centers every thing in himself, and neither loves nor hates, but for his own Sake," a new moral basis is posited, in which

[e]very individual is a little World by itself, and all Creatures, as far as their Understanding and Abilities will let them, endeavor to make that Self happy: This in all of them is the continual Labour, and seems to be the whole Design of Life. Hence it follows, that in the Choice of Things Men must be determined by the Perception they have of Happiness; and no Person can commit or set about an Action, which at that then present time seems not be the best to him.[55]

The shared strong evaluations of familiarity are thus shattered and replaced by the morality of self-regarding individuals who—if there is to be any social order at all, any law (in Maitland's sense)—must come to trust one another.

Individualism as the unconditionality of self-regulating market exchange thus brings in its wake the concomitant idea of trust as an element of such unconditionality. This development is not unilinear or homogeneous across societies or markets. Rather different mixes of familiarity and trust have developed differently in different historical contexts. To return to our earlier example of contract: indications of this difference can be found in the different attitudes to the contract of the common or civil law traditions, whether based on a "promise" or on an "agreement," as well as attitudes to the different types of limitations on contractual agreement provided in each tradition.[56] In broad historical, ideal-typical terms, what modernity has involved has been precisely the replacement of the criteria of familiarity with those of trust in and of the individual as an aspect of social unconditionality.

Having established this new form of generalized exchange as it developed in Western European societies, we must nevertheless note that the idea of the individual and of the recognition of individual agency is not the only possible foundation for the social order—or even for modern social orders. Such is the case for Japan and other southeast Asian countries within which a familiarity based on generalized kinship ties also correlated with high levels of modern economic performance (though playing different roles, more or less saliently at different levels of economic organization and complexity, as Fukuyama's comparison of China and Japan indicates). Familiarity as the ability to establish strong evaluations based on kinship is only one possible form of familiarity. Again, the case of Germany, according to Fukuyama, illustrates another form of familiarity, of a communal tradition not based on such ties.

Some recognition of this difference is inherent in Fukuyama's own statement that

> there are three broad paths to sociability: the first is based on family and kinship, the second on voluntary organization outside of kinship such as schools, clubs and professional organizations, and the third is the state. . . . The first and third paths, it turns out, are closely related to one another: cultures in which the primary avenue toward sociability is family and kinship have a great deal of trouble creating large, durable economic organizations, and therefore look to the state to initiate and support them.[57]

Our interest here is not with models of economic modernization, but with the terms of unconditionality, and in this sense Fukuyama presents what are really two, not three, models, one based on the familiarity of kinship and one which encompasses that element of trust which is an aspect of voluntary associations. Note the necessary correlation between the agency that must be an aspect of any voluntary association (what makes it voluntary) and the correspondent existence of trust in what is essentially the voluntarism of other social actors. It is, recall, precisely this trust (defined albeit as sociability) that the Scottish moralists saw as so central to the existence of polished or civilized societies. Recall, too, that familiarity as shared strong evaluations does not have to be based solely on ascribed criteria. It may have other sources, which is what Durkheim attempted to provide in his definitions of the term of modern solidarity (based on the individual) and what Putnam has studied as at work in northern Italy. Indeed, the development of capitalist economic relations in Western Europe has on the whole been characterized by the replacement of kinship-based forms of familiarity with those based on a civic consciousness. (It is, as noted above, precisely within this latter form of familiarity—and only within this form—that trust can be seen to emerge.) Where this did not take place, such areas or regions failed to modernize (again Bainfield and Putnam on southern Italy). Thus the terms of familiarity were transformed from those based on kinship to those predicated on a shared civic consciousness. This is not the only road to modernity, as the case of Japan proves. (How to explain this difference is another matter entirely and would take us beyond our current concerns with trust into a comparative analysis of family structures and their transformation.)

Here the astute reader may well remark that we have again lost hold of that elusive entity of trust (in the fundamental opaqueness of the other) since it seems to be reducible to familiarity (based on the ability to impute shared strong evaluations of precisely this orientation, what may be termed civic consciousness, Durkheim's forms of modern solidarity, and so on). This, however, is to confuse two very different meanings of familiarity. *The one is a form of unconditionality in its own right* (which would hold true in the case of kinship-based systems, or those organized on shared religious belief), *and the other is a mechanism for maintaining system confidence* (under any and all definitions of generalized exchange and unconditionality). It is this latter case that is of greater interest to us. In opposition to Durkheim, who sought to reformulate the terms of familiarity in modernity (based on the idea of the individual), what we are arguing is that these very terms of familiarity, precisely because they are based on the agency of individual actors, must include an element of trust between actors as a principle of society's unconditionality. Thus it is not only the familiarity of shared strong evaluations (those of individualism) that define the unconditional in modern life, but also the existence of trust necessitated by these very terms of familiarity. In modernity, then, the terms of society's unconditionalities go beyond those of shared strong evaluations (i.e., of familiarity) to include trust in what, in the final analysis, cannot be reduced to familiarity alone (i.e., the agency of the other). This is the real challenge of modern forms of social organization and one that we may not be capable of meeting. Trust may be too demanding, even more demanding than faith (and hence the current return to different forms of familiarity, such as religion, kinship, gender, or ethnicity, in its stead).

Whatever the terms of the current crises in trust (which will be dealt with in our last chapter), the particular terms of the unconditional in modernity do set up an interesting dynamic in respect to the workings of familiarity *as a mechanism* for enforcing society's unconditionalities. For if, as we have argued above, friendship (or even love relations) provides the model for that pristine form of trust we associate with modern forms of unconditionality, it is also the case that, as remarked on by Geoffrey Hawthorn, "interpersonal trust itself cannot, as it stands, be a model for enduringly cooperative and trusting relations between strangers . . . this is possible if, but perhaps only if, the relations are simplified, stylized, symbolized and given ritual expression: if, that is, they are coded in convention."[58] That means only when they are institutionalized into a system of mutual expectations, which is exactly what the principles of generalized exchange as limitations on free market exchange accomplish. When such a system betrays its own inherent limits (role conflicts, differential commitments, etc.), we supplement our confidence in it with an assumed familiarity (in the second sense, i.e., *qua* mechanism only) based on the imputation of strong evaluations of a shared unconditionality (in this case, the recognition of individual agency, i.e., trust). What enables the projection of these strong evaluations (based on shared moral commitment to the unconditional principle of individual agency) is the existence—on the level of individual action and not of system organization—of familiarity in the second sense (that is, as a mechanism for the inculcation of society's unconditionalities). Shared structural positions in the division of labor thus allow the use of familiarity in the second sense to project the unconditionality of trust and agency to one another.[59]

Note carefully the argument proposed as it is somewhat complex. Familiarity, it is claimed, exists in two forms: Form #1, as itself a basis for social solidarity; Form #2, as no more than a mechanism, rooted in the structural composition of the division of labor, allowing the imputation of whatever unconditional principle binds society together, i.e., its terms of solidarity. In modernity, due to its high degree of system differentiation and advanced division of labor, the terms of social solidarity include: *(a)* the familiarity of shared strong evaluations (in this case the evaluations of moral individualism, civic consciousness, and the other unconditionalities of modernity that we associate with individual agency) but also *(b)* an element of *trust* in what cannot be taken as shared. Here is where modernity distinguishes itself so forcefully from all previous forms of social organization. For while the terms of familiarity are indeed different in different social formations (recall how this familiarity may be based on tribal kinship, on transcendental religions, or on shared orientations to individual valuation and agency), modernity is the only form of social organization whose basis of social solidarity rests not solely on the familiarity of shared strong evaluations (Durkheim's individualism) but also on trust in an unknown and (structurally) unknowable other. Both these aspects of modern solidarity are different from the existence in modernity—as in other modern forms of social organization—of familiarity as a mechanism for the inculcation of system confidence.

Some realization, though not fully developed, of these two senses of familiarity was, I believe, implicit in Durkheim's own understanding of the workings of social solidarity in the modern world. For Durkheim not only posited a new definition of familiarity in the first sense, that is, a new definition of the terms of strong evaluations or unconditionalities at work in society based no longer on kinship but on a civic consciousness organized around the appreciation of the individual as value. He saw these new strong evaluations as arising out of the division of labor and differentiation of roles, and he was well aware of the need to institute organizational frameworks that would make it possible to use familiarity in the second sense, as a mechanism, to impute the new terms of unconditionality (what Durkheim would term solidarity). This was the role to be played by secondary groups and intermediary associations, "family trade and professional associations, Church, regional arenas and so on [which would] . . . absorb the personality of their members" and thus inculcate them with the new terms of solidarity (or unconditionalities) based on the individual as moral value.[60] These associations would thus act as sources of familiarity in the second sense, as a mechanism to establish those strong evaluations based on individual agency and autonomy which Durkheim saw as constitutive of modern solidarity.

Thus trust in the agency of individual actors as an aspect of unconditional general exchange must rely on familiarity (in the second sense) in order to work as precisely that lubricant, that form of social capital, that allows for associational life. This is why it is so difficult to grasp as a particular form of unconditionality and so often posited as a general model for all unconditional generalized principles of exchange (it also explains why familiarity, whether based on kinship or other forms of association, is so often confused with it). Moreover, it is this "reliance" on familiarity that makes of it so problematic a model in a number of contemporary societies.

The "intrusion" of familiarity into the workings of trust also serves to obscure the difference between pristine or pure trust and trust as a mode of generalized exchange. It was in his failure to note this difference that Durkheim, I believe, went wrong. For these two manifestations of the principles of unconditionality in society (of its terms of generalized exchange) are not reducible the one to the other, nor do they exist without conflict and tension. Durkheim, in positing a precontractual basis of solidarity founded on individual autonomy and agency (and, as we would note, on the mutual trust this implied), did not adequately address the fact that the representation and symbolization of this trust in the more informal contexts of social life (for example, in the private realm of friendship) are of a different order than its function in regulating the flow of resources in society. The first refers to its pure or pristine embodiment and the second to its institutionalized form as a regulatory mechanism. When we referred above to trust as existing *in minora*, in some contexts of interaction, this referred to an awareness not of its role as an unconditional principle of generalized exchange but as a recognition, however oblique, of its pristine role in the recognition of another's agency. Hence our only passing need to register its existence in most contexts; in most cases, familiarity in the second sense is sufficient.

Durkheim's own failure to register this difference in the two senses of trust thus led him to conflate the terms of society's unconditionalities (i.e., its precontractual beliefs) with the workings of familiarity as a mechanism for ensuring the shared nature of these beliefs; that is, he conflated trust as familiarity (*qua* mechanism) and trust as a basis for modern forms of solidarity. Some latent realization of this difference was evident, though, in the importance he attributed to the establishment of intermediary groups as providing that familiarity necessary for the establishment of modern forms of solidarity. Membership in these groups, we recall, was meant, in some way, to overcome the process of social differentiation, which in itself made it increasingly difficult to posit precisely those shared strong evaluations of individual actors as a basis for solidarity. As a mechanism for the provision of social solidarity they were thus meant to circumscribe that very differentiation (and concomitant freedom of the other) engendered by the modern forms of the division of labor (and differentiation of roles). However, as we have noted in our prior discussion of Durkheim, that freedom of the other and the risk it implies are fundamental aspects of modern social relations and cannot be "defined away" through membership in intermediary associations. The recognition of their existence is not an aspect of our quotidian life, of the confidence of role expectations and the principles of generalized exchange that structure them, but lies solely within those interactions defined by its "pristine" presence (most generally in the informal realm of friendships and private relations). Thus the reason behind Durkheim's failure to register that trust in the opaqueness of the other's will as a fundamental aspect of modern solidarity lay in his failure to differentiate between the principles of generalized exchange and its pristine form, since only in the latter realm can it make its appearance.

Not only are the phenomena of pristine trust and trust as a principle of generalized exchange not reducible the one to the other, they exist in tension with one another as well. The tension is that between any representative ideal vision of the moral bonds of community and its institutionalized form. The same tension exists between, say, the idea of society represented in the Sermon on the Mount and the institutional workings of the medieval Catholic Church or between the Brahmanic ideal of renunciation and the daily organization of the division of labor in the caste system, between any ideal of kinship and its concrete role in the organization of economic relations. As noted above, it is precisely this tension that leads to periodic ritually institutionalized moments of communitas (whether in the form of pilgrimages, the shared Eucharist, rites of transition, and so on) that reassert those constitutive terms of community that are, by their very nature, vitiated by the quotidian workings of that division of labor based—we stress again—on these very principles.[61]

The need to reassert these fundamental terms of solidarity, to make the unconditional visible, also brings a different aspect of its existence to light: that we do not live our daily lives on the basis of a continual awareness of its presence. The networks of exchange and reciprocity that we daily engage in are not governed by a direct conscious awareness of those principles upon which they are based. And while all social systems have institutionalized some realms of action as defined by the direct connection to the unconditional principles of solidarity (whether in the type of rituals studied by Victor Turner or in certain social roles themselves, of the renouncer in Hinduism, holy man in Islam, shaman, and so on), they cannot for all that subsist solely on a direct connection to such unconditionalities. Such attempts are damned by their own antinomianism (pardon the pun) and examples abound throughout history (we may recall the example of the hippie movement for a contemporary illustration). Augustine's struggle with the Donatists may be understood as just such a struggle over the workings and place of unconditionalities as directly present in the definitions of role, in this case of the priest (the Donatist position) or as mediated by the institutional structure of the Church (Augustine). Augustine betrayed a sharp awareness of the inability to build a perduring social order (in this case of the Catholic Church) on the basis of any continual, direct definition of social roles based on their constitutive terms of unconditionality. The subsequent development of Christendom and of the heterodoxies it spawned have proved Augustine correct. The most singular success of the heterodoxies, the Protestant Reformation, faced the same crises of institutionalization which, in its very success, transformed its original ideas of community and its constitutive bonds.[62]

With Augustine we would thus assert that while the terms of unconditionality in society define its modes of solidarity and principles of the division of labor, they cannot in themselves replace the division of labor. As Marx succinctly put it: "The Middle Ages did not live by faith alone." That is to say, they did not live by the terms of unconditionality as such but by its institutionalization into a system of roles and principles of generalized exchange: institutionalization into precisely those system rules in which confidence may be placed (and social capital seen to exist) and from which a return to the pristine forms is necessitated with the emergence of what we have termed system limits (what we termed above its existence *in minora* within the complex of our daily interactions). Just as the Middle Ages did not live by faith, we do not live by trust. Its existence as an unconditional principle of generalized exchange does not make of it a daily facet of our lives. Indeed it could not be so given the inherent tension between it and its institutionalized forms—that division of labor upon which social life is based.

This brings us to the first contradiction of our contemporary position: that the very success of modernity as a civilization, its successful institutionalization, has led, for reasons adduced above, to a greater and greater need to rely on trust (to refer to the unconditional) at precisely the same time that the conditions for this reliance (familiarity in the second sense) are diminishing (i.e., more interstitial spaces with differentiation of roles combined with less ability to impute a familiar basis of strong evaluations, these strong evaluations being that *conscience collective* based on the idea of the individual and the trust it necessitates). There is also a second contradiction, or perhaps only tension (though it does seem an irresolvable one), and that is between the symbolization of the unconditional in its "pristine" form and its role in the organization of the division of labor: in S. N. Eisenstadt's terms, between those "interactions that symbolize and legitimize the process of unconditionalities and of the establishment of conditions of trust and of the precontractual elements of social life."[63] It is, I would hazard, this contradiction that stands at the core of the existing debate between communitarians and liberals in their different visions of the Public Good and perhaps, just perhaps, by rephrasing the issue in these new terms, we may be able to see the road to the solution.

For the issue of private versus public goods, which stands so centrally at the core of current debates in political philosophy, is, if we think it through sociologically, really an issue of the symbolization of the pristine terms of modern unconditionalities (based on the idea of trust and of the individual) as opposed to its institutionalized forms. The symbolization of the modern terms of solidarity is best represented in the private realm of intimacy and friendship, in the informal and generally considered private realm of interaction. Intuitively, it is there that we seek the warmth and embrace of unconditional solidarity, of trust as shared strong evaluations, and not in the wiles of the marketplace, mall, or stock-exchange (in those areas system confidence usually is sufficient). It is in such more private spaces that we can, following Seyla Benhabib, assume a willingness and capability of individuals to act in terms of the highest ethical standards of our culture (i.e., of its terms of unconditionality) and where, together with others—very concrete others with whom we share mutual ties of history, ideas, love, care, and friendship—we generally seek the locus of that solidarity based on the representative idea of trust which we posit at the core of our culture.[64] This is the source of a particularly modern paradox: the representation, the very constitution, of an ethical space as representative of the unconditionalities of cultural life as apart and in contradistinction from the realm of its organizational effects as a principle of generalized exchange— the opposition of the private and public realms. The "strong ties" of trust in the personal realm thus stand in opposition to the "weak ties" of the workings of trust as a principle in the organization of the division of labor.[65]

This opposition is a developmental one and like the first contradiction in the terms of modern unconditionality (trust), its progress is an aspect—an unintended consequence—of its very successful institutionalization. For at its origins not only was such a contradiction between private and public realms not felt, but it was the very new terms of unconditionality (based on trust) that permitted the establishment of commercial society through the development of similar modes of interaction to "out-groups" and "in-groups" alike. This development was paralleled in both economic and political arenas. Its political expression was best captured in Burke's famous quote on the "little platoon" where he states that "To be attached to the subdivision, to love the little platoon we belong to in society, is the first principle, the germ, as it were, of public affections. It is the first link in the series by which we proceed toward a love to our country and to mankind."[66] Its importance for modes of economic action was much studied by Max Weber, who stressed its debt to the religious codes of Reformation Protestantism which led to the "disappearance of the dualistic ethics, of the distinction between a universally binding morality and a specifically advantaged code for the virtuosi."[67] Hence his famous remark that

[t]he universal reign of absolute unscrupulousness in the pursuit of selfish interests by the making of money has been a specific characteristic of precisely those countries whose bourgeois-capitalistic development, measured according to Occidental standards, has remained backward. As every employer knows, the lack of *coscienziosità* of the labourers of such countries, for instance Italy as compared with Germany, has been, and to a certain extent still is, one of the principal obstacles to their capitalistic development. Capitalism cannot make use of the labour of those who practice the doctrine of undisciplined *liberum arbitrium*, any more than it can make use of the business man who seems absolutely unscrupulous in his dealings with others.[68]

Not, then, the establishment of voluntary associations *per se* (*pace* Fukuyama and others) that stands at the root of capitalist entrepreneurial success, but the terms of these associations, their moral codes or unconditionalities are the central issue. When these ties have been based on trust (and not on familiarity, as in Japan, for example), the development of these codes was concomitant with the strong ties—weak ties dynamic noted above (and hence, as we shall see, with the developing contradiction between the private and public realms). As Benjamin Nelson pointed out: "It is a tragedy of modern history that the expansion of the area of the moral community has ordinarily been gained through the sacrifice of the intensity of the moral bond, or, . . . that all men have been becoming brothers by becoming equally others."[69]

Yet such definitions of moral community (and hence of the unconditionalities of exchange) were necessitated in the West by the two fundamental tenets of modern capitalism: the separation of business from the household and the rational organization of free labor. The idea of a moral community of virtue *qua* trust remained problematic and perhaps untenable. For the selfsame vision of trust that plays so much a part in the classical republican tradition and which in Anthony Pagden's terms "makes it so peculiarly suited to capitalism, or to use the contemporary term, to the commercial society" divides precisely along the fault line of the representation of pristine trust, which is overwhelmingly conceived in terms of the private realm.[70] Eighteenth-century America can perhaps be taken as the exemplary case of both these issues: the correlation between classic republicanism and the growth of commercial society; and the representation of this virtue upon which society is based in terms of private selves rather than public persona.[71]

Thus, where originally public trust was seen to rest on private trust (just as the "freedom of contract" and the guaranteeing of the "personal autonomy" of contracting parties was enshrined in nineteenth-century contractual law), today the relation between these two forms of trust is more conflictual: the "freedom of contract" has been circumscribed by its many restrictions and the privileging of the autonomy of the parties made more and more subject to principles of public order. It needs to be stressed that these restrictions on contract are themselves consequent on the contradiction between the terms of pristine trust as "personal autonomy" and their institutionalized form in the entitlement and rights of individuals and groups that circumscribe the "free" workings of the contract. Note the seeming contradiction here—for it will take us to the heart of the matter at hand. In the nineteenth century the principles of generalized exchange guaranteed the freedom of contract, while in the twentieth century the very same principles limited such freedom by providing for the rights and entitlements of working people and extending the social dimension of citizenship beyond the gentleman class; and affirmative action laws do the same to other groups. Thus, the greater *institutionalization* of the idea of the individual as source of the moral order—within the workings of the society and the economy—led to restrictions on that very personal autonomy of the individual (here the contracting parties) that had, in the mid-nineteenth century, represented the idea of society's unconditionalities par excellence.

These issues arise again and again in Atiyah's influential study of contract law, *The Rise and Fall of Freedom of Contract*. He shows how in classic nineteenth-century liberal theory public trust in the "performance" and "fidelity" to promises did indeed rest on private trust in the same:

> It was an important principle of social life amongst "gentlemen"; it was an important commercial principle, for businessmen had to rely on the promises of others; it was an important principle of social behavior and discipline, for the public, who had to learn that once arrangements had been made, they must be observed; it was an important principle of justice too, for justice required that every man be given his due, and what was more obviously due than what had been promised?[72]

Atiyah also demonstrates how by the end of the century these principles had changed and freedom of contract and the autonomy of contracting parties had become more and more subject to public restraints. These restraints rested on new principles of distributive justice which came to subject the contract to more and more qualifications. Interesting is the fact that these new arguments were legitimized by principles of marginal utility (one hundred pounds to a millionaire was worth less than ten pounds to a working man), which, I believe, illustrates how they continued to invoke the same unconditionalities (of the moral idea of the individual as value) or principles of generalized exchange, but now formulated in more generalized social, and societal terms and, crucially, institutionalized to a greater extent within the workings of economic life.[73] It was precisely this institutionalization that pitted the public, social, and instrumental aspects of what have become the principles of generalized exchange in Western modernity against their more pristine, pure, and private aspects.

And it is through this process of institutionalization of the unconditionalities, or principles of generalized exchange, that, I believe, we can best understand some of the most pressing problems in contemporary political theory and their relevance to the problem of trust in the contemporary world. For as we have attempted to argue, this tension or contradiction in the very different realms that "pristine" trust and trust as a principle of generalized exchange are seen to operate is in fact the operative principle in the current and often remarked-upon conflict between the private and the public realms—especially as this is represented in current political theory and in the conflicting vision of liberals and communitarians respectively. To these more symbolic and ideological aspects of this conflict we must now turn.

Part Two

THE REPRESENTATION OF TRUST AND
THE PRIVATE SPHERE

Four

Public and Private in Political Thought

ROUSSEAU, SMITH, AND SOME CONTEMPORARIES

THE CONCEPTS of public and private, like the idea of civil society, associational life, or the public sphere, are, at present, undergoing a minor renaissance and are the subject of innumerable books, essays, conferences, and symposia. They are not, however, new concepts or new ideas and have in fact been integrated into the work of anthropologists, political scientists, and sociologists for some time. From Hannah Arendt's *The Human Condition* (1958) through Charles Maier's influential volume on *Changing Boundaries of Public and Private* (1987) and down to the appearance in English of Jurgen Habermas's *The Structural Transformation of the Public Sphere* (1989, which played a major role in refocusing scholarly interest in this direction), the concepts of public and private have been gaining saliency and prestige in scholarly circles. The recently edited volume by Jeff Weintraub and Krishan Kumar, *Public and Private in Thought and Practice: Perspectives on a Grand Dichotomy* (1997), is ample evidence of the new awareness scholars in different disciplines are bringing to this subject.

Given this extensive interest and the frequency with which these terms appear, not only in scholarly books and articles, but in popular debates as well, it is interesting to note that the ideas of public and private are surprisingly undertheorized concepts within the field of sociology. This situation is quite the reverse of the current interest in the issue of public and private found in political science or anthropology, where these concepts have been subjected to rigorous scrutiny and debate. In neither case is this interest surprising. Liberal political theory rests, after all, on the separation between public and private realms—and indeed lives; and from Karl Marx and Benjamin Constant in the nineteenth century down to recent debates between communitarians and liberals over the definition of the public good, the issue of public and private—their boundaries, content, interpenetration, and so on—have been the subject of intense interest and debate. In recent years, this debate has been joined by feminist scholars who, like many theorists of republican democracy (such as Quentin Skinner), are offering a critique of the liberal distinction between home and market (private and public spheres) and challenging the classical liberal distinction between public and private realms.[1]

Moreover, the current interest in civil society and the idea of the public sphere—sparked by the events of 1989 in Eastern Europe and, to some extent, by Habermas's *Structural Transformation of the Public Sphere*—have led to renewed interest in the very idea of public and private, its historical, comparative, and analytic dimensions. All these factors, together with the current debates on privatization and the role of the public sector in the organization of the polity and collective life, feminist critiques of the "patriarchal" project hidden at the heart of the modern liberal vision, struggles over the multiculturalist agenda and what have been termed "political correctness," have contributed to a sophisticated and highly articulate attempt to theorize the issues of public and private in the fields of political science, political philosophy, and public policy.

In a similar vein, these issues of public and private have, for some time now, played an important role within the discipline of anthropology, where the encounter with other cultures has led ethnographers to explore the similarities and differences of these categories across different cultural contexts. In this realm, the work done by Jane Schneider on the structuring of gender relations in North African and Middle Eastern communities, or the research by Leslie Haviland and John B. Haviland on privacy in a Mexican village are but a few examples of the continuing interest of anthropology in understanding the dynamics of public and private in different societies.[2]

Given this situation, it is somewhat surprising to find that there has not yet been any synthetic attempt to theorize the issues of public and private; that is, to unite the different perspectives and definitions currently being propounded in political philosophy, anthropology, or feminist theory into a comprehensive statement. Such a statement should be able to provide a classificatory scheme that would hold across cultures and historical epochs and so allow for further inquiry into the uniqueness and specificity of different forms (and ideologies) of public and private in different cultural settings. In a sense, such a project should be the concern of sociology, which has, however, shied away from any such attempt. This reticence is surprising not only given the increasing saliency of the terms in both popular and academic discourse, but also—and even more importantly—given the very diverse and sometimes opposing meanings and definitions attributed by different theorists to these concepts.

One glaring example of this type of divergence among existing perspectives can be found in Hannah Arendt's very conception of public and private, which in her reading begin to disappear in modernity with the "rise of the social," a concept which in her usage subsumes the very distinction that had previously existed (in antiquity, for example) between public and private. This very compelling account stands in contradiction to that of most other theorists, from Marx and Constant down to Habermas, all of whom see in the eighteenth century and the beginnings of modern capitalist culture the very origins or emergence of that distinction between public and private realms whose demise Arendt posits in the selfsame period.

Or, to take yet another example, Norberto Bobbio's now classic piece on "Public and Private/The Great Dichotomy," where he classifies these concepts in relational terms of inequality versus equality and of relations between the parts and the whole versus relations among parts.[3] His scheme would appear somewhat as follows:

PUBLIC	PRIVATE
unequal	equal
relations between:	relations between:
parts and whole	parts
God	brothers
State	kin
family	friends
	citizens
	enemies

Here we have the beginnings of a fascinating cross-cutting categorization but one laden with problems as soon as we leave the field of political philosophy and enter the minutia of daily life. Thus, relations between God and man, while certainly unequal and pertaining to the relations of the part to the whole, are also often defined within the privacy of conscience and in many circumstances the privacy of a home or other secluded space (at least since the Protestant Reformation—a point we will have occasion to return to often in our analysis). So too the family, in modernity, has entered into the private realm as the State has penetrated into the regulation of private lives and agendas. On the other side of the balance, the relation between brothers is characterized by equality only in some cultures and not in others (primogeniture being a good example of the inequality reigning between brothers). In tribal societies kin systems may be ordered according to principles of equality or hierarchy, and one does not take analytic preference over the other. Friendship, too, as an informal relation between equals is a most modern phenomenon with vast variations across cultures and historical periods. What does remain of Bobbio's definitions is the crucial (somewhat Hegelian) and thought-provoking identification of public with the relation between the parts and the whole, and the private with the relations among the parts.

Such a definition is indeed tantalizing in its implications not least in the sphere of trust and its relation to issues of social solidarity. For example, we have already stressed the need to distinguish between trust in its "pristine" form and as an institutionalized model of generalized exchange. We have also seen how this distinction bears on the relations between the public and the private realms: how in modern societies the realization of trust in its "pristine" form is seen as the preserve of the private realm (what Bobbio defines as the one of relations among the parts) as opposed to its institutionalized expression in the public realm (where the relations of the parts to the whole are articulated). By supplementing our own insight with those of Bobbio we thus begin to appreciate the problem of maintaining social solidarity, or associational life, in societies where the principled articulation of its unconditionalities is reserved for the private and not the public spheres. It becomes manifest (or rather exists as potential) in the relations among the parts and not in the relations between the parts and the whole. In different ways this is the tension that we shall be exploring in this section of our inquiry.

We will begin with a brief inquiry into two traditions of political thought whose moral imperatives bear directly on these two very different realms of public and private and have, consequently, over the past two hundred years, posited the one or the other set of relations as constitutive of the Public Good. Thus before entering into more analytic dimensions of the public/private issue as they turn on matters of confidence and trust, we think it wise to explore first certain aspects of their role in political or moral philosophy. For the argument that I wish to develop is that if we explore the two political traditions of what I will call for brevity's sake "civic virtue" and "civil society" respectively, we can find two very different visions of public and private as sources of virtue and morality. Ultimately these two political visions privilege two very different sets of relations—those between the parts and the whole and those among the parts—as constitutive of the very terms of mutuality and of the moral order, essentially as I will argue, of trust.

These two traditions represent what are, basically contrasting models of citizenship and so, what are ultimately contrasting visions of the social good. Indeed, many of the current debates over citizenship in the West as in the East, whether of a highly principled nature (e.g., the liberal-communitarian debate) or inherently practical (over multiculturalism, language instruction in schools in some North Atlantic communities, the status of Russian minorities in the Baltic states, or the status of ethnic minorities throughout Eastern and East Central Europe), are rooted in principles that derive from these two political traditions principles that tend, as I shall argue, to privilege different conceptions of trust as aspects of the public and private realms respectively.

To some extent, this insight is not terribly new. In fact Benjamin Constant's 1819 speech given at the Athenée Royal on "De la liberté des anciens comparée à celle des modernes" is precisely an explication of some salient differences between the traditions of civic virtue and civil society, though not expressly presented in those terms.[4] Given the tenacity of current debates in political theory (and their oft-times polemical character) as well as the much more critical practical challenges facing societies in both Eastern Europe and the West at the end of the twentieth century, it may not be imprudent to review some of this territory once again and attempt to isolate those areas of convergence and, perhaps more importantly, of divergence, in these two traditions within whose contrasting desiderata our own ideas of the social good are so deeply rooted.

Both civil society and civic virtue are concerned, as is all political theory, with defining relations between the individual and the social, and positing this relationship in normative as well as descriptive terms. Both are firmly rooted in the intellectual traditions of Western Europe, in the doctrines of natural law, the political philosophies and images of ancient Greece and Republican Rome. Both played a considerable role in the early modern era when with the breakdown of the feudal order and the universal Catholic Church a new basis was sought for the organization of society.[5] Both continued in different (and often interwoven) forms into the eighteenth—and to an extent into the nineteenth—century among different thinkers, making it difficult (and in the space of this chapter, impossible) to give a full history of these terms. What is possible is the abstraction of some of the core analytic ideas which more or less defined the respective traditions in their different attitudes toward the social good. Both are concerned with providing the foundations of what could be termed a "moral community" as the foundation of social life. And in both traditions the idea of "virtue" is seen as central to the existence of this moral community.

Similarly, both are concerned with the forces of "corruption" threatening this moral community, forces posited in strikingly similar terms of luxury, envy, avarice, and what we would term the growing differentiation of society (and, by the end of the eighteenth century the growth of the market and ties of pure, instrumental exchange between social actors). Similarities notwithstanding, there are important differences, both historical and analytical in nature, and both are to some extent related.

Civil society was more an Anglo-American tradition embodied most saliently in thinkers such as Francis Hutcheson, John Millar, Hugh Blair, Adam Ferguson, and Adam Smith, whom we identify with the Scottish Enlightenment. By contrast, the tradition of civic virtue would seem more continental in nature, our immediate associations running from Machiavelli through Jean-Jacques Rousseau (though the importance of civic virtue in England among "neo-Harringtonians" and as an influence on colonial culture in the decades of independence is critical).[6] The civic virtue tradition was more immediately rooted in the political philosophy of ancient Greece and Rome and in this sense more "backward looking." Taking the ancient city-state as a model of republican virtue, it sought (and in some sense still seeks) to return to that definition of citizenship embodied in the Athenian polis or Roman republic. It thus seeks to return to a definition of man as citizen where, following Aristotle, man's (and now presumably woman's) telos was to be found in and only in the sphere of political activity.

This concept of man as the "complete citizen" or what can be alternatively rendered as the "totalization" of man as citizen was far from that tradition of social thought that we associate with the idea of civil society, as least as it developed in the eighteenth century among the Scottish moralists.[7] While recognizing the virtue of ancient republican government, these thinkers were more sensitive to the irremediable nature of historical change, and their thought was, consequently, more attuned to positing a new foundation for reciprocity, mutuality, and cooperation (and so, ultimately for virtue) and less to a return to a form of social organization whose efficacy in the support of virtue in eighteenth-century commercial society was increasingly in doubt.

In some sense, these latter assumptions of the Scottish moralists would seem to have been vindicated by the passage of time, for, by the last third of the eighteenth century and more definitely in the early nineteenth century—insofar as we can distinguish between both traditions—the civil society tradition begins to take the place of the civic virtue tradition. This becomes clearer as the nineteenth century progresses and the ideas of civil society are in some sense institutionalized within the growing struggles over citizenship.

These historical differences, however, can serve as no more than an introduction to what are the crucial differences between both traditions. And our interest, fed as it is more by current concerns and less by a purely theoretical interest in the history of ideas, must thus focus on what are the crucial analytic differences between these two traditions in their vision of human endeavor within society.

These differences turn on what are essentially different definitions of virtue, or, in somewhat broader terms, different conceptions of the moral order. In more sociological terms these can be expressed as different conceptions of solidarity where the moral sense is a function of public or private morality respectively (in the civic virtue and civil society traditions). We need only recall Durkheim's analysis and comparison of repressive and restitutive law as characteristic of mechanical and organic solidarity to apprehend the immediate parallels with the very different moral visions represented by these two political traditions.[8]

In the civic virtue tradition from Aristotle (man's telos in polis) through Machiavelli, the neo-Harringtonian (fear of corruption in the eighteenth century), Rousseau (surrender of all natural liberty to community), and even into Hannah Arendt's philosophical vision (where human realization can only be in the participatory light of the public realm), the moral idea is a *public* one.[9] It is defined by the *conscience collective* or, to use Rousseau's famous expression, the *volonté générale*.[10] Morality, or the stuff of virtue, is less a private attribute and more a public or communal enterprise. It is realized by the active (and continual) participation of collective members in communal affairs and can, following Machiavelli, be abstracted and removed from all elements of private morality.[11] With Rousseau, "virtue" is succinctly defined as the "conformity of the particular wills with the general will."[12] This is congruent with his overall moral vision where what is regulated and subjected to authority is not only man's "actions" but also his "will."[13] The sovereign authority in question is not that of the despot but of the community, that community constituted, as Rousseau explains in *The Social Contract*, by "the total alienation of each associate together with all his rights to the community."[14] That community where "each of us puts his person and all his power in common under the supreme direction of the general will, and, in our corporate capacity, we receive each member as an *indivisible part of the whole*" (emphasis mine) is not only a model of that type of solidarity which Durkheim termed mechanical, but is, in essence, a model of citizenship which most closely approximates the ideal society in the civic virtue tradition.[15]

Rousseau describes, then, a community of a totally unmediated relation between the parts and the whole, where "private interests" and "partial associations" are condemned and where the relation "of the members to one another" are "as unimportant" and the relation of the member "to the body as a whole" are "as important as possible":[16] a moral community where what is moral is precisely the community. Once we have abandoned a transcendent morality (and if we remain unenticed by utilitarian theory), we have few choices but to follow Durkheim's strictures on the communal nature of all morality. I note this only for the purpose of keeping a crucial distinction in mind—that between community as the source of morality (a sociological truism) and the notion of community as morality (to put it somewhat starkly). The latter idea is at the heart of the civic virtue tradition, where a community of virtue (to use a more emic term) is one in which the social good is defined solely by the subjugation of the private self to the public realm.

We are now entering somewhat tricky ground, for the boundaries, indeed the very definition of the public and private, are not only continually changing but, in the eighteenth century, are only beginning to emerge as a distinction worthy of thought.[17] Thus, before discussing the other distinctive characteristics of the civic virtue tradition (which, I would maintain, follow from this defining trait), it may be wise to contrast its very public character with that of the civil society tradition as exemplified by the Scottish moralists. For, in the civil society tradition, especially as it differentiates itself from civic virtue (in the second half of the eighteenth century), the moral basis of society becomes more and more a *private* ideal. This private idea (and ideal) of virtue stands in such marked contrast to the public character of virtue in the former tradition as to exemplify what is, as noted above, a fundamentally different model of citizenship and of the social good. In fact, the move from virtue as an attribute of the public sphere to one of private morality was a crucial development in the making of modern liberal individualism and its models of order. It is, as such, worthy of our attention. The juxtaposition of these two traditions, moreover, will aid in our understanding of each in its own right.

The tradition of civil society is, as I have argued elsewhere, first and foremost an ethical edifice.[18] From Anthony Shaftesbury's *Characteristics of Men, Morals, Opinions, Times* (1711) through Francis Hutcheson's *Inquiry Into the Origins of Beauty and Virtue* (1725), Adam Ferguson's *An Essay on the History of Civil Society* (1767), and until the 1790 edition of Adam Smith's *The Theory of Moral Sentiments*, it is concerned with positing the moral sense or a "universal determination to benevolence in mankind" as a fundamental given of human nature.[19] It was this moral sense that assured mutuality, compassion, empathy, and so a basis for human interaction beyond the calculus of pure exchange. In Adam Ferguson's words:

> If it be true that men are united by instinct, that they act in society from affections of kindness and friendship, it if be true, that even prior to acquaintance and habitude, men, as such, are commonly to each other objects of attention and to some degree of regard . . . it should seem that . . . the foundations of a moral apprehension are sufficiently laid and the sense of a right which we maintain for ourselves is by a movement of humanity and candor extended to our fellow creatures. [Consequently, Ferguson goes on to note] Mankind, we are told, are devoted to interest, and this, in all commercial nations, is undoubtedly true: But it does not follow, that they are, by their natural dispositions, averse to society and mutual affection . . . human felicity does not consist in the indulgences of animal appetite, but in those of a benevolent heart; not in fortune or interest but in contempt of this very object, in the courage and freedom which arise from this contempt, joined to a resolute choice of conduct, directed to the good of mankind, or to the good of that particular society to which the party belongs.[20]

The definition and conceptualization of this moral sense was different among the different thinkers of the Scottish Enlightenment. Shaftesbury's "natural affections," which discerns "the amicable and the admirable," is not the same as Ferguson's "moral sentiment" or "principle of affection to mankind."[21] Nor were either of these as developed philosophically as Adam Smith's principle of "sympathy and approbation" which for him provided the driving force of "all the toil and bustle of the world . . . the end of avarice and ambition, of the pursuit of wealth."[22] They are all, however (with the partial exception of Smith, whom we will discuss in greater depth), strikingly similar in positing an innate moral sense whose existence is both independent of reason and a function of individual (moral) psychology.[23] The "conscience" that the thinkers of eighteenth-century Edinburgh and Glasgow were struggling toward was one of individual mores rather than public commitments. It was rooted in the individual self rather than in a social being. If for Rousseau the moral sense in the form of the *volonté générale* can be said to arise sui generis out of society, for the thinkers of the civil society tradition, it also exists sui generis and beyond reduction to other interests, reasons, and passions. Yet in struggling to posit an autonomous grounding to moral facts they had recourse not to the social, but to the individual self as guarantor of the moral order.[24]

The idea of civil society maintained elements of the civic virtue tradition, that is, of the communal locus of individual life (especially when we consider the later development of liberal theory and "methodological individualism"). The ideas of "vanity" for Ferguson and "approbation" for Smith play this role and provide the basis for natural sympathy and moral affections upon which moral community is predicated.[25] Both posited what we have termed earlier an "interactive" self whose existence is social in nature and constituted by the refraction of our actions in the eyes of the other. Both link us to the social whole as we become who we are through the other's perception of us (a sort of Meadian social self *avant la lettre*). Yet, crucially here the communal or social "other" is internalized in the self, which remains inviolate though not abstracted from community. This, however, is very different from—if not diametrically opposed to—the classical tradition which saw the individual as human only within the polis and through activity in the public realm (and which, in ancient Rome, even saw the intimate activity of procreation as a fulfillment of civic duties) or Rousseau's ideal where only the replacement of the individual personality by a "corporate and collective body" with its own communal identity, life, and will can guarantee civic virtue, and human realization.[26]

Interestingly, both models are to act for the protection of moral, communal ties against corrupting influences and against, in Rousseau's terms, the "cheapening of virtue," but whereas the first achieves this by rooting communal virtues in individual selves, the second seeks to achieve this by restricting individual virtue to the public realm.[27] A good example of this difference, as well as of the fact that the principals involved were well aware of this difference, can be found in the question posed to the Edinburgh Belles Lettres Society in the early 1760s—"Whether the Character of Cato or that of Atticus is most excellent?" i.e., public or private man. From this followed the true residency of virtue, which for the literati of Edinburgh society was to be found in Atticus's role as a virtuous individual, impartial and sympathetic observer of the public realm.[28]

This emphasis on private morality as a guarantee of public welfare was a common feature of eighteenth-century thinking on civil society, especially in Scotland where it was propounded by such thinkers as Hugh Blair and the Moderate Preachers, enjoined in such publications as the *Edinburgh Magazine* or the *Caledonian Mercury*, and debated in such societies as the Mirror Club and the Parthenon Society.[29] Thus it was precisely in those social organizations of the public realm (where civil society is today, somewhat nostalgically, seen to reside) that argument was most forcefully presented for the necessary foundation of public order on private morality.

In slightly different terms, and if we think back to the tradition of civic virtue, "sociability" (or, with Adam Smith, "interactive sympathy") can be said to replace "virtue" as the foundation of moral community. This is at one and the same time a more differentiated and sophisticated theory of the moral community and rests on a very different conception of the social enterprise. Put more strikingly and remaining with Adam Smith, whose psychology is perhaps the most sophisticated within the civil society tradition, the idea of conscience as the internal impartial spectator takes the place, as it were, of the *volonté générale* since virtue is defined as that which is approved by the impartial spectator.

This juxtaposition of the internal, impartial spectator against the idea of the *volonté générale* is, I would claim, the very heart of the issue at hand and adds both a historical specificity and analytic sophistication to our prior contrast of private and public conceptions of virtue. For while subjection to the *volonté générale* is a rational act that guarantees (public) virtue by the suppression of all partial (private) interest (through, we may add, the creation of a new *corps collectif*), the idea of the impartial observer is but an individual (psychological) mechanism through which, for Smith, the workings of mutual sympathy progressed.[30] Smith, it should be noted, did not share with Hutcheson, Ferguson, and others the idea that "sympathy" or "mutual sympathy" was a particular type of emotion, irreducible to any other—a psychological datum, as it were.

Rather, he saw sympathy as a function of that practical virtue termed "propriety" which was assessed by the "impartial spectator." Without entering here into Smith's complex and subtle psychology of interactive emotions, it is sufficient to point out that "propriety" (and so the workings of sympathy) turn on the idea of the impartial spectator, conceived as impartial, informed, and sharing in the common standards of the community. Through assuming the position of the impartial spectator, we judge both our own conduct and that of others. In Smith's words:

> We endeavor to examine our own conduct as we imagine any other fair and impartial spectator would examine it. If, upon placing ourselves in his situation, we thoroughly enter into all the passions and motives which influenced it, we approve of it, by sympathy with the approbation of this supposed equitable judge. If otherwise, we enter into his disapprobation and condemn it.[31]

This exercise both aids us in bringing our own passions in line with acceptable common standards, (propriety) tempering the intensity of our own felt experience to fit common standards and more importantly, creates an independent moral standpoint detached from any given social morality.

The idea of propriety as a standard to judge both our own actions and those of others is, for Smith, rooted in "the eyes of a third party," that impartial spectator, "the great inmate of the breast" who "judges impartially" between conflicting interests.[32] As Smith advises us when assessing our interests in opposition to those of our fellows:

> Before we can make any proper comparison of opposing interests, we must change our position. We must view them from neither our own place nor yet from his, neither with our own eyes nor yet with his, but from the place and with the eyes of a third person, who has no particular connection with either, and who judges impartially between us.[33]

As convincingly argued by Knud Haakonssen, it is the continual search for this neutral third-party position, for the standards of this impartial spectator, that makes social life possible, in that it provides the foundation for a morality higher than the changing whims of any given set of social mores.[34]

It is with this insight that Smith breaks with both the preceding tradition of civil society, with its naive anthropology and notions of an innate sympathy, as well as with any attachment to collective norms and mores (what may perhaps be termed today, in the language of republican citizenship, the "latent community") upon which the civic virtue tradition is based. For in revising the sixth (1790) edition of *The Theory of Moral Sentiments*, Smith abandoned his idea of a harmonious society in which public opinion can be seen as a guide to moral action (or virtue) and proposed in its stead a psychological mechanism for the development of an internal conscience. As the "man within the breast" takes the place of the man outside—or public opinion—as the source of virtue, a new foundation is posited for the pursuit of the social good. In the move from the first to the sixth edition of *The Theory of Moral Sentiments*, the impartial spectator is internalized, removed from any facile identification with public opinion, and virtue casts off its moorings in the public sphere.[35] While men are, in this reading, still social beings, what permits sociability is not the dissolution of self (in the *volonté générale*) but the constitution of self through that higher morality imparted by the impartial, internal spectator (higher, that is, than the mere motive of recognition and approval on the part of "high society," a motive that Smith was to view with increasing apprehension through the closing decades of the eighteenth century).[36]

Here then, I submit, we have a very different model of virtue, of social mutuality, and of the common good than that presented in the different thinkers whom we associate with the traditions of civic virtue. In that tradition, the public good is one which overrides all private goods and rests, ultimately, on the overcoming of self-interest for public concerns. This is not simple public-spiritedness, but rather a vision of humankind that sees in the public arena the only possibility to realize and fulfill the self-identity of the private citizen. By contrast, the ethical idea in the civil society tradition is a private one, realized within the hearts, minds, and acts of exchange of individual social actors. To be sure, after Hume's critique of the Scottish Enlightenment view of reason, it became increasingly difficult to posit an innate propensity toward mutuality and sympathy among humans, as had stood so well for the likes of Shaftesbury, Hutcheson, and Ferguson.[37] In the works of Adam Smith, however, a new prop is added to the armature of civil society which was not only more sophisticated and supple, but also served to ground interactive sympathy in individual virtue (specifically, by the final edition of *The Theory of Moral Sentiments*, in that of self-command).[38] These differences between the two traditions of political thought can be outlined—somewhat schematically—as found in the table on page 115.

From these fundamental distinctions on what may be termed the nature of virtue other distinctions follow. They are, I believe, of less analytic importance than the prior distinctions noted (and of less relevance to current concerns), and so we shall summarize them rather than submit them to analysis.

a. Attitude toward the "distinction of talents."
The civil society tradition has a more moderate (or perhaps ambivalent) attitude toward the processes of social differentiation. On the one hand, social differentiation is seen as leading toward civility and the civilizing process; this is as true of Ferguson as of Smith. On the other hand, when it is too great and is combined with too enlarged a territory, producing the loss of a small community (and of face-to-face interaction), it is viewed as a source of corruption. In Ferguson's telling words:

> [T]he separation of the professions, while it seems to promise improvement of skill, and is actually the cause of why the productions of every art become more perfect as commerce advances; yet in its termination and ultimate effects, serves,

	Civil Society	*Civic Virtue*
Realm of Virtue	private	public
Definition of Virtue	moral sentiments; natural sympathy, attention, and approbation	shared community
Mechanisms of Virtue	impartial spectator	*volonté générale*
Model of Self	divided (and so), reflexive (relatively differentiated)	constituted by *conscience collective* (relatively undifferentiated)
Orientation of Self	inward	outward

Source: From Adam B. Seligman, "Animadversions upon Civil Society and Civic Virtue in the Last Decade of the Twentieth Century," in *Civil Society*, ed. John Hall (Oxford: Polity Press, 1995), 210.

in some measure to break the bonds of society, to substitute mere forms and rules of art in place of ingenuity and to withdraw individuals from the common scene of occupation, on which the sentiments of the heart and the mind are most happily employed. . . . In proportion as territory is extended, its parts lose their relative importance to the whole. Its inhabitants cease to perceive their connection with the state and are seldom united in the execution of any national, or of any sanctious designs. . . . It is even remarkable, that the enlargement of territory, by rendering the individual of less consequence to the public, and less able to intrude with his counsel actually tends to reduce national affairs within a narrow compass, as well as to diminish the numbers who are consulted in legislation or in other matters of government.[39]

Within the civic virtue tradition (especially with Rousseau), social differentiation is also seen as the source of corruption, perhaps the major source, and for Rousseau virtue is indeed the only alternative to the falseness of life that this had led to. It is, for Rousseau, the distinction of talents which as a function of life in society is the cause of inequality and the loss of virtue.[40] We should note too that the tradition of civic virtue is in fact predicated on the idea of the city, a "closed" society or community of nonanonymous individuals for whom mutual trust and responsibility presupposes mutual acquaintance.[41]

b. Source of corruption.
This has been viewed very differently by different thinkers, especially within the civic virtue tradition, which is historically older. Yet, to a great extent the source (in addition to the very differentiation of society noted

above) of corruption is seen as rooted in external factors (this was very much the case in eighteenth-century England and America).[42] In its most classical form (ancient and medieval), this external force took the form of *fortuna*, whose influence on human affairs could be mitigated only by the possession (or pursuit) of *virtu*.[43] In the civil society tradition there is a greater appreciation of internal corrupting influences—internal to society and, even more, internal to the individual. This is perhaps most evident in Adam Smith's increasing ambivalence to wealth and to "our disposition to admire, and consequently to imitate, the rich and the great," which is for him "the great and most universal cause of the corruption of our moral sentiments."[44] Thus the problem of *fortuna* gives way to the problem of market ties, the pursuit of particular interests, and, ever so much more interestingly with Adam Smith, the corruption of individual conscience. The concern with particular interests, cupidity, and the problem of wealth is also present in the civic virtue tradition, especially with Rousseau, but note an important difference: the problem exists at analytically different levels in both traditions. For Rousseau it is a constitutive (I am almost tempted to call it an ontological problem) of our very being in society that can be overcome only by the pursuit of virtue through submission to the general will. In Rousseau's words: "All the inequality which now prevails owes its strength and growth to the development of our faculties and the advance of the human mind, and becomes at last permanent and legitimate by the establishment of property and laws."[45] In the civil society tradition, the problem of particular interests is more "tactical"; it becomes a problem only when it takes an extreme form, and covetousness is a threat only when it is unmediated by conscience and the workings of the internal, impartial spectator. Particularity, privateness, and the individual have, as we have seen, a validity in this tradition—as individual/private/particular—that they lack in Rousseau and in the whole tradition of civic virtue of which he is a part.

More "etically," more sociologically, with more historical hindsight and with an eye to current concerns (in both the West and the East), we must query the moral basis of social solidarity in both traditions: what keeps society civil and/or virtuous, as the case may be? The ramifications of this question on the current debates between universalists and communitarians, on advocates of liberal or republican versions of citizenship, and, more crucially, on the current political situation in many parts of the world should be clear.

For the debate over liberal or republican versions of citizenship is, in many respects, nothing but a contemporary reformulation of the contrasting visions of citizenship, of the individual and of the public good contained in the two traditions of political thought we have been discussing. Liberal (or what Charles Taylor has called "procedural") theory views society as an assortment of morally autonomous individuals, each with his and her own concept of the good life, with the function of society being limited to ensuring the legal equality of these individuals through a procedurally just (or fair) process of democratic decision-making in the public sphere.[46] It is concerned with ensuring the continued operation of universally valid principles of justice (or right) rather than with imposing any particular moral vision on the individual social actors who make up society.

Republican versions of citizenship posit, by contrast, a conception of society as a "moral community" engaged in the pursuit of a common good, whose ontological status is prior to that of any individual member. In this reading, the terms of selfhood no less than those of community are transformed, since—following Sandel's critique of Rawls—there can exist no "radically situated" or "unencumbered" self free from the morally binding and constituting ties of a particular community.[47] Even without further explication, it is not difficult to hear the (slightly modified) echoes of Smith and Rousseau resonating in these different positions across two hundred years.

However, what is debated in highly principled terms at Harvard, McGill, or Princeton is, in other parts of the world, a subject for less civil and studied debate. Throughout Eastern and East Central Europe, in Hungary, Slovakia, the Baltic States, the Czech Republic and elsewhere, the emergent civic polities are all struggling to define new principles of social organization and solidarity along a fault line of what can roughly be termed the principles of either a "demos" or an "ethnos," principles that draw on either of the two models we have been analyzing.[48]

As was tellingly argued in a recent article by Yoav Peled on the terms of citizenship in contemporary Israel, any given polity may be defined not solely by its acceptance of one or the other of these models, but—and especially in ethnically heterogeneous societies—by a mixture of both: and so by differential definitions of the terms of mutuality and solidarity, as well as the obligations and rights of citizenship of different ethnic groups within society.[49]

Of great importance to this debate (regardless of whether it is carried out in the West, East, or Middle East), therefore, are those terms of solidarity or membership which inhere to the different models of political theory and so of citizenship represented by the traditions under discussion. This draws on the different conceptions of self and society represented by both traditions. And if, for the liberal-individualist (or universalist) tradition which emerges out of the idea of civil society, the model of solidarity is one of acts of exchange between morally autonomous and agentic individuals, for the communitarian tradition, or that of republican citizenship, it is one most often rooted in primordial or ascriptive criteria. This is so even in Sandel's description of individuals "as members of *this* family or community or nation or people, as bearers of *this* history, as sons and daughters of *that* revolution, as citizens of *this* republic" (emphasis mine), to whom, it may be added, I owe "allegiances" and "obligations" that go beyond those that "justice requires or even permits."[50] Note, then, not only the particular conditions within which every self is situated, but also the overwhelmingly primordial or ascriptive nature of that condition.

This, I would venture, is the real problem not just with the idea of republican citizenship, but with all traditions of political thought rooted in the traditions of civic virtue, especially when viewed as an ongoing concern and disconnected from military exploits (courage being seen, not surprisingly, as an essential component of civic virtue). For despite its very strong affective elements, seemingly cogent solutions to some of the pervasive problems of citizenship as we know it today, and strong appeal both in the past and the present, articulation of a model of civic virtue free from primordial referents is virtually impossible. Indeed, the (albeit halting and partial) development of universal principles of citizenship following the French Revolution may thus go some way in explaining the gradual replacement of this strand of social thought by ideas stemming from the tradition of civil society.

Not surprisingly, the consistent articulation of a model of solidarity based solely on the principles of political virtue posed a continual problem to thinkers working within this tradition. In the early modern period, this was evinced in the problematic interrelation of "providence" and *fortuna*, "grace" and *virtu*—relationships explored most fully by Pocock, who stressed the pervasive difficulty of how *virtu* could succeed unaided by prophetic grace.[51] We may note that the only actual example of "institutionalized" *virtu* is in eighteenth-century America where—and this is crucial—it was not unaided by (an albeit secularized and nationalized) grace.[52] This is a key point, for if we remove the affective commitment engendered by either revolutionary upheavals or foreign wars and if we accept the existence of highly differentiated societies where the nonmediated existence of the citizen in the polis is no longer possible (and if we discount the totalitarian implications of a public will), what remains to provide basis for virtue? The fact that this problem was solved only—and only partially—in eighteenth-century America is of great importance. For there, lacking an ascriptive or primordial conception of the community (notions which—as we have seen in the Sandel quote above—remain important for republican conceptions of citizenship), an "ideological community" was constituted; it was one that owed much to preexisting Puritan traditions of the community of believers, that is, to some secularized idea of a community of grace.[53] How *virtu* can be institutionalized without such a referent remains an open but critical question—ultimately, I would claim, undoing the ideal of civic virtue. Here a necessary clarification must be made. This is a problem (or more properly an insurmountable problem) only when we (norma-

tively) reject a primordially defined basis for the political community—
that is, when virtue is to be effected solely by the participation in shared
political institutions. Indeed, among contemporaries, the only one to posit
this ideal (in a somewhat utopian fashion) was Arendt. All others, including contemporary accounts of republican citizenship, maintain the element
of ascriptive membership as a necessary component of the civic virtue tradition (the early modern version of which, for Rousseau and others, was
that of a small community of shared history, interaction, etc.).[54] Why or
whether this need be so is another matter, ultimately depending on one's
own philosophical anthropology. Yet historically and theoretically, the
construction of a binding "tradition" and so of a community (moral or otherwise) existing over time, without some referent to primordial "givens,"
has proved a fruitless enterprise.[55] Again, the partial exception is the
United States, and more particularly eighteenth-century America, where
the primordial element was replaced, though only partially, with a "transcendent" grounding of political institutions in a polity of grace and the
traditions of the community of saints. Without either of these principles as
supports of virtue, the constitution of a moral community (one based, let us
say, solely on the principles of participatory politics) has proved untenable.

Interestingly enough, the idea of civil society as it developed in the second half of the eighteenth-century in Scotland arose out of a need to posit
a model of solidarity and mutuality freed from primordial attributes. The
failure of the Jacobite uprisings of 1715 and 1745 and the memories of the
battle of Culloden in 1746 were all telling reminders of the inadequacy of
existing national (or ethnic) solidarities as foundations for political identity
in the increasingly differentiated and interlocking commercial economies
of eighteenth-century Scotland and England.[56] Thus, from Ferguson to
Smith we find a new "universal" and increasingly "individualistically"
defined basis for the construction of communal life: what ultimately would
emerge as the basis of liberal-individualistic principles of citizenship.

The models of solidarity and mutuality contained in this ideal carried
with them, however, their own set of contradictions that were somewhat
different in nature from those studied above in the civic virtue tradition.
Ultimately, as we know, the idea of civil society came to rest on the idea of
the autonomous, moral, and agentic individual as standing at the foundation of the social order. (Hegel and Marx rejected this outcome but in so
doing also rejected the idea of civil society as an ethical ideal and, in their
different ways, went quite beyond it.) This idea of the moral individual
became the basis of liberal political beliefs and, as such, was institutionalized within liberal-democratic polities. In the process of institutionalization the earlier and rather labile concepts of mutuality and, by implication,
civic equality between individuals were replaced with formal, legal, and, to
different extents, in different countries, economic guarantees. These are, in

effect, the attributes of citizenship as developed by T. H. Marshall, extending and formalizing, as it were, the mutuality of the autonomous individual in different realms of shared, public life.[57] Current concerns over entitlement can be viewed as the continuation of this process in different realms.

The developmental logic of this process, however, is paradoxical. For the more the relations between individuals are defined by abstract, legalistic, and formal criteria (what Giddens calls "abstract systems"), the less the public realm can be defined by a shared solidarity based on concrete ties of history, ideas, love, care, and friendship.[58] As the public space of interaction is increasingly defined by the workings of an abstract, rationality (what Weber would term "instrumental" rationality), the less the concrete concerns for mutuality and trust are realized (or perhaps seen to be realized) in the public realm. One consequence of this is the increased difficulty of re-presenting social life in terms of the public sphere and (most salient perhaps in the United States), the positing of sometimes private, sometimes simply particular, entities and interests as public concerns—as actually defining the public good. In fact, I would hazard the claim that the whole emphasis on multiculturalism, on the maintenance of (often ethnic) group solidarities in contrast with the prior ideology of the "melting pot" (based on the ideology of the individual as moral absolute), is part of this dynamic. In short, as a shared public sphere recedes from the affective grasp of the citizenry (through its very formalization and increased institutionalization) the particular and often the private are posited in its stead as an alternative mode of symbolizing society. The renaissance of arguments based on the "republican" conception of citizenship by Sandel, MacIntyre, and others is rooted in the selfsame dynamic as these somewhat less theoretically principled developments.

We are thus left with the problem of how to articulate citizenship in terms of participation in the public realm (virtue tradition, republican citizenship) without stressing primordial, ascriptive elements of communal identity. (How, for example, could we even begin to discuss a "latent community"—that favorite expression of the Western republican citizenship tradition—of the Danube nations without Jews?) In slightly different terms we are left with the problem of the maintenance of virtue—but through the conceptual and institutional venues as presented in the civil society tradition. How then to provide a definition of virtue which, while maintaining the moral suasion of the civic virtue tradition, would root it in individual selves and in the organizational mechanisms of interaction that we have come to associate with the tradition of civil society?

In slightly different terms and as will, I believe, by now be clear to the reader, we are left with the problem of generalized trust which, as hinted at in the previous chapter, is precisely what the conflict between liberals and communitarians, proponents of the civil society and civic virtue traditions, has come down to. Let us then attempt to bring together both perspectives—those drawing on our analysis of trust and those rooted in this (albeit brief) history of political thought.

The crux of the issue—the historical (and to some extent contemporary) debate over models of virtue—is, as we have seen, its residence in the public or private realm respectively. Virtue here is taken to be that model of social solidarity—what Durkheim termed the precontractual—at work in society. This becomes clear when we translate virtue into the contemporary idea of citizenship and the different types of rights and obligations envisioned in either model.

What is the meaning of the precontractual? In current scholarship it is understood as the principles of generalized exchange or unconditionalities in society which regulate the workings of the market. It is, as we have seen and in S. N. Eisenstadt's terms, those "limits to the free exchange of resources in social interaction and the concomitant structuring of the flow of resources in such a way that differs from free (i.e., market or power) exchange."[59] This structuring takes different forms, primary among which are the creation of Public Goods and the public distribution of private goods, both allocate resources according to criteria other than those of pure market exchange. It is these principles that provide that "symbolic credit" upon which all interaction (even the most instrumental) turns—supplying that "social capital" that Coleman, Arrow, and others have seen as central to economic well-being.

The principles upon which these unconditionalities are founded can be many: they can be predicated on ascriptive ties of kinship or the familiarity of dense social networks (as for example among RCAs), or they can be based with Durkheim on a civic consciousness predicated on the mutual recognition of the agency and autonomy of the individual as the source of the moral order. This latter model, we recall, was that posited by Durkheim as at the heart of modern, organic forms of the *conscience collective*.

What Durkheim posited and what has in fact come (to a different extent) to characterize the terms of solidarity in the West has been the positing of the individual agent and his—and increasingly her—autonomy as that unconditional principle of generalized exchange that regulates and structures the flow of resources in society. This has been manifest in myriad and contradictory forms. First among these was the very development of contract law and the freeing of the contract from restrictions and encumbrances in the heyday of laissez-faire capitalism, privileging the autonomy and freedom of choice of the contracting parties. But it is also manifest in the wealth of entitlements that today do in fact restrict the very workings of contract (minimum-wage regulations, child-labor laws, even affirmative-action criteria).

Recall now the seeming contradiction referred to earlier: how the growing institutionalization of the idea of the individual as source of the moral order led to restrictions on the autonomy and freedom of individual agents (as parties to contract). Thus, the very process of institutionalization, of, in other words, the concrete organization of the division of labor on the basis of society's unconditionalities or principles of generalized exchange, has led to the currently perceived tension between the noncontractual forms of relations posited by the communitarian tradition and the types of encumbrances and restrictions placed on the contract in the liberal tradition—*in the name of the very same set of principles*: those predicated on the idea of the individual as source of the moral order. The communitarian tradition privileges and attempts to integrate the "pristine" form of these relations into the public realm while the liberal tradition values, and, in some cases apotheosizes, its institutional expression.

Here a word of clarification is in order; for some may object that I have only been able to develop the foregoing analysis by imputing to communitarianism a concern with the individual actor that does not really reflect its thought at all and is rather the preserve of the liberal tradition alone. This argument must, however, be rejected out of hand. For if we are to see the individual as something beyond a simple bundle of infinite desires, that is, as one imbued with agency and able to make, in Charles Taylor's terms, "strong evaluations," endowed with what Philip Selznick has called "moral competency," then we must admit that the agentic individual has stood at the core of the classical republican tradition since its inception.[60] Indeed agency itself and, crucially, the mutual recognition of agency are at the heart of those very noncontractual relations posited by the communitarian tradition—in fact, must be so, or else there can be no meaning to such social bonds and relations. Contrariwise, contractual relations can be seen as those where agency is severely circumscribed by formal rules, regulations, imposition of sanctions, and the whole web of systemic injunctions in the fulfillment of role obligations and expectations. They are characterized less by trust than by the threat of sanctions (trust, as we have seen, is only meaningful where agency is operating).

The problem, however, is one of the arena where this agency is effected, and again I would claim we come to the problem of institutionalization. For, as we know now, in contemporary societies that social arena where agency is most recognized and consequently trust in its "pristine" form (as unconditionality) seen to reside is not in the market place, mall, stock exchange, or other public space but in the private realm of friendship or love relations.

In a sense both communitarian and liberal positions recognize this fact but value it differently. The liberal position—at its principled extreme—accepts this as the cost of the modern division of labor and is content to let the chips fall where they may. That is to say, the liberal position is content to let the public realm (that defines the relations between the parts and the whole) be defined solely by the institutionalized workings of society's unconditionalities, preserving for the private sphere its most valorized "pristine" articulation. The republican and communitarian traditions (though they cannot in truth be so blithely equated) are less willing to accept this principled distinction between the two realms. (Nor were the early proponents of the civil society tradition who, with Ferguson, mourned the loss of that particular form of solidarity whose passing was occasioned by the modern division of labor.) What was lost and what contemporary republicans attempt to reintroduce into the public realm are precisely those forms of what we have defined as familiarity (see Sandel quote above), which they see as a necessary precondition for the existence of trust (and indeed that agency upon which trust rests).

In some sense, then, they wish to reintroduce an element of "pristine" trust into the public sphere but can do so only by reformulating trust in terms of familiarity. (There can be some rather nasty unintended consequences from this move into the political realm because it may be perceived as legitimizing particular backward-looking political groupings and movements. This is not our concern at the moment, nor should responsibility for such groups be placed at the door of communitarian thinkers.) My own position is that when one stands back from the current political fray and analyzes the situation with some measure of objectivity, one comes to understand that the contradiction between public and private (between virtue and civility, between communitarian and liberal) is but a mirror of the contradiction between the realm where our principled unconditionalities are symbolized and legitimated and the realm of their institutionalized workings. The issue then is not one of voting for Democrats or Republicans nor of supporting a communitarian agenda or a liberal platform. The issue is one of institutionalization, of an inexorable process that always involves a transformation of the ethical principles upon which it was founded—a process that also relegates its intestine debates to the dustbin of history. (Who today studies the debates between Armenian and strict Calvinists over the terms of sanctification· and regeneration in Congregational theology?)

Agency remains and with it the idea of the autonomous individual around whom the private realm is defined. To this individual and the constitutive terms of agency we must now turn.

Five

The Individual, the Rise of Conscience, and the Private Sphere

A HISTORICAL INTERPRETATION OF AGENCY AND STRONG EVALUATIONS

THE FOREGOING identification of the private realm as one where individual agency is realized par excellence cannot go unsupported. Nor can it be abstracted from our prior argument on the intimate connection between the realization of individual agency (beyond systemically mandated role expectations) and the development of role complexity and segmentation. Such a mode of characterizing and defining the private realm would, on first sight, seem quite idiosyncratic and opposed to more accepted definitions. There are, as noted in the previous chapter, myriad ways to conceptualize the issues of public and private. Indeed, the categories seem to accumulate dichotomies in almost too facile a manner: government/economy, market/family, sociability/domesticity, political community/household, and so on. Different scholarly traditions, such as those represented by Jurgen Habermas, let us say, or by contrast, Philippe Aries, approach the matter in varied, though I would argue, ultimately compatible ways. What I wish to present here is a historical argument for the type of definition offered above, to be supplemented in the next chapter with a more analytic inquiry into the same theme.

We may note at the outset that the very construction of that eighteenth-century "publicness" that was theoretically articulated by Habermas and admirably charted by the work of such historians as Robert Chartier (on the development of a literary culture in eighteenth-century France) or Sarah Maza (on the increasingly public nature and representation of private court cases in the same period) had its complement in the very definition and isolation of the private as a realm of value that we find in the writings of Philippe Aries and other Annaliste historians.[1] Not surprisingly, both realms can be seen as defining themselves concomitantly and in mutual recognition. Ultimately, I will argue, both rested on the newly emergent *idea* of the individual and of individual agency as coming to exist beyond the normative expectations of what we would term status and role.

Necessary for this development was a reformulation of the reigning terms of sociability and of the laws governing such sociability. As Aries himself has noted, "The entire history of private life comes down to a change in the forms of sociability."[2] Habermas too notes the intimate connection between the emerging universalistic codes of public communication (i.e., the new terms of sociability) and the constitution of private individuals—of what may be termed socially recognized and (legally) validated selves:

> The criteria of generality and abstractness that characterizes legal norms had to have a peculiar obviousness for privatized individuals who, by communicating with each other in the public sphere of the world of letters, confirm each other's subjectivity as it emerges from their sphere. . . . These rules, because they are universally valid, secure a space for the individuated person; because they are objective, they secure a space for what is most subjective; because they are abstract, for what is most concrete.[3]

Inherent to the eighteenth-century change in the terms of sociability was a reformulation of the terms of familiarity (in the sense of strong evaluations used above), which essentially saw the gradual transformation of the meaning of the private from that which was hidden and withdrawn (either on account of shame or the *imperia arcana* of royal justice, for example) to that which pertains only to the individual. To be sure, both meanings continue to be used today, often contributing to much confusion in our understanding of the phenomenon. Yet an understanding of the modern distinction between these realms and of its specificity in terms of other forms of social organization rests, I would maintain, on an appreciation of this historical dynamic. The often-remarked-upon lack of a "publicness" (in the Habermasian sense) in premodern European culture (allowing for such exceptions as Renaissance cofraternities in Italian city-states, for example) rests on a conception of privateness as that which was hidden and beyond the gaze of a society where the public itself (the whole) was constituted solely in transcendent terms (the corpus mysticum of the Church, universal and apostolic). Only the disembedment of the whole (society) from this transcendent matrix allowed that differentiation of realms through which the idea of public and private in their modern senses emerged. In this differentiation a new whole (in Bobbio's sense) was constituted which turned on the very privileging and valorization of private selves that the new definition of privateness involved. This was reflected, for example, in the development of modern natural law theory, as manifest in the quote of Habermas above.

But what of familiarity? How, in the reconstruction of the whole in terms less than (the) universal(ity of the Church), was familiarity to be maintained? The answer, as we all know, was in the universalization of the law as represented and maintained by the edifice of the State (Durkheim's strong evaluations predicated on the shared orientations to the value of the

individual that we noted above). However, as we have seen, the very institutionalization of this principle led not only to an attenuation of the relation
between the part and the whole (Sennett's *Fall of Public Man*, and the
current *cause célèbre* of the communitarian critique of liberalism, as well
as a concern which we have seen was saliently felt in the eighteenth century), but also to increasing difficulty in maintaining confidence among the
"parts." The new terms of familiarity in modernity thus engendered that set
of problems, that peculiar type of "risk" (to use Luhmann's nomenclature)
for which trust emerged as an (albeit partial) solution.

So much we have already established, together with the peculiar and
contradictory dynamic that the very institutionalization of trust (as principle of generalized exchange) involved: that is, the distinction between its
pristine representation in the private sphere of interpersonal relations and
its more formal, public and institutional expression in the laws regulating
the division of labor in society. This distinction turns, to no small degree,
on agency, on what some have termed "voluntarism" (as willed activity,
rather than as a candy-striper in the hospital, though the parallels are striking) and the realm of its actualization. For as we have argued above, the
forum most amenable to the workings of agency, understood as the ability
to negotiate role behavior and expectations, is that of private life[4] and, not
surprisingly, of the individual agent who stood at its heart. (This is the only
definition that maintains a relatively sophisticated social conception of human life but can still see the individual agent as apart from and not reducible to the internalized role expectations of the social structure—what Dennis Wrong long ago termed the "over-socialized" conception of man.) If we
think back to our prior discussion of Adam Smith, we can see this gradual
privileging of individual agency (in the crucial realm of conscience, that is,
of strong evaluations) over any attempt to root virtue (or for that matter,
strong evaluations themselves) in the familiarity of the public realm.

Thus we have seen how for the Smith of the sixth edition of *The Theory
of Moral Sentiments* the public nature of individual validation gave way to
a much more private locus of virtue and ethical realization.[5] In this move
the idea of the "impartial spectator," the "great inmate of the human
breast," as adjudicator of competing moral goods ultimately broke with the
naive anthropology of Ferguson and Shaftesbury, with all ideas of innate
sympathy as well as with any allegiance to collective norms and mores
(with familiarity per se, as principle of generalized exchange), or with what
may be termed in the language of republican citizenship the "latent community" as repositories of virtue.[6] Rather than being identified with public
opinion and a "propriety" rooted in the common standards and social morality of the public sphere, the impartial spectator is internalized (in the
sixth edition of *Theory of Moral Sentiments*). As the "man within" takes
the place of the "man without"—or public opinion—as the source of virtue

(i.e., of familiarity *qua* principle of generalized exchange), a new, much more private and individual foundation is posited for the pursuit of the public good, and virtue casts off its moorings in the public sphere. Henceforth the realm of virtue was to be located in the individual citizen himself, that citizen for whom the abstract and impersonal laws of justice (*pace* Habermas above) provided the necessary framework for interaction and exchange.[7]

I would thus maintain that Smith at the end of the eighteenth century has given us one of the earliest and most insightful understandings into the new terms of privateness, defined as individual agency, which has come to characterize the modern era. He has posited this agency as conscience and placed it at the center of modern ideas of virtue, that is, of the organizing principles of generalized exchange. The only thing left to add to Smith's analysis remains the historical conditions of this development, which, admittedly, if developed in full, would constitute a book in itself. Yet, for all that, some appreciation is needed of the growing identification of the individual as both *(1)* imbued with agency and *(2)* manifest in the workings of conscience if we are to fully appreciate the centrality of the individual to our contemporary ideas of the private and the problematic nature of trust that it involves. Such an inquiry, structural in nature, will of necessity refer back to our earlier analysis predicated on the ideas of role and role differentiation in the making of human agency.

Thus, what I wish to offer here is no more than a brief précis of a possible history. As I can neither reconstruct the history of Western individualism, nor for that matter, of conscience and agency in their relation to the private realm, what I will try to argue—through a few brief examples—is the historical and analytical connection between these developments and the type of role differentiation discussed above.

It is in quite conscious rejection of the intellectual history of ideas and rather in the structural conditions of social existence that I would like to seek an explanation of that development of human agency (as an aspect of individual valorization) out of which the problem of trust emerged. Note then, at the outset, the different components of the analysis that we wish to address. Our starting point was the development of trust as a specific modern form of social relations incumbent on the generalization of agency within more and more arenas of the social structure (the afore-noted problem of system limits occasioned by the proliferation of complex roles). Thus, as we have already established, the problems of agency and of trust are intimately connected. We have also explored (in our chapter on trust and generalized exchange) the workings of this connection in the public realm and through that analysis have come to understand the abiding contradiction between public and private spheres in the institutionalization of trust and agency as the unconditionalities of modern exchange relations.

Having briefly explored this contradiction in the realm of political philosophy, we must now supplement our earlier understanding of the public, institutionalized role of trust with an appreciation of its more "pristine" existence in and as an aspect of private life. It is here that we hope to pick up the thread left by Adam Smith in seeing this private realm of "pristine" trust as constituted by our ideas of the individual as moral matrix of the social order. This connection is most clearly felt in the development of the idea of conscience as the central arena for the workings of agency. Thus the earlier definition of the private realm as that centered on the individual is further specified as that realm wherein the workings of agency *in the form of* conscience must be at play and so trust evoked.

Our attempt to treat the individual as constituted by the workings of agency in matters of conscience is thus very much an attempt to treat the individual as a very special "category of mind," part of the structure of belief, indeed, of the moral sentiments of a very specific cultural form. For, though the idea of the person may well be, as P. F. Strawson has claimed, one of the fundamental categories of human thinking "which has no history," the idea of the individual as unconditional principle of generalized exchange in the West does, very much, have a history, one rooted, as I will claim, in some very specific types of structural developments.[8] And it is by concentrating on the analytic aspects of this development—as manifest in the growing transformation, complexity, and hence indeterminacy of role expectations—that we can isolate the growing awareness of both the individual and the private sphere of his (and increasingly her) agency and so come more fully to understand the problem of trust as derivative of these developments. In sum, the development of a private sphere characterized by labile and relatively indeterminate role expectations was itself part of the developing idea of the individual who, I would argue, developed very much in same manner, arising very much as a Durkheimian social fact out of the different role-sets acquired by the person.

To a great extent, the emergence of a private sphere as somehow separate from systemically defined role expectations rested on the prior disengagement of the individual from collective identities. This development can be understood both analytically and historically. Analytically, it involves the multiplicity of roles and so the unique configuration of role-sets that becomes every "individual identity." Connected to this is the developing propensity to negotiate the contents and expectations involved in each role. Moreover, these developments allow the crucial possibility to judge one role (or role-set) from the perspective of another (or others). As the person becomes a vector of more and more roles, the very idea of the individual becomes a means to specify the unique aggregation of roles that every social actor bears. This very multiplicity of roles carries with it the potential for the mediation and blurring of the boundaries between roles in a singular manner and for the progress of an almost infinite self-reflexivity since each role can become the Archimedean point from which others can be judged, negated, modified, and so on. Connected to this process (and facilitating its progress) is the fact that as roles and role-sets proliferate within social formations, the boundaries between the roles become more permeable and the moves from one to the other less structured by formal (ritualized) criteria. There is then more negotiability not only in the definition of each role but also in the moves from one to the other. This too becomes a process that each social actor negotiates alone, in private, rather than within the confines of normative group-held injunctions.

While these analytic traits characterize social formations from Papua New Guinea to Los Angeles, U.S.A., the degree of differentiation between roles and the specific type of roles defined are crucial variables in the development of individual and collective identities. While some notion of the individual and of the private sphere as separate from the group exists in all known societies, there is little doubt that the type of individualism that we associate with Western European civilization (i.e., the civilization that developed from the Judeo-Christian and Greco-Roman foundations) is a relatively unique phenomenon: it sees in the individual the locus of the moral and political orders, the fount of agency and intentionality, a transcendental subject invested with transcendent rights. It is, moreover, one which came to invest the private sphere with a unique and moral priority.

While the uniqueness of this phenomenon has been studied by scholars ranging from Max Weber and Marcel Mauss down to contemporaries such as Charles Taylor and, in a very different mode, Louis Dumont, the above-noted perspectives on role open some imposing questions for existing traditions and understanding Western individualism and its concomitant ideas of the private sphere as realm of value.[9] To a great extent, these traditions see Western individualism as rooted, in one form or another, in the soteriological assumptions of Christian belief. That is to say, the very positing of a monotheistic creator God and—especially with Christendom—the "personal" relation of the "individual" to the godhead are, to a large extent, the foundations of our notions of individualism and of the transcendental subject. In sum, this tradition sees the constitution of the individual in, as Troeltsch put it, man's essence being that of an "individual-in-relation-to-God." Christianity is thus, in Dumont's terms, "the emancipation of the individual through a personal transcendence, and the union of outworldly individuals in a community that treads on earth but has its heart in heaven."[10] At present I am not concerned with specifying either the precise origin of such beliefs (whether in the Jewish idea of creation in the image of God or in Christian doctrines of grace) nor in the varieties of its development and transformation (in Kantian ideas of the transcendental subject, for instance). All those aware of this tradition of sociological thought can easily delimit its contours. What I am interested in exploring, however, is the notion that it is not solely in Christianity per se, that is, in its soteriological doctrines, that the origin of modern individualism is to be found. Rather it is the specific differentiation, division, and definition of roles that Christianity brought to the cultural, political, social, and economic arenas that are perhaps at the core of our own understanding of the individual.

Let us, for the sake of argument, take only three historical periods that, in the past, have been seen as critical points in the development of Western ideas of the individual: Late Antiquity, the renaissance of the twelfth century, the Protestant Reformation. All have been identified with the development of Christian individualism through the refinement of Christian salvational doctrines. Is it not possible that the individualism that we identify with these eras is an outcome not solely of the changing content (soteriology) of religious civilization but of its changing form (in the nature of group affiliations)?[11] Thus while Late Antiquity is the period of the emergence of Christianity as a world historical religion with its own salvational dogma of grace, it is also the period of the emergence of a whole new set of roles and role definitions identified with Christianity (as, for example, in the transformation of sexual relations from a public matter to the private concern of individuals).[12] This is, after all, the central dynamic behind the replacement of kinship identities with membership in a sacramental community.[13] Similarly, the positing of the City of God provided a most central counterfactual reality from which the City of Man could be judged, negated, or affirmed. It injected a dimension between social reality and ontological reality (through the redefinition of the latter in terms of transcendence) that gave to the former a lability and negotiability not hitherto existent.[14] The argument I wish to make, however, is that perhaps it is less in transcendence itself, and more in the radical breaking and making of social bonds that accompanied it, that the origins of Christian individualism are to be found.

For the very Christian vision which posited new models of bridging the "transcendental chasm" through a greater interweaving of this- and other-worldly activities, a new stress on individual salvation, and a linear and telic time perspective which posited both a definite beginning and an end to historical time also demanded new modes of social organization.[15]

Thus on the institutional level, the development of early Christianity saw the construction of a new "moral community" of believers differentiated from the societies in which they lived and united by bonds of exclusive communal fellowship.[16] These groups of early Christians, scattered across the Roman Empire, were united by social ties of a charismatic nature. Cutting across existing solidarities of kith and kin, the message of the early Church was one of a social solidarity rooted only in a shared experience of the sacred. In the words of Saint Paul: "There is neither Jew nor Greek, there is neither bond nor free, there is neither male nor female: for ye are all one in Christ Jesus."[17] These new communities epitomized that "communitas" which stood at the root of the Christian charismatic organization.[18] Explicitly enjoined to see themselves as a community apart from the social world in which they existed, the early Christians shared a tie rooted in their immediate relation to that ultimate source of meaning and values beyond the immediacies of everyday life. This tie to the transcendental locus of meaning was expressed in the Christian context in the mystery of the *Corpus Christi*:

> For as the body is one, and hath many members, and all the members of that one body, being many, are one body: all also is Christ. For by one Spirit are we all baptized into one body, whether we be Jews or Gentiles, whether we be bond or free; and have been all made to drink into one Spirit.[19]

It was symbolized ultimately in the sacrament of the Eucharist wherein "each individual formed a part of the community of true communicants, sharing together the promise of eternal life."[20]

Early Christianity thus presented an alternative locus of social identity and of community that was rooted in the experience of grace. The bond established between communal members was one rooted not in primordial givens, but in an immediate connection to the fount of transcendental order. The new locus of communal solidarity and of the moral order was epitomized in St. Paul's rejection of the "ascriptive confines of Jewish ethical monotheism."[21] This redefinition of the terms of community in the experience of grace and a direct relation to the source of cosmic order and salvation (and not in legal prescriptions or primordial networks) allows us to speak of the Early Christian ties of community as essentially a reformulation of existing roles and role definitions within the social world of Late Antiquity.

These new roles were those of members of a new corporate body (the Church) which subjected the *nova creatura* to the new laws of regenerate man. What this new *congregatio fidelium* implied was precisely a transformation of the terms of the *fidelis* "now subjected as far as his social and public life went, to the law as it was given to him, not the law as it was made by him. The consequence of the incorporation was that his *fidelitas*, his faithfulness, consisted precisely in his obeying the law of those who were instituted over him by divinity."[22] The very absorption of the individual in and by the new corporation of the Church was thus a transformation not only of the terms of familiarity (and the strong evaluations that went with them), but also of those social bonds, roles, and role-expectations that had hitherto defined the social world.

With time and the growing needs of maintaining an institutional structure, the early organizational structures of the Church underwent a fundamental transformation. The dynamics of institution building, of establishing pervading and long-lasting definitions of communal membership and equally hegemonic structures of authority, resulted in what was essentially a process of routinization. This process saw, in the early Church of the second and third centuries, the development of fixed points of dogma, established models of social action, and with the office of the bishopric, a hierarchic structure of roles and offices.[23]

With the growing institutionalization of Christian life there thus emerged new structures of authority: bishoprics and holders of priestly office as well as of communal membership and identity. These specific institutional roles were a crucial component in the transformation of primitive Christianity into an institutionalized religion capable of "world building," organizational expansion, and, in the final analysis, construction of civilization. They also set up the constitutive dynamics of public and private with which we are concerned: that which rooted the private in the workings of individual conscience and began that valorization of the private realm whose consequences we live today. While the specific terms of Christian soteriology were no doubt essential in this development, I wish to stress their evolution together with the process of role differentiation and system complexity which, I maintain, was the hallmark of all further progress in these matters.

We may thus note a similar emergence of role differentiation and the development of individual identities, especially in the refinement of ideas of conscience and agency, which characterized what has been termed the renaissance of the twelfth century.[24] Not—or not only—the recovery of spiritualism in that era, but also the establishment of new social groups through which it emerged is responsible for the growing individualism of that period. The very differentiation of corporate bodies engendered by the Papal Revolution (Investiture Conflict) and the development of myriad new roles as group identities proliferated in this era were central to the development of ideas of an inner life and of intentionality (as opposed to action) as an aspect of the individual agency and morality. In fact, this period was characterized not solely by the growth of different group identities (of which the new corporate identity of the clergy was by far the most important) and by the increase in horizontal mobility as the immediate family differentiated itself from wider kin groups but also by the very emic recognition of different orders of knights, clerics, priests, married men and women, widows, virgins, soldiers, merchants, peasants, and craftsmen—each with their different talents, institutions, and roles in society. Central here was the growth of different religious orders.[25] All these developed concomitantly with the growth of individual and private modes of self-expression through the revival of the religious tradition of autobiography, confessional literature, and courtly love poetry, as well as the emergence of legal differentiation, of a legal corpus no longer bound by custom or Germanic tribal ideas of honor and fate.[26] This last development stressed the legitimacy of enacted, objective law over the consensual mold of tradition and custom. In so doing, the new legal system of the twelfth century set up a generalized conceptual legal system that broke with existing group (clan and household) loyalties and posited new corporate definitions of what were, essentially, new social roles and role expectations.[27]

In a manner both reminiscent of the development of early Christianity and foreshadowing the Protestant Reformation of the sixteenth century, the twelfth century was thus also characterized by a convergence of a specific set of structural and symbolic features. All coalesced around a greater appreciation of individual identities as central and focused, interestingly enough, on the ideas of agency or voluntarism and the workings of conscience. As Benjamin Nelson noted: "The extraordinary stress on the responsibility of each individual for the activity of his will and the state of his soul attained its height in the High and Later Middle Ages."[28] It was not simply Abelard in his *Ethica seu Scito te ipsum* (*Ethics: or Know Thyself*) and *Sic et Non* (*Yes and No*) who stressed inward intentionality in the conceptualization of spiritual life. Such a reorientation was evinced in the writings of others, the School of Laon, for example, and upheld even by such critics of Abelard as Bernard of Clairvaux. Its institutionalized expression was in the decree of the Fourth Lateran Council of 1215, which required an individual confession for communicants at least once a year. As Colin Morris has noted: "The attempt to make intention the foundation of an ethical theory is a striking instance of the contemporary movement away from external regulations toward an insight into individual character; a movement which finds its widest expression in the acceptance of private confession as the basis of the Church's normal discipline."[29] Its other institutional expression was in the developing science of causistry and the proliferation of "specialized treatises tracing the obligations of conscience in the here and now, spelling out how individuals were obligated to act in every case they encountered in the conduct of their lives. . . . In these works conscience extended into every sphere of action, ranging over the whole moral life of man."[30]

Importantly, the idea of intentionality was not limited to the religious realm alone; it both appeared in courtly poetry, for example, in such writings as Chrétiens de Troyes, *The King of the Cart*, and resonated in the developing genre of autobiography as well as in the changing representation of portrait painting.[31] In the following discussion of portraiture by Harold Keller we can find an appreciation of precisely that idea of the individual who exists beyond roles and role expectations that we discussed earlier, drawing from sources as diverse as Montaigne and Musil to grasp that elusive entity:

> The portrait, as we understand it today, is one of the new concepts of the late Middle Ages . . . The characterization of a man, absolutely and unchangeably by his particular physical peculiarities, especially his face, and not by the insignia of his office or rank or by his weapons—that is a concept of the portrait which in the second century A.D. came into question in the West and which was progressively lost from the time of Constantine onwards. Only about 1300 did the new conception of man lead to the recovery of the old idea of the portrait.[32]

Not surprisingly, the new valorization and representation of a self apart from social roles saw too the valorization of personal relations not so defined. Hence there emerged tentative and nascent ideas of friendship (albeit still within the boundaries of the Church), on the one hand, and the conceptualization of love advanced by the troubadours on the other. Both of these, in Morris's terms, "desired to make personal experience and personal relations the focus of life," through, it should be added, the process of self-discovery and analysis.[33]

Of crucial sociological importance is the fact that these developments all took place against a backdrop of increasing structural differentiation. Central to this increasing complexity of the system were: *(1)* the separation of the nobility from the rest of society through its increasing tendency to be defined in hereditary terms; *(2)* the growth of commerce and of cities with the vast degree of internal differentiation among the different urban orders that characterized their growth; *(3)* the post-Gregorian Church which not only freed episcopal elections (and elites) from political impingement but "created a clergy that was set apart much more radically than before from ordinary Christians."[34] As Caroline Bynum has noted, the Gregorian Reform not only separated the clergy from the laity, most especially through the campaign for clerical celibacy, but also led to a vast proliferation of new institutional (and sometimes only semi-institutional) religious orders or roles, most formidably in the development of the friars (for men) and in the creation of new roles for women, such as the begunie, which was, in its essence, "opposed to complex institutional structures."[35]

Note then the very "Durkheimian" correlation between the development of individual identities together with the ever-growing complexity of social organization and its roles and role expectations. The same period that sees the "fundamental religious drama" relocated into the self is the period that sees a proliferation of religious orders, vocations, "callings," and "lives." The same period that sees a growing literature of private passion and theories of love, in R. W. Southern's terms, of "the enlargement of the opportunities of privacy, in the renewed study of the theory of friendship, of conscience and of ethics," is also a period marked by a greater social differentiation, complexity, and distinction in the forms of social life.[36] Curiously enough and as Southern emphasizes, the greater differentiation—and so what is essentially an establishment of ever more numerous particular identities—was also marked by a "changing emphasis from localism to universality," most especially in the rise of the science of logic which, by subsuming all particularities, made recourse possible to a whole beyond an increasingly particularized conceptualization of space and time.[37]

As Bynum has noted, this period was characterized by a proliferation of the forms of institutionalized religious life as well as a greater degree of social differentiation in other realms; also by an intense awareness of this differentiation, an "urgency, unlike anything we see in the early Middle Ages, about defining, classifying, and evaluating what they termed "orders," or "lives," or "callings" (which includes what we would term both voluntary religious associations and social roles)."[38] But unlike Bynum we do not believe that the vision of the twelfth century that emphasized inwardness and conscience must be "modified" by an appreciation of the growth and diversification of the forms of social life.[39] These phenomena are, as we have attempted to argue throughout, not contradictory but complementary, the latter being the preconditions for the former. For only in the developing complexity of social identities (what sociologists so unfelicitously term role incumbencies) can a sense of individual identity flourish. Central to this individual identity as it developed in the West were the idea of conscience, expressed most saliently in this period in the idea of intentionality in religious life, and the gradual construction of a private realm, beyond formal role obligations, where such intentionality and conscience came to the fore, whether in the rites of courtly love, the developing genre of correspondence between friends, or in the individual Church confession.

If Caroline Bynum is correct and the discovery of the individual in this period proceeded together with the discovery of the group (and the new role relations this entailed), we would stress too the concomitant sense of the individual as bearer of different roles in different groups and the disengagement of these groups from existing sacred and customary matrixes—a development which, together with the emergent idea of privacy, progressed apace in the following centuries.[40]

The importance of the Protestant Reformation, especially of its sectarian variants in the developing idea of conscience, is so well studied as to need almost no explication. Through it, in Benjamin Nelson's words, there

developed a new integration of life, both personal and political, through the rearrangement of existing boundaries ... older maps were redrawn, fixing new co-ordinates for all focal points of existence and faith: religion-world, sacred-profane, civil-ecclesiastical, liberty-law, public-private. [In this rearrangement] new scope and authority were given to the Inner Light, sparked by the Holy Spirit. This was the Holy Spirit within each individual and within groups. This inspiration came to serve as the basis for vastly expanded involvement of new participants in a variety of different relations of self and world: charismatic activism, quietistic mysticism, covenanted corporate consensualism, natural rights individualism, a religion of Pure Reason."[41]

Here then was the return to Augustinian piety, the breaking with the sacraments and mediating structures of the Church (as well as its symbols of the Virgin Mary and the different saints) to reassert unmediated access of the believers to the deity within what became the private space of individual conscience.[42] But here too were the radical, painful, often violent breaking of established group identities and the reestablishment of new group solidarities and new role definitions (through, among Puritans, for example, the whole covenantal theology).[43]

The new bonds forged under sectarian Protestantism were a recasting of the bonds of "community" as a shared tradition into new bonds of "communality." These bonds of a new "communion," in Herman Schmalenbach's sense, were to be the basis of the new communities forged by religious virtuosi throughout European societies.[44] The social restructuring of the bonds of communality (and, we may note, of authority) was part of the restructuring, effected by the Reformation in general but specifically in ascetic Protestantism, of the relation between the Church and the world. Within medieval Catholic Europe, the only "life calling" legitimized in sacred terms was that of the monastic orders. As noted by Weber and others, the importance of the Reformation lay precisely in its "endowment of secular life with a new order of religious life as a sphere of 'Christian opportunity'."[45] It was thus only with the Reformation that secular callings were given a religious legitimation and were perceived as possible paths to salvation.

This orientation toward a greater this-worldliness, toward the "justification" of the whole person and his everyday life in terms of salvation, was at the center of Weber's famous Protestant Ethic thesis. Its implications, however, are broader (as Weber himself realized) than simply the rationalization of economic activity. For with the "demise of the older images of 'Religion' and World, Law and Grace" and with mundane life imbued with soteriological efficacy, the way was opened for rebuilding secular society in the selfsame image of perfection that had characterized monastic life.[46] To quote from Nelson's work once again:

[A] fundamental reorientation of the social and cultural patterns of the Western world could not occur until the medieval administration of self and spiritual direction fell before the onslaughts of Luther, Calvin and their followers. So long as a distinction was made between the special calling of monks who lived "outside the world," systematically observing a rule in their pursuit of the status of perfection, and everyone else in the world, who lived irregularly, without benefit of a rule, in the midst of continued temptation; so long was there a brake on the incentive of ordinary men and women to forge integrated characters with a full sense of responsibility. The Protestant notion of disciplined character nourished by a resolute conscience replaced the medieval sense of life as a round of sin and penance."[47]

This new sense of responsibility and moral authority was expressed in a pursuit of the status of perfection within the orders and institutions of the world.[48] What this implied (and if we take Calvinism as the "ideal type" of these religious beliefs) was the establishment of a new type of moral bond between communal members, and so of a redefinition of the terms of group membership. More than Luther's "priesthood of believers" who while positing a break with the Church, did not posit a similar break with the overriding social definitions of community, followers of Calvinist doctrine in England, Scotland, the Netherlands, France, and Geneva tended to be bounded by new ties of fellowship as well as by notions of a new type of moral authority based on inner conscience.[49]

Calvinism was thus integral to the construction of new symbolic definitions of collective identity which developed in sixteenth- and seventeenth-century Europe. The basis of this new ideal order, the new *ecumene*, was henceforth to be the "Holy Community" of "saints," voluntarily participating in Christ.[50] This new definition of community was to form the basis of a new, ideal model of Christian society. Henceforth, the boundaries of Christian community were not those of common participation in the sacrament of the Eucharist, but a common and voluntary subjugation of each individual will to the Will of God. By *willful* participation in the Body of Christ, a new community was defined, one which, like that of the early Church, existed in the body of the old but was distinct from it. Such a code of conduct led to the effective separation within each parish of two bodies of communicants: "on one side there were the true, genuine, faithful and active Christians, and on the other those who were merely nominal and worldly." There thus was effected, in Troeltsch's words, "the separation of the pure body of communicants from the impure."[51]

While this separation was not always explicitly enacted in the congregant's behavior, it did imply a fundamental reorientation in the definitions of social roles and role expectations. Such a reorientation of role definitions may, for example, be seen in the changing definitions of ministerial authority and in the relations between congregants and minister. Thus the voluntary nature of the true Christian community was expressed in the covenantal or consensual nature of the ties assumed by its participants. This new community, based on a consensual notion of membership, was to be governed by elected officials whose authority was rooted in "the general voice" of the community.[52] As the role of the ecclesiastical official was one of *administratio spiritus* and of building the community, his election or "calling" by the "elect" was essential, "not to diminish any part of the common right and freedom of the Church."[53] In this conception the role of the ministry underwent a fundamental change, from a hierarchic position mediating between communicant and the deity, to assuming a purely functional and administrative role.[54] Through such doctrines, Calvinist thought prepared the way for a breakdown of the existing solidarities of Christian society and posited a new set of ties between people—in Donald Kelly's telling phrase, "a kind of sublimation of blood into belief."[55] In so doing, it redefined the nature of society and of its constitutive relations.

These new conceptions of the social order implicit in Calvin's "active ideal of holiness," tied, as they were, to the "ideal of the Holy Community," developed differently in different historical communities.[56] We will restrict this brief survey to the Puritan context, if only for the privileged position it has had within the sociological tradition. Thus, the development of novel forms of social organization following on the return of the Marian Exiles took in the context of Elizabethan England, a particularly intense expression.[57] There developed new forms of religious expression, as well as of communal bonds, both characterized by a break with existing models of social organization. More than in any other social act, the drawing up of "covenants" between and among Puritans in Tudor England provided the basis for the reworking of the terms of social life in line with a new model of social organization.[58] In the covenanted communities and the "gathered churches" of the later sixteenth and the early seventeenth century, diverse groups of English Puritans laid down, as it were, the blueprint for a fundamental reorganization of the principles of collective life.[59]

The institutional aspects of this new conception of social order have been attested by historians from William Haller and Patrick Collinson to William Hunt and J. G. A. Pocock, and we need only summarize them here.[60] On one level, they were manifest in a new mode of religious expression characterized by lay preaching and "prophesysings," as well as by what later would be termed an "enthusiastic" religiosity of popular piety and noninstitutionalized manifestations of grace.[61] On the level of social organization, the covenanting of communicants implied primarily a break with existing solidarities of both Church and neighborhood.[62] Covenanting together, the Puritans also covenanted themselves off from the major existing institutional loci of solidarity—the Church, village, or parish—and so of those social identities which prevailed in English society.[63] The withdrawal from existing loyalties both national and ecclesiastical to the Church of England and the growth of a new set of commitments, loyalties, and identities to the individuals covenanted together in pursuit of a new spiritual and moral life were fundamental elements in the construction of new loci of social life and individual identity.[64]

The Puritan movement was thus an attempt to build a new set of communal bonds within English society through a redefinition of individual selves and of the organizational structures of their interaction.[65] This fact amply explains their constant reference to the early Church as a legitimizing body of practices—at odds with existing solidarities. Both groups defined themselves solely by the establishment of new institutional nexi. In the case of the early Church this was accomplished in the rites of the Eucharist and in the case of the Puritan communities, in the ritual of the covenant. Indeed, the idea of the covenant, as it developed among certain groups of self-governing Puritan churches, effectively replaced the sacraments, especially that of the Eucharist, as the primary mode of establishing and asserting the development of these new ties within the emerging communities of Puritan "saints." The covenant was then both the institutional locus and symbolic expression of a new moral community, bounded by different institutional and symbolic parameters from that of the society within which they coexisted.

These developments represented, in fact, new definitions of the social order and the parameters of social interaction. Symbolically this was evinced in the reinterpretation given to the Eucharist, no longer an entity in its own right, but a "seal of the covenant," which itself represented the new sacred dimension of existence. It is in this context that we must view the specific changes instituted in Puritan churches in the manner of administrating the Host. For the destruction of altar rails and the change from altar to table, level with the congregants, represented in symbolic terms the destruction of that sacred space within which the sacred had been confined.[66]

From a Durkheimian perspective, the symbolic and institutional relocation of the sacred was totally congruent with the changing boundaries of collectivities, with the new ties engendered among and between Puritan communicants.[67] For the new social covenant, in the words of Richard Rogers, "did knit them in that love, the bond whereof could not be broken either on their part which now sleepe in the Lord, whiles they heere lived, nor in them which yet remaine, by any adversarie power unto this day."[68] It was, in fact, the organizational form taken by a new "moral community." As new forms of solidarity emerged and were constituted, new definitions of the sacred—as expressions of this solidarity—were proffered. The desacralization of the sacraments, and of ritual in general, is but the symbolic concomitant of the establishment of new ties or affinities between social actors leading to the establishment of new collective entities (as in New England), or to the redefinition of existing ones (as was the case among Puritans in England).

And this brings us to the point of the whole foregoing exercise. For once again we witness the correlation of a specific set of structural factors with the developing ideas of conscience, privateness, and individual valorization. The role of the Protestant Reformation in general and of ascetic Protestantism in particular in the development of these orientations within the culture of Reformation (and for that matter, Counter-Reformation) Europe is a standard of historical and sociological research. What we have attempted to emphasize, however, is that these orientations developed together with a proliferation of new role identities within society. The very transformation of personal relations in the making and breaking of social roles—between communicants, between communicants and their ministers, between Protestant communities and the broader society—was, we argue, essential to these developments. Similar in some ways to events of the twelfth century, it was the establishment of new group identities and the very conscious awareness, recognition, and representation of these new identities—not least as these were constituted by the growth of representative political institutions in mid-seventeenth-century England—that led (however counterintuitive it may seem) to an increasing recognition of the privacy of each individual as manifest most especially in the privileging of conscience as an aspect of individual existence.[69]

Interestingly enough, as Puritan communities underwent a process of institutionalization in the late seventeenth and early eighteenth centuries, the privileging of conscience and individual agency in the definition of the moral life (i.e., as an attribute of virtue) became a constitutive component of many such communities. Institutionalization, essentially a move from what Herman Schmalenbach has characterized as a "Bund" type of solidarity to that of "community," was typified by a particular set of structural changes.[70] These can be broadly defined as the breakdown of a society characterized by intensive commitment to collective values; small size; social homogeneity with an absence of functional differentiation and institutionalization and with a strong overall emphasis on collective solidarity and communality, denying legitimacy to subgroups. Structural differentiation and the development of subgroup loyalties, as well as broader sets of individual commitments beyond confessional boundaries, developed in many Protestant communities of the late seventeenth and early eighteenth centuries. With these structural changes there developed as well an ever-increasing stress on the individual, the individual conscience, and the realm of the private as *the* arena of religious activity.

Perhaps more than anyone else, Margaret Jacob has developed this argument in respect to English Unitarians, Dutch Collegians, and the increasingly secular French Freemasonry. (It also emerged among different groups of English Puritans of this period, such as the Cambridge Platonists, noted above.) Perhaps the central tenet of these groups' religiosity was, as

Andrew Fix has described in his study of the Dutch Collegians, the fact that they "rejected the authority of ecclesiastical institutions and based religious life on the individual believer and his inner ability to know religious truth."[71] By the second half of the seventeenth century this conception, wedded to a belief in the workings of natural reason in the apprehension of truth, led to an emergent belief in the "principle of individual conscience."[72]

Jacob's own work has in fact stressed the role of religion—or more properly a particular form of privatized Protestantism that developed among certain groups of elites—in the construction of that private and individual sphere oriented around personal autonomy which we identify with bourgeois culture:

> At the heart of this experience lay the encouragement it gave the individual to conceptualize and to experience himself and herself as an ethical being equally engaged in the private and public spheres. . . . This was religion prescribed for the mind where in effect the public disciplined the private, where standards of conduct drawn from social experience and rational argumentation, and not from dogma, ordered and admonished the conscience. In its internalization of ethics and belief drawn from lived social experience, the new religiosity sacralized the public as much as it sanctioned private autonomy.[73]

A further and interesting example of this new religiosity with its deep concern for "creating the conditions for ethical and virtuous conduct" and one not studied by Jacob, was the case of the New England Congregationalists who, by the end of the seventeenth century and beginning of the eighteenth had transformed a deeply communal, public, and eschatological religion into one of a privatized morality characterized by that "internalization of conscience" noted previously.[74] Thus if, in the early decades of settlement, the sacred locus of existence was effected in the public sphere, in the communal rite of the test of relation, by the end of the century it was carried out within the private soul of the individual communicant. Similarly, whereas the earlier decades symbolically objectified the boundaries of the community as those running between the regenerate saint and unregenerate sinner, by the early eighteenth century, the broadened (more inclusive) definition of communal boundaries was conceptualized as being within each individual. Integrating all communal members in one collective definition, the boundaries between insider and outsider no longer ran through the community, but rather through each individual member. As a result, the crossing of a boundary in the move from profane to sacred and from outsider to insider—to membership in the collective—became less a public ceremony and more a private rite. This process, in its more analytic moments, has been noted by Roger Caillois, who termed it the "internalization of the sacred" and described it as the state where "any external criterion seems inadequate, from the moment that the sacred becomes less an objective manifestation than a pure attitude of mind, less a ceremony than a profound sensation."[75]

This "internalization of the sacred" progressed together with two related developments. The first was an increased privatization of the religious experience evinced in the growing "sacramentalism" of this period (i.e., the communicant's private meditations prior to approaching the Host) and, more significantly, the growth of what has been termed the "new Baptismal Piety" and the practice of private baptism. Originally proposed in 1700 by Stoddard in his *Doctrine of the Instituted Churches*, the first private baptism was administered in 1718, thus breaking with the New England doctrine that a sacrament must be a "visible gospel addressed to a faithful congregation."[76] The recognition inherent in this practice (and doctrine) of the private nature of the sacrament of baptism, devoid of its public function, is of a similar nature to the privatization of the Lord's Supper. Through being open to all communicants, these previously publicly constituted rituals had, by the early eighteenth century, lost their public and communal function and become a matter for the individual conscience.

The second important development was a transformation in the terms of communal and individual identities oriented toward an affirmation of normative principles, (as opposed to the prior criteria of evincing the workings of regenerate grace), as the basis of communal membership. Paul Lucas, who studied the admittance practices of the Churches of Connecticut in the period between 1670 and 1725, found a marked increase in the use of "moral behavior," as opposed to conversionary experience, as the means of judging an applicant's suitability for admittance to the Church:[77] "Moral behavior gradually replaced conversion experience as the most important criterion for membership—and moral behavior was determined by the applicant's ability to abide by the standards of the group."[78]

Here too, then, as in those cases studied by Margaret Jacobs, we see the concomitant rise of three related phenomena: the increasingly private nature of religious experience; its reorientation around rational-normative lines; and the growth of a secular rather than a religious morality as foundation for individual and collective identities. Important for our more structurally orientated argument is that these changes in the nature of religious experience developed as a response to the process of institutionalization, that is, the growing diversification and the multiplicity of social roles congregants began to assume at the turn of the seventeenth century. Margaret Jacob, to be sure, sees the growth of cities (with populations over 30,000) as integral to these developments. Yet while she stresses the anonymity of city life in providing the necessary protection for the development of new and unorthodox religious orientations, we would stress the very complexity of its social organization as conducive to these changes.[79] This is why the case of New England is so instructive. For there the development of the new religiosity was much more of a public and, if we may use the term, mainstream, phenomenon, supported by dominant religious elites and cutting across doctrinal differences in different congregations. It was also not an "urban" phenomenon in the European sense, but it did reflect a similar transformation in the terms of social life and the social differentiation inherent to the growing mercantile economy.

Behind these transformations was, clearly, what may be termed a transformation in the terms of familiarity, the shared sets of "strong evaluations" that make a community. We may recall here Fukuyama's quip regarding Mormons and Methodists to appreciate the underlying dynamic. For the type of strong communal ties characteristic of Fukuyama's Mormons or Jehovah's Witnesses were no longer adequate to the changing terms of the division of labor, that market economy for which he prescribes greater "trust." What emerged in their stead, in the wake of the breakdown of the religious sect or "Bund," were the new terms of religion (in fact of familiarity) oriented around the individual and the conscious workings of individual conscience as providing new terms for familiarity. Thus the universal subject *qua* individual emerges as the new locus of solidarity, orientated around new definitions of economic unconditionality (as explicated above in our survey of contract law), predicated on the autonomy of this individual. Significantly and as Stephen Darwall has explained in his recent work on seventeenth and early eighteenth century moral philosophy, "the most significant development of this period was the fashioning of the concept of autonomy *in tandem with* philosophical speculation about moral obligation (emphasis in original).[80] Here too we see the necessary concomitance of doctrines of agency and action together with ideas of moral obligation and the workings of conscience (as opposed to action being based on either the force of sanctions alone or Aristotelian versions of any natural teleology and the coincidence of duty and interest in human life).

While the Durkheimian resonances of this analysis are clear, they are less our concern at the moment than our wish to establish, in however brief a historical sketch, the correlation between the growing appreciation of the private realm as realm of value and as pertaining to the individual, and the growth of structural differentiation and, by implication, of complex social roles. We have thus attempted to present a brief historical backdrop to the analytic points made in our earlier sections. Although our discussion of agency has been circumscribed within the religious realm and limited to the phenomenon of conscience, we have, I hope, seen how the moral valuation of the private and of the individual agent who stood at its core developed (albeit haltingly) in periods of greater structural differentiation to become, with capitalism and the culture of modernity, constitutive of both our political principles and our individual selves.

Here we should note that I do not mean to offer a unicausal explanation of the development of Western individualism predicated on structural factors alone. Structural differentiation and role complexity did also develop in other societies and civilizations without the same growth in individual identities and their moral valuation. I would maintain however that the greater structural differentiation that characterized the growth of Western Christendom provided the necessary conditions for the full realization of that reflexivity (and so also agency) that was, to some extent, built into the soteriological premises of Christianity. The very positing of a monotheistic, creator God and the inherent tension between the City of God and the City of Man provided the potential for a radical reflexivity in the evaluation of social roles that could develop and progress only within a certain set of structural conditions. The very different developments of the Eastern Church provide ample illustrations of such alternative routes where similar religious premises failed to develop anything approaching Western individualism.[81]

Finally, beyond Christian civilization proper we may look to eighteenth-century bourgeois society with its doctrines of civility and moral individualism—those beliefs given philosophical form by Kant and embedded within our own sociological understanding by Durkheim. Here the idea of the individual sheds its religious garb and is no longer constituted by relations with the transcendent but achieves its meaning in the autonomy of the individual conscience. Here too, contemporary social thinkers, from Adam Ferguson in the eighteenth century to Benjamin Constant and Alexis de Tocqueville in the nineteenth, all noted the importance of what we would term role differentiation in the making of bourgeois culture.

In all periods we witness a number of similar, related and central developments: (a) the breaking of existing group bonds and their replacement with new ones, including new roles and new definitions of existing roles; (b) the move from fewer roles to more roles and more complex and multitudinous role-sets and status-sets; (c) the move from more rigid, publicly sanctioned modes of role transition (and definitions) to ones less anchored in public constraints. Tribal, civic, fraternal, and later, confessional, boundaries between roles are replaced by actor-orientated ones: for example, sexual practices among early Christians; twelfth-century religious orders; the "internalization" of conscience among late seventeenth-century Puritans; and the role of civility—as opposed to honor—in the discourse of the Scottish moralists.[82] In all of these, the idea of the individual emerged slowly from increasingly labile and ultimately negotiable definitions of social roles, as did the idea of a private sphere set apart from systemically defined and publicly sanctioned role injunctions. Both would only begin to be fully articulated in the eighteenth century when, not surprisingly, the tension between them and more public (i.e., systemically defined and sanctioned) modes of role expectations became apparent. This tension is perhaps most accessible in the literature of the period, and its resonances are manifest in works such as Defoe's *Roxana*, Richardson's *Clarissa*, and Fielding's *Amelia*. In all of these mid-eighteenth-century novels, the hero and heroine need to come to terms with the new distinctions between public and private, between law and morality—essentially between formal relations regulated by public law and the search for new bases of individual trust and a matrix of interpersonal relations beyond contract and law. As succinctly stated by John Zomchick, "In Fielding law and virtue remain divergent."[83] In this divergence lies, we might add, the developing tension between public and private existence as they became apparent in this period.

This tension, as we have endeavored to explain, rested in no small measure on the contradiction inherent in: *(a)* the institutionalized, publicly sanctioned role expectations of the division of labor, defined "in the last instance" by the legal system and orientated around the actions of individual selves and the workings of their agency (most crucially in the economic realm); *(b)* the preserve of that "pristine" form of this autonomy and (we mustn't forget) the mutuality between autonomous selves in what has come to be defined as the private realm of existence. This latter realm, where the workings of agency attain their most visible form (as we negotiate role expectations and incumbencies with much greater aplomb than in the public sphere), has thus come to exist—or seems to exist—in opposition to the public realm where our actions are circumscribed that much more by systemically imposed definitions of role behavior. The public realm is indeed characterized more by confidence (or lack thereof) in system than trust in the agency of the individual actor. And while the structural limits to this system are, as we have seen, inherent to it, the resulting lacunae are "filled in" most often by what we have described as familiarity. Trust remains visible only *in minora,* in what we have come to realize is nothing more than a reference to its pristine expression in the private realm.

The emergent paradox is a vision of the individual agent whose agency and intentionality can be most fully realized in the private realm and not in the realm of social affairs. It is this individual and the structural (as opposed to ontological) agency of his (and in modern Western societies, increasingly her) social positions that, as we have stressed again and again, necessitate the granting of that "trust" whose loss is so lamented at present. But the very emergence of this trust has, as we have seen, no great history. If, as we have argued, trust emerges at system limits, the private realm too must be seen as one coming to exist at the limits of system—as, in fact, defining these limits in ideal-typical terms, exemplified in the growing importance of individual conscience beyond ecclesiastical hierarchies and institutional roles. A more precise analysis of the relations between these two aspects of our existence and their implications for our understanding of confidence in the construction of the public realm will be the subject of our next and final chapter.

Six

Spheres of Value and the Dilemma of Modernity

IT WAS to a great extent an awareness of the growing divergence—indeed a realization of the very distinction—between public and private lives that, as we noted above, characterized so much of the social and political thought of the eighteenth and nineteenth centuries. One could claim that the core of all eighteenth-century attempts to articulate a notion of civil society lay in this recognition of the problematic relation between the private and the public, the individual and the social, public ethics and individual interests, individual passions and public concerns.[1] For if constitutive of the emergent eighteenth-century notion of civil society was some sense of a shared public, so was the very existence of the private. It was, after all, the very existence of a free and equal citizenry—that autonomous, agentic individual, the private subject—that made civil society possible at all. The public space of interaction could be conceived as a public space only in so far as it was distinguished from those social actors who entered it as private individuals. Where there was no private sphere, there was, concomitantly, no public one: both had to exist for sense to be made of either one.

We have already seen that it was precisely those eighteenth-century moral philosophers of civil society who first posited a personal or private sphere, of friendship and trust (as opposed to interest) as one of the unalterable benefits of "commercial" (what we would term "modern") society. In premodern and feudal society bonds of personal affinity were rooted in codes of status and honor, while in the court societies existent from the sixteenth century they were tied to a personalized politics of court status. Freed from the constraints of calculation and interest, the private sphere became in the eighteenth century a realm where the personal nature of individual relations (i.e., friendship) was freed from concerns of social station. Thus, just as the individual emerged through the myriad of new and impersonal role relations in the public sphere, the very idea of the private emerged concomitantly as a realm of trust and mutuality existent apart from the systemically defined role relations of the public sphere.

If with the Scottish moralists, the idea of civil society emerged as a way to bridge the two worlds of public and private, of interest and trust, of less and more labile role expectations, we have seen too how the realm of the private, founded on individual conscience, took a certain moral priority, constituting, with Smith for instance, the true residency of virtue (or with

Immanuel Kant, the realm of the ethical).[2] Here, however, a new dynamic evolves. For the very emergence of a realm of trust as an (ideal) potentiality of true mutuality also makes of trust something problematic. Just as the potential for trust emerges when mutual role expectations are no longer determined by public norms, so does the potential for mistrust. With the ability to negotiate roles and role expectations, an element of risk enters social relations that was, to a great degree, absent when roles (and hence role expectations) were perceived as embedded within strict normative definitions. If we follow Giddens's framework and contrast trust between individuals and confidence in abstract system—as two modes of negotiating risk—we see that where relatively strict definitions of role behavior apply, the mutuality of roles is embedded, as it were, within the overall social system. One need not develop trust within particular role-sets because the relationship between role incumbents is structured by the existence of an overriding systemic logic. Rather than trust between individuals, what anchors the mutuality of the relationship is confidence in the system. The specific normative values of said system are, of course, variable. They can be organized around the certainties of kinship (honor), a transcendental religion (faith), or the logic of market exchange and the principles of abstract, rational, and universal rights of the individual (contract). These inform the system of modern social relations. In the last case, however, the issue of trust does become a problem.

The move, if you will, from faith (confidence plus sacrality) to trust, which brings with it a heightened degree of indeterminacy, also fundamentally transforms the nature of social relations, engendering, in modernity, the very particular distinction and tension between public and private which has become a hallmark of modern civilization. Thus, in ideal-typical terms, modern societies are characterized by the existence of two types of relation, those defined by public, formal, relatively determined (and often increasingly legally defined) roles and those defined by negotiable, labile, and relatively indeterminate role expectations. Whereas earlier societies tended to subsume the vast majority of role-sets (and so of interaction) within the parameters of determined, normative, and publicly sanctioned expectations, the specificity of modernity is precisely the emergence of a realm of interaction that, while not so defined, is nevertheless seen as a repository of value: the realm of the private.

To put the issue somewhat starkly, we are thus identifying the public realm with the phenomenon of confidence in systemically enforced expectations and the private with those of trust, individual agency, and a space for the negotiation of role expectations. Rather than making an absolute distinction, I would suggest envisioning these as existing along a continuum where the more negotiation, agency, and trust existing in an interaction, the more it can usefully be conceived as being of a private nature and the more confidence in systemically mandated (and sanctioned) forms of interaction, the more public its nature. (We may, just for example's sake, take the interaction between a father and his six-year-old daughter. The same father and daughter will interact differently in their living room and in the mall. This difference is the difference between the public and the private, between less and more negotiable forms of role incumbency that I am indicating above).

One could certainly argue that while these characteristics may adhere to interaction on the micro level, they do not hold in the aggregate of collective action on the macro level. Argument may thus be made that the great class struggles of the nineteenth century (the period of high modernity par excellence) were nothing less than the public, often violent, negotiation of role expectations. What after all are worker's rights and entitlements if not specific sets of universally recognized (within the nation-state) role expectations that only emerged following a period of intense negotiation between the relevant social actors (employers, workers, government agencies, and other corporate actors)? But such a criticism would miss its mark. For precisely what I would wish to argue is for the ways in which different forms of micro interaction inform and structure the manner of the macro public contest. Thus, in Europe and to some extent in Latin America, where the public/private distinction is quite developed, the social actors who entered the public arena to negotiate different role expectations did so as *public* actors and not as private selves. They entered the public realm of social action, precisely in their public capacity as representatives of workers' councils, employers' associations, and the like. Moreover, we should not forget that the *struggle* over role definitions is different from a process of *negotiation* within and between different agreed-upon accepted definitions of role behavior. In the second case, a given set of definitions, or at least their outer boundaries, are accepted by role-set members, and negotiation progresses within these boundaries. This is very different from a struggle (especially a violent, not to mention a revolutionary, struggle) over the very definition of a role or, in the case of revolution, its negation.

Interesting to note, if only in passing, is the comparative perspective that emerges from these remarks. In Europe, where the public/private distinction was more absolute and so the definition of roles more structured, so the establishment of accepted role definitions (in the field of production) was less violent than in the United States. There, by contrast, where the public/private distinction was more mediated and fluid, more labile, the process of establishing new role definitions in the sphere of industrial production was characterized by a process of more violent negotiation.

In explaining this divergence of labor violence in the United States and Europe, I would think that we would do well to look at the extent to which different roles and, most especially, the distinction between private and public realms was institutionalized. In Europe, where this distinction was highly institutionalized, a given structure of reciprocal expectations tended to mediate the violence of the "negotiation" process; while in the United States, the very lability of boundaries and the inability to posit or assume shared expectations between contesting parties gave to the labor struggle its especially violent characteristics. This, despite the fact that in the United States (as opposed to Europe) the working class was never excluded from membership in the collective, and so labor struggles were never over identity and membership as they were in Europe (as represented by the struggle over the franchise—a fact which would have led one to assume more violent rather than less violent struggles).[3]

The corollary to this in the realm of social movements and organizations is that in the United States the public sphere is warrened coast to coast by a multitude of private organizations which continually remake the public realm. In Europe this process is much more the work of State/administrative directives and hence the realm of the State per se, which is consequently seen as the public space par excellence; as such it is the object of contestation by, as just noted, individuals acting as public personae. Thus, I am not claiming that a public realm of systemic definitions and confidence (or lack thereof) is not a contested one; but, rather, that the very nature of this contestation may be differently constructed by either publicly or privately defined individual actions. In Europe it is more the former and in the United States the latter. On the other hand and as part of the same dynamic, what are most often defined as private affairs, morals, attitudes, and behavior—of the everyman and woman—have a much more "public" resonance in the United States than in Europe and as such are more of an issue of public regulation: from prohibition to today's moral crusades against smoking, certain forms of language use (what is termed political correctness), and so on. In this context it is useful to recall the great reticence of the French press to discuss François Mitterrand's mistress and their daughter as well as the rather unproblematic nature of their appearance at his funeral alongside his more publicly recognized family, an appearance that would certainly have been impossible in the United States.

One of the interesting derivatives of this particular American propensity to blur the boundaries of public and private realms is the way this exacerbates the difficulty modern societies have with the existence of ambiguity, both conceptually and, more importantly, in the field of human relations.[4] For with the increasing difficulty of modern societies to construct a shared world of life experience (i.e., familiarity) and with trust increasingly less capable of complementing confidence in universalistic, univocal, and abstract systems (of increasingly instrumental nature) as the basis of social life, ambiguity becomes intolerable and often unacceptable. The existence of situations of interpersonal indeterminacy thus becomes not something to be navigated through but an aspect of life to be restricted to the greatest extent possible.

In the United States this has in fact emerged as an increasingly salient concern of both the public and private realms. In the latter context I suggest recalling some of the stories told by the French-born anthropologist Rahel Wasserfall, who when visiting this country as a Fulbright Fellow found that the very American academic valuation of pluralism seemed to lead to a uniquely American obsession with ambiguity, especially in relations between the genders.[5] Ambiguity in gender relations, she noted, was not tolerated at all and the type of "flirtation," "letting things happen," that she was familiar with in other cultures was not countenanced in the professional, American academic environment. Rather, at the very beginning of any interaction, even the most innocuous and professional, her interlocutors (regardless of their own gender) felt it imperative to establish almost immediately the boundaries, potentialities, and restrictions of the interaction. Thus, for example, she notes:

> I was meeting a male anthropologist who was about my age, and we were on our way to have lunch. Almost immediately he said something about going with his wife to Washington over the weekend. I myself found a way to answer a few sentences later that, "I will be going to visit my partner in LA next month." After this (in my view strange) dialogue, we went on talking about anthropology and his interests.[6]

Wasserfall's fears that she was unwittingly giving off sexual messages to men (and hence the above interaction) were soon set to rest when she realized that women too (albeit gay women) also immediately on meeting proclaimed their willingness (or lack thereof) to enter into a new relationship. As she notes, she soon learned that men and women both were very concerned to know "not my class, my kin, my religious or political beliefs, or the origin of my family, but my marital situation."

This mode of behavior is, I would claim, directly correspondent with the analytic claims made above: The interstitial spaces of system can no longer be easily "filled in" by structures of shared or imputed familiarity (which did, in fact, once define the culture of American universities—white, male, Protestant, and from the leisure class) which would have allowed one to trust. (Trust, we recall, can only be proffered or accepted against a background of indeterminacy, what is termed here ambiguity.) In its stead, there is then an attempt, in Wasserfall's terms, to "tailor," or explicitly define crucial (though not immediately relevant) aspects of one's status. As we can only "trust" to other's agency, we seek to delineate the precise contours of the potential interaction through an explicit (if subtle) recitation of our place in the world (at least in terms of this discrete set of factors). All in all, this is not that different from—indeed, is but a Western, individualist variant of—the contemporary Bedouin who upon meeting strangers establish one another's lineage relations, the better to know if they are friends or enemies. Perhaps many of the most "burning" of contemporary issues revolving around political correctness, new norms of interpersonal behavior, and the almost obsessive concern with explicating (often legally) gender roles and role expectations are to be viewed in this light: as an attempt to reestablish familiarity rather than trust as the basis of social unconditionalities, as providing the ground of interaction.

This is a process that takes place not only on the level of individual or private interaction, but it is becoming an important component of public culture as well. Those problems of indeterminacy and ambiguity that bedevil the private sphere are also making themselves increasingly felt in the public realm as well. Both manifestations result from that particular definition of society's unconditionalities where the very institutionalization of the rights of man and citizen (as public values) increasingly leaves the realm of the private as the paramount realm of value and meaning (and ethical action).[7] This process has been most accomplished in the United States, though aspects of this trend were already present in the eighteenth century and can be found in the foundation texts of political liberalism as well as in the thought of the Scottish moralists. So, for example, and as noted above, the very idea of civil society contains a stress on the private realm as that of value and ethical action as opposed to the public stress of other political traditions such as those of civic virtue.

Within this developing dynamic of public and private, and the increasing relegation of meaning and value to the realm of the private the problem of trust takes on an added dimension because it is only in the negotiation between private realms—those occasioned by trust—that shared value can emerge. The problem of shared value (or lack thereof, which is precisely what stands at the core of current debates between communitarians and liberals on the definition of the public good) brings us directly to the problem of the collectivity—of defining its boundaries, criteria of membership and participation and, most especially, modes of representation. It is this problem (or set of problems) that stands behind much of what is currently termed "the culture wars," analysis of which will in fact provide a useful introduction to the crises of familiarity and trust that we seem to be facing at the close of the twentieth century.[8]

To appreciate the sociological aspects of this debate we should return to the distinction made by Norberto Bobbio between relations among parts (private) and between the parts and the whole (public). What will be argued is that whereas Bobbio's distinction holds for premodern and classical modern culture where the public realm was one that included the relation between different roles (and structures or institutions) and the representative social whole, the very logic of modernity, resting on the idea of the individual as moral absolute, fundamentally transforms this set of relations. For with the terms of representation increasingly being defined by the autonomous, rights-bearing individual, the representation of the public sphere (and so of relations between public and private) becomes increasingly problematic. This problem is essentially that noted by Luhmann of the part (the private/individual) supporting the whole (the public/collective).[9] With the realm of value relegated to the sphere of the private, it becomes increasingly difficult to represent the collective whole, the realm of the public (especially when we consider the moral or value-laden aspect of every representation). In this sense and very tersely we may note that the loss of honor as a category of public value represents the triumph of the private. Contrariwise, such a radically constituted private cannot support itself, cannot, in fact, represent itself: this is the situation at present.

If we bear in mind the legal aspects of any process of representation, we find one particularly salient illustration of this process (and one not unconnected to the loss of honor) in the field of family law where, as Mary Glendon has noted, "the emergence of new legal images of the family . . . stress the separate personalities of the family members rather than the unitary aspect of the family."[10] Quoting the 1972 *Eisenstadt v. Baird* court decision which stressed that "the married couple is not an independent entity with a mind and heart of its own, but an association of two individuals each with a separate intellectual and emotional makeup," she argues that the new family law "holds up self-sufficiency [of individual members] as an ideal and is somehow degrading and implicitly denying the importance of human "inter-subjectivity."[11] Thus, even the legal idea of the family as a social and moral institution has been replaced by those discrete and particular individuals who comprise it. The case of the family and its legal representation (or lack thereof) is but one aspect of a trend whose inherent logic is diametrically opposed to the type of communal affirmation characteristic of the communitarian tradition noted above.

The sociological consequences of this situation are of a dual and related, even if seemingly contradictory, nature and of great importance to understanding the current and reigning confusion in matters pertaining to the public and the private. The one is the phenomenon of projecting the private into the public realm as an attribute of representation. The other phenomenon is the reimposition of public definitions onto the private realm. This dual moment is in a sense the core dynamic of what Arendt referred to as the "rise of the social" and the loss of all distinction between public and private realms.[12]

As illustrations of the first, we may think of the inordinate importance awarded to the drinking or fornication of public officials in the United States or of talk shows dedicated to sexual infidelities, incest or penile implants, or, for that matter, the bumper stickers one passes on the highway proudly proclaiming the owners to be the parents of a child on the honor list at some elementary or middle school. And while the latter case may leave us wondering why the validation and recognition of the child's accomplishments within the private circle of the family is not sufficient (or perhaps nonexistent, or, as I believe, tied to the changing nature of the family), the former leaves us wondering why the most weighty of public matters (such as the confirmation of a Supreme Court justice) are debated almost exclusively in terms of personal sexual ethics.

And if in the former set of cases the public realm seems to be reduced to a movie screen for the projection of private lives and interests, it is, to a great extent the logic of the latter development that defines much of what we refer to so often as multiculturalism (a development classical liberals view with some approbation, marking as it does an attack on that distinction of realms which stands at the heart of the liberal political philosophy and *lebenswelt*). Behind the development of multiculturalism (and much of present struggles over political correctness) stands the defining premise of modernity—value as an aspect of the private. The multitude of private realms, each a value in itself, can no longer be negotiated without the imposition of public, normatively standardized role definitions. Without a shared universe of expectations, histories, memories, or affective commitments, no basis of familiarity can exist. In a situation of radically incommensurate life-worlds (or even their potentiality), that familiarity necessary to negotiate role expectations (that is, familiarity in what we have termed above its second sense, as mechanism only) is lacking, and beginning to emerge in its place are the increasingly public definitions of roles and role expectations (defined, most saliently in this country, through its legal culture). In the absence of trust, indeterminacy becomes intolerable, hence the continued promulgation of "speech codes," housing association regulations, smoking laws, and other forms of formal regulation (and sanctions) of interpersonal behavior.

This logic goes much further than simply interpersonal relations. The world of private philanthropic foundations, for example, is currently being reorganized to meet standards of "diversity" and "multiculturalism"—a subversion of their private purpose (of aiding, let us say, artistic excellence, expression, and performance) in the name of currently salient public desiderata.[13] The fact that much of this is framed in terms of collective identities (ethnic, gender, or even sexual preference) is, I argue, indicative of the fragility of collective representation based solely on the private. It is a return of collective identities rather than individual selves as modes of representing public culture.

It is this dynamic that explains so many of the contradictory features of modern social and political life in the United States: not only increasing regulation from the top (as social actors can no longer negotiate their own role behavior) but a rise of affective group identities from the bottom. The politics of gender and of sexual preference, the whole multicultural agenda and the very strong feelings it evokes both among its adherents and its more conservative opponents, points, I would claim, to a reemergence of group identities that take the place of those individual identities that we had come to equate with the progress of modernity. Ethnicity, race, gender, sexual preference, "new age," and so on, are not simply separate interests akin to corporate groups acting in the public arena. Nor are they simply what is so tellingly termed "lifestyles." They are rather lifestyles which represent a mode of identity contrary to those classic ideas of the individual that we associate with bourgeois political forms and that were indeed essential to that mode of social organization. They are also, as we shall see, attempts to reconstitute the ties of familiarity, within a social structure that has seen, the almost total erosion of all basis for such familiarity. As it becomes more and more difficult to "impute" shared strong evaluations to other social actors and hence maintain interaction on the basis of an assumed familiarity, we are more and more led to rely on trust, alone which, as we have seen, is too fragile a phenomenon, too fleeting and labile a basis upon which to construct enduring structures of interaction. What is taking its place as the basis of solidarity is thus a return to the terms of familiarity *qua* unconditionality and not *qua* mechanism. It is almost as if trust, which is predicated on individual agency and the negotiation of role fulfillment inherent to such agency, is too demanding an unconditionality to be maintained over time (especially given the increasing complexity of roles that have come to define contemporary existence in the West). Trust is thus being replaced by decidedly premodern forms of solidarity and of self, oriented not toward the agentic or intentional self but toward group loyalties, many of which are defined in the most premodern of terms possible (i.e., on the ascriptive or primordial bases of gender, race, and ethnicity). That these developments have increasingly come to characterize aspects of social and political life in the United States, France, and Germany, and not just Moldovia, Romania, or Turkmenistan is an indication of precisely how mediated and difficult it has become to maintain the unconditional principles upon which modernity has been seen to rest from 1789 onward.

In this context, there is a good deal of irony in the fact that the current, much heralded postmodern era is characterized also by a return to the quintessential modern notion of civil society and its search for a solution to a problem which has, in effect, defined modernity since its inception. However, given the above analysis, we are entitled to query this renewed concern with the basis of trust and mutuality among our contemporaries and question the solutions posited. We are moreover compelled by the logic of the foregoing analysis to provide some explanation for this reemergent concern with the basis of what is termed trust but is in fact an attempt to return to bases of familiarity in postindustrial and postmodern societies. We must also explain why this reemergent concern with the problem of trust is being phrased in the idiom of the eighteenth-century idea of civil society and not in the generation of new analytic models for understanding the problem. I would claim that this return to what are still relatively unsophisticated ideas of civil society in the current scholarly (and civic) discourse reflects a change in those very structural features upon which we have based our analyses of trust, its emergence in modernity, and its analytic dimension. For if the current return to the idea of civil society reflects anything, it is, as noted, the heightened saliency with which we, today, feel the social construction of trust as problematic. The reasons for this, I believe, are rooted in the changing nature of social roles and role negotiation through which we have come to understand what is involved in the act of trusting. In brief, the transformation of the economies and societies of many Western European and North Atlantic societies over the past few decades—most especially in the United States but not uniquely so—have "forced" us to rely more and more on trust as a mode of negotiating risk. The problem is that trust, as we have indicated above, is at best a fragile and limited commodity. Rather than that agentic "leap of trust" which can emerge in the interstices of role expectations, the very heightened differentiation of roles that characterize contemporary societies makes such an orientation incumbent on more and more types of interaction, and such a generalized diffusion of trust cannot, it would seem, be maintained. What has taken its place is a return to different types of familiarity based on the ability to impute shared strong evaluations to one another, evaluations based more and more on ascriptively defined terms of community. Having viewed some of the more obvious political or symbolic aspects of this development, we must now take a closer look at the structural conditions of its emergence.

The argument here is simple and turns on the ability of both trust and familiarity to "fill in" the undefined "spaces," those interstitial points of system limits when confidence in role fulfillment is itself insufficient to maintain interaction. Familiarity, as we have seen, turns on the ability to assume (or impute) shared moral commitments to the other and so to negotiate the structurally determined agency of the other on the basis of assumed shared moral commitments (or strong evaluations). This, we recall, was Durkheim's point in relation to the establishing of familiarity based on the shared recognition of the individual worth of each social actor. However, the very heightened degree of role differentiation, which for Durkheim stood at the center of the new models of social solidarity, does in fact undercut the ability to base social solidarity on familiarity alone (however defined, including in terms of a shared normative orientation to the sacrality of the individual).

This progress of social differentiation and its emergent problems, which was perhaps still obscure at the end of the nineteenth century, is today more than obvious; in fact, I would claim it to be one of the defining characteristics of the postmodern condition. And it is in the understanding of this phenomenon that I believe Durkheim went wrong (though of course he cannot be blamed for failing to predict the future any more than Marx could). For the changing terms of solidarity in late-nineteenth-century France were such as to necessitate a transformation in the terms of familiarity and not in their replacement by trust (which is the situation we are facing at present). This is eloquently expressed, for example, in V. Wright's analysis of the foundations and crystallization of the French Third Republic where the compromises (and contracts) between fervently opposing ideological elites have always presented a problem for historical analysis.[14] What Wright and others have maintained is that however opposed the economic and political elites of the Third Republic were in ideological terms, they did share a common "metaphysical universe" (in Taylor's terms, strong evaluations) that made compromise possible. Frequenting the same cultural establishments, involving one another in business transactions, and often intermarrying their progeny, the elites shared a common set of orientations or preferences. It was this that made the political compromise of the Third Republic possible. Not trust but familiarity provided the foundation of the social and political order. This accords well with our own understanding of trust as a relatively labile and rare phenomenon, in itself insufficient for the construction of long-lasting social relations.

What I wish to claim, however, is that the condition of late- or postmodernity makes this type of familiarity an exceedingly difficult matter to maintain (or even to project on the other) and so intensifies our need to trust; this condition pushes the problem of trust into the forefront of our consciousness as a norm of conduct that cannot be met. For all its irony, the current attempt to resurrect the idea of civil society as an analytic concept in the social sciences—and, we may well add, as a political slogan by interested parties of almost all political hues—is a veiled indication of precisely this problem, an attempt to resurrect the original language of trust and sociability in our current condition where the problems of risk are even more salient than they were to the Scots of the eighteenth century. Perhaps unknowingly we are returning to the sources (when the problem of trust first emerged analytically) to find a language in which we might express a most contemporary dilemma: the diffusion of risk—and hence the need to trust—throughout increasingly significant networks of our social relations.

What emerged in the eighteenth century as a potential orientation, one whose realized form was represented in the rather circumscribed realm of friendship, has become today an imperative of broad gamuts of interaction, imposing upon us a continual negotiation and lability of expectations that are ever harder to bear. Behind these contemporary developments is the continued progress of system differentiation which structures our lives in terms of an ever-increasing heterogeneity of roles, making confidence in system increasingly difficult to maintain since this heterogeneity implies more and more interstitial spaces between role expectations and involves us in ever more complex patterns of role relations with potentially conflicting role-set members. The same structural process of role differentiation thus exacerbates the problem of trust in two distinct ways: *(a)* it increases the potential for role conflict and so the inability to maintain confidence in the given system of role expectations; but *(b)* it also makes it increasingly difficult to supplement confidence by (real or assumed) familiarity because the very progress of role differentiation and segmentation makes it increasingly difficult to assume shared moral commitments or strong evaluations with other social actors. It is this latter development which remained unaccounted for in Durkheim's theories and it is one whose contours have only become obvious in the past few decades as the idea of postmodernity has gained in prominence. It is, moreover, crucial to our understanding of the contemporary issue of trust.

The connection between the increased division of labor (and so also the differentiation of roles and role involvement) and the increased difficulty to maintain familiarity at the close of the twentieth century is rooted in Durkheim's own idea of collective representations as shared normative orientations to the structures of social life. For if we are to abjure any idea of "collective mind" or similar notions of the collectivity as constituted as such and not of its individual members, the only possible explanation of these shared orientations is in the structural conditions of social existence. These structural conditions are themselves in the final analysis, nothing but the social roles we assume in the division of labor. The more roles we share, the more we can impute familiarity, indeed the more we also share a familiar universe with others occupying the same statuses in society. This is what was behind the growth of working-class solidarity and the development of the union movement in large factories, where shared positions in the division of labor allowed the construction of class solidarity. This is the case recently made by Barry Barnes in his analysis of the formation of status groups and classes: that it is the context of a shared experience of the conditions of existence and not the play of any "objective" forces that allows the mechanisms of resource mobilization and so the overcoming of the collective action problem in the construction of associational life. Familiarity—what Barnes often refers to as participation in a shared tradition—is what allows the construction of social solidarity (and by implication, the establishing of the social order *tout court*).[15] In terms of more traditional sociological categories what this familiarity is based on is nothing other than a common position within the division of labor. Workers shared this position with other workers, priests with other priests, industrialists with other industrialists, and so on. The existence of these common positions allows social actors to impute familiarity to others in similar positions, notwithstanding the development of role conflicts and system limits that progress together with the diversification of roles.

Thus while I am fully aware of the potential for role conflict to exist with others in my status-set, well aware that in my relation with the colleague in the department across the hall, she may be hiding or highlighting certain aspects of her behavior (of the normative orientations guiding that behavior) with me or with the Dean (as we both compete for scarce resources); I also (correctly or incorrectly, as the case may be) impute to her certain shared normative standards (strong evaluations or moral commitments) of what it is to be a professional social scientist. On the basis of these attributes, which I assume will condition her behavior or at least provide certain limits, I can continue our interaction, sometimes even in the realm of resource mobilization and engage with her in collective action. Different levels of collective action (from sitting together on an undergraduate honors committee to drafting a protest letter to the university president) will demand different "mixes" of confidence, familiarity, and trust. In most of our interactions, however, I do not need to rely on trust and certainly not on trust alone or to a significant degree. The parameters of confidence in the normative expectations of role fulfillment together with the ability to impute familiarity or shared moral orientations will suffice for most forms of daily interaction. Thus, on the honors committee I can expect certain behavior and a certain commitment on her part to the student's fulfillment of his scholarly obligations as reflected in the grade she will recommend: role expectations. I also know that as this student is her own, she has a vested interest in the student's attainment of the highest grade possible: role conflict. (In this case within her role as university professor, she is committed to both maintaining the standards of the profession and rewarding excellence only and not mediocrity; but also in her pursuit of more particular "careerist" goals, she has an interest in having graduated a student *magna cum laude* on her own vitae.) If we are aware of this conflict (and anyone who has ever sat on a university committee of any nature surely is), our collective effort to come up with a consensual grade for the student can more or less be encompassed by my reliance (i.e., confidence) on her maintaining the normal standards of role fulfillment attended by my ability to impute a shared orientation toward professionalism which, I believe, will limit at least the most flagrant violations of her role fulfillment. In most cases these two aspects of our experience are sufficient to maintain interaction and so provide a solution to the collective action dilemma. Moreover, when we are mistaken (i.e., when we attribute too much force to the familiarity of shared strong evaluations), we are generally mistaken in the degree to which we attribute this force and not absolutely.

Thus in the progress of social solidarity, trust enters into the matrix of social interaction but only *in minora*, only minimally, and it is rare that we are dependent on its workings alone to maintain interaction or solidarity. But if such is the case, why the current and growing concern with social trust? Why the reemergence of the idea of civil society as a solution to a problem perceived as growing almost daily? Why the almost obsessive concern with reestablishing the bases of trust in society as evinced in the communitarian movement? Why indeed if it is not all that central to the constitution of society? And here, I believe, is precisely where the condition of postmodernity—what is now better characterized as late-modernity—diverges from the conditions of modernity simple, or classical-liberal modernity. This divergence, as noted above, is in the changing nature of social roles and the growth of role differentiation incumbent on the changing modes of production and the organization of labor (as well as other modes of social life, such as the family); these have undergone a qualitative transformation in recent decades which seems to be characteristic of the future as well. In brief, the thesis I wish to develop is that the rising concern with trust is a response to the fact that in the current situation we are more dependent on trust (and less on familiarity) to supplement those interstitial points where system confidence is not sufficient; this is occurring at the same time that these points become more numerous with the ever-increasing differentiation of roles.

Take, for example, the current concern in the United States with the "disintegration of the family," expressed most often in the rise of divorce—a constant theme of Republican legislators and other conservative groups concerned with the "saving" of marriage and the family.[16] This theme is a well-known one in contemporary politics in the United States and while it is true that divorce rates have risen—from 15% of white women married in the early 1940s to over 50% of those married in the 1970s and now includes something like 30% of all women in the United States—it is also the case that more than half of those divorced have also remarried.[17] With this the social scientists usually rest their case and rue the ignorance of the masses and their failure to appreciate statistical data. That, however, is to miss the point. For while marriage, per se, the "sanctity" of marriage, may be the concern for some on the Christian right, the growth of both divorce *and* remarriage nevertheless does imply the growth of new roles and role commitments (divorced, remarried, second, third, or fourth husband) and with them, an increasing difficulty in imputing familiarity (with the stress here on shared strong evaluations) to other married actors. The experience (expectations, normative orientations, shared moral commitments, interests even) of marriage becomes fractured with divorce, as does that of the children's own expectations (of relations, family, role models, modes of conflict resolution, etc.) which will no longer be shared with those from families that did not experience divorce.

I mean here to make no moral judgment, only to point out, in this one small case, how an experience (of marriage, or with children, or family life) that once could provide the basis for the imputation of familiarity can no longer do so. Even when family structures perdure in new forms (single-parent families, same sex couples, and so on), seemingly similar roles no longer carry with them the same meanings. Indeed the same social status (husband, child, wife) carries with it very different role-sets in different cases which makes the imputation of familiarity based on shared structural position even more difficult. Crucial here are the implications of these developments on children and so on the socialization of coming generations. For as Ronald Ingelhart's research on the development of post-materialist values has shown, the experience of one's formative years seems to be even more critical in the development of value orientations than experiences in later life.[18]

The family is but one example among many and arguably far from the most important. We may look to the changing nature of production—again in the United States—to see a structurally similar development. The drop in manufacturing employment (from 27% in 1970 to 18% in 1990 to an expected 12% by the end of the century), the shift from heavy industry to microchip and computers, and the fact that 75% of the labor force are in the service industries are all developments that fracture the shared nature of the work experience and make it more and more difficult to impute familiarity to actors in structurally identical status positions.[19] When workers are no longer sharing a spot on the production line or meals together or work breaks, the experience of work is more and more personalized and individualized. Many of the elite of this new work force work at home and can work anywhere there is a fax machine, modem, and airport. While Christopher Lasch has seen this situation leading to the disembedment of these elites from their local communities (and hence leading to a crisis in the provision of Public Goods), it involves first and foremost a differentiation of the work worlds, of those cognitive universes that make the imputation of familiarity possible.[20] Thus software consultants or market analysts have both more differentiated role-sets than production workers and less ability to assume familiarity with other software analysts working from home than industrial workers in close proximity to one another. More and more positions in the division of labor are coming to resemble the former.

Similarly and perhaps even more importantly, the changing nature of production and the new flexibility of labor contracts and employment conditions have produced an ever-shrinking minority of workers' benefits from full employment (prestige or status, health benefits, pension plans, etc.) and an ever-growing majority of workers employed on a temporary (rather than part-time) basis. This too significantly changes the nature of employment roles and the experience thereof. Note: this development does not necessarily correlate with high levels of worker dissatisfaction but it does make the experience of work very different for different segments of the work force, even for those working in the same industry, or the same company.[21] Again, the different definitions of similar statuses make the work experience something very different for different people and so make the ability to impute familiarity to those in the same status increasingly difficult. As David Harvey has pointed out:

> Class consciousness no longer derives from the straight class relation between capital and labor, and moves onto a much more confused terrain of inter-familial conflicts and fights for power within a kinship or clan-like system of hierarchically ordered social relations. Struggling against capitalist exploitation in the factory is very different from struggling against a father or uncle who organizes family labor into a highly disciplined and competitive sweatshop that works to order for multinational capital.[22]

Our concern here is less with class solidarity and more with the structure of familiarity and trust in society but the parallels, I believe, are obvious. The difficulty of establishing solidarity in the workplace is met by the difficulty of imputing familiarity in the subway. So too the dispersal and geographic mobility of production—what Daniel Bell has termed "distributive manufacturing"—where the same company may have productive facilities in dozens of countries also undermines the ability to impute familiarity, as the workers engaged in the same productive process (making zippers for men's trousers, say) are not working across the bench from one another but across the world.

Decline in plant size, movements of capital from the center to the periphery, geographic—in fact, global—division of labor, flexibility, small-batch production, personalized payment systems, labor diversification, specialization of services in industrialized countries: all aspects of the modern system of production that, whatever they may mean for the development of capital and labor relations, do combine to differentiate the organization of productive roles, defining more and more of such roles in idiosyncratic and particularized ways that make it less and less plausible to assume that we share strong evaluations or commitments with others in what may seem to be similar structural positions.[23]

To reiterate our original point: the division of labor under late-modernity has been characterized by an exponential growth in the number of roles we fulfill in society (thus, a similar growth in the potential for role conflict and, therefore, limits to confidence in the system of role expectations), but at the same time, it has seen an increasing difficulty in maintaining a sense of familiarity with others in similar roles. Hence the growing perception of trust as a problem—as we are more and more forced to rely on its presence to maintain interaction and so the foundations of social order.

On the cultural and symbolic levels these developments have led to a new "structure of feeling" (to borrow Raymond Williams's felicitous phrase in dealing with the now long gone eighteenth century), one characterized by the porousness of experience, by the fracturing of cognitive worlds, by the catch-words of discontinuity and difference—by an acceptance of all that is ephemeral and fragmented, by all that is diverse and polymorphous. The whole postmodern jargon of "local determinisms," "particular interpretive communities," "hyper-realities," and the reduction of experience to "a series of pure and unrelated presents" where "the image, the appearance, the spectacle can all be experienced with an intensity (joy or terror) made possible only by their appreciation as pure and unrelated presents in time" and where "the immediacy of events, the sensationalism of the spectacle (political, scientific, military, as well as those of entertainment), become the stuff of which consciousness is forged" is the symbolic reflection of just these developments.[24]

Consciousness forged from the immediacy of events and one that abandons all sense of historical continuity (recall here the postmodern abjuration of all "meta-narrative") is precisely a consciousness that is no longer forged through the matrix of either role expectations (system confidence) or the mutuality of shared moral commitments (strong evaluations) that make familiarity possible. I can no longer assume that Fred played stickball in his youth on East 13th street, thus our interaction is defined solely by this moment. This privileging of the ephemeral by the postmodernists is nonsense and makes of my interaction with a friend or colleague something analogous to my interaction with the neighbor's dog. However—and this is the crucial point—if I can no longer assume stickball, I have to rely on trust (to fill in the lacunae of system), and that is the problem. Perhaps here (and in the context of stickball) we should note the importance of baseball to American popular consciousness and the extent to which the baseball strike of 1994–95 was a blow to so many people. Baseball is, after all, the symbol of shared familiarity, the icon upon which we can hang our sociability, our familiarity: in a sense we all played stickball as children and thus we can all maintain a certain degree of familiarity.[25] However, as baseball becomes—like so many other aspects of our "shared" world—the play of different forces of capital transfer, individual salary packages (free-agent contracts), and so on, it too threatens to lose this iconic status. Hence the pain of so many citizens as the economic forces of diverse interests revealed the nature of the game as something not at all "familiar" in the sense of representing shared strong evaluations (a preview of which had already been experienced in 1989 with the scandal surrounding the betting of Pete

Rose who represented for many, not only in his native Cincinnati, precisely this shared, familiar aspect of the sport).

More examples of this type of transformation in the nature of social roles could be presented though I believe the point has been made. We should also note the important and growing role of computers and Internet as a means of communication which makes the imputation of familiarity and shared moral commitments increasingly difficult. This has been the subject of a study by Deirdre Boden, who analyzed how the increasing spatial and temporal distance between interlocutors undermines that sense of what she terms "trust" (and what we term familiarity) that is a function of face to face communication. Interestingly, this relation between the extent of communication and the level of trust between actors has been the subject of a number of game-theory studies showing how the greater the degree of directness and the less the degree of ambiguity in communication, the more beneficial the outcome of the interaction. Similarly, studies of ambiguity per se have stressed how in the Con Game, which was designed to evaluate manipulative and unscrupulous behavior "when the game was played such that each player knew exactly what resources the other had and there was minimum ambiguity," the devious players could not exploit the situation to their own advantage.[26] The ability to reduce ambiguity is, according to Boden and others, a prime characteristic of what she terms "copresent" interaction and is itself an outcome of those qualifying moments in discourse that Garfinkel has termed "practical ethics." These tend "to maximize the tendency for socially solidary actions to take place."[27] These too are lost in the spatial and temporal separation of computerized interaction.

Perhaps one of the most important insights of David Harvey's study of the postmodern condition is precisely how the development of the production processes in late-modernity fractured our sense of time and place and has made of these most fundamental coordinates of social life highly diversified (if not yet individualized) matrixes of behavior and position in the world. Thus, even on this most fundamental level, it is becoming more and more difficult to assume (with Durkheim) a shared normative set of orientations and thus to maintain the solidarity of a *conscience collective*. The constitutive aspect of this, our current condition (though not shared equally in all postindustrial societies nor in all areas of the same country, hence the crisis of the nation-state as locus of solidarity), is our increasing need to rely on trust as the shared and familiar aspects of our world are progressively shrinking.

As the conditions for this trust are increasingly diminishing, what is replacing trust is, as noted, a return to different forms of familiarity as a means of negotiating those increasingly interstitial moments of system's own making. The situation of post- or late-modernity is thus one where the very nature of confidence in mutually articulated role expectations is itself ridden with the potential for role conflict. The endless privileging of some aspects of role over others is a fundamental and necessary aspect of the heightened degree of role segmentation that constitutes our social selves. Moreover, as analyzed above, and in contrast to high-modernity or modernity *simpliciter*, the conditions for trust as a mode of negotiating these interstitial points are also rapidly diminishing. We are thus forced to rely more and more on trust at the very moment when its presence (and even potential) is receding.

The crisis of trust thus rests on several interrelated developments. The first is the problem of maintaining conditions of familiarity as a mechanism for the establishment of trust (as an unconditional principle of interaction). As we have seen, this problem is rooted in the very heightened degree of change and transformation that characterizes the current, global division of labor. The second is the institutionalization of trust as a component of modern principles of generalized exchange which, through its very realization, leads to an ever-increasing divergence between the institutionalized and "pristine" forms of this unconditionality. Unlike other institutionalized unconditionalities (that of medieval Catholicism, say), those of modernity (based on the idea of the individual and the trust that is its necessary corollary) suffer from a peculiar paradox—that of representation. For precisely those symbolic moments where the "pristine" form of society's unconditionality is celebrated as a shared social orientation (i.e., shared strong evaluations, familiarity as a mechanism), rituals such as the Eucharist Mass, for example, or tribal rites of passage are in modern circumstances within the private realm and do not allow representation of the whole. The "pristine" form of society's unconditionality is, as it were, *by definition* permanently removed from its more public social and institutionalized expression (recall here remarks above on liberals and communitarians).

Would it be going too far to say that the era of modernity which emerged with the crisis of trust is closing with the selfsame crisis? Would it be an exaggeration to claim that trust as the defining conceptual problem of society both opened and now closes the era of modernity? Surely this would provide new light on Foucault's claim, quoted above, that "man is an invention of recent date, and one that may well be coming to an end."[28] Like the very idea of man, trust circumscribed the modern era but has become—as unconditionality—too demanding to be maintained.

However, if the above holds then so must its corollary. Trust, after all, is intimately tied to the issues of negotiation, agency, and the individual, indeed, to the very idea of the individual as the center and moral locus of autonomous willed activity. Hence, if trust as a matrix of social interaction is receding, what of those individual selves who make this trust possible?

Does a return to familiarity rather than trust as a mode of negotiating system complexity not raise questions as to the constitution of that very self upon whom trust was based?

Briefly, I would like to posit as a hypothesis to be explored that at a certain level of complexity within the progress of role differentiation (i.e., within the growth of organic solidarity and of structural differentiation), the nature of what Ralph Turner has called the "fit" between the role and the person changes.[29] At a certain stage the role becomes more and more affect-neutral (to use Parsonian terminology), more instrumental (in Weberian terms and in those currently behind much of the social and rational-choice research agenda). The very progress of role negotiability and differentiation—and so also of self-reflexivity—leads to "role distance," an idea which stands behind Goffman's penetrating work on front- and backstage (as well, if more latently, behind David Riesman's now classical distinction between other-directed and self-directed selves).[30]

While some degree of role distance and instrumental attitudes toward role-taking no doubt existed in all social formations (concomitant with the more generalized ability to move between and negotiate roles), it would certainly seem that the greater degree of differentiation and complexity which characterizes postmodernity brings with it a much greater role distance and looser "fit" between any particular social role and the social actor. Perhaps this very critical point reached by role differentiation is itself a product of the conditions of late-modern division of labor discussed above. Thus, when the progress of role segmentation reaches a point where familiarity between social actors can no longer be assumed, then the nature of the "fit" between role and actor reaches a turning point. Such an argument would accord well with a Meadian perspective on the self as existing only in and through the gaze of the other.[31] When there are no longer such others through whose gaze the self can be constituted, the social component of the self does indeed fracture.

If, however, the "fit" between actor and role is loose, by what—we may well ask—is the actor constituted? In premodern societies, however much the actor may have interpreted and negotiated social role, the self was (by all historical and anthropological evidence) still deeply embedded within collective mentalities. Identity was still a collective attribute rather than an individual one. The period of classical modernity, or what may be termed high bourgeois culture, was, by contrast, characterized by what I would call a "strong" fit between role and person. The social actor was seen (and saw himself or herself) as fundamentally constituted by the different role complexes which in turn made up the components of personal identity. This premise stood at the heart of all legal, social, and economic relations and is expressed in the literature of Fielding and Richardson through Balzac, Zola, and Thomas Mann.[32] In this period, the era of the individual par excellence, the idea of the individual and the uniqueness of each rests not only on the progress of role differentiation, negotiability, and reflexivity noted above, but on the fact that roles were viewed (by the person and society both) as constitutive of each unique individual identity. Behind whatever front stage was presented (at theater, stock exchange, CGT meetings, or Republican clubs), there stood a backstage which was perceived as a self, an identity, deeply rooted in one's social role complex (hence the primacy of the private as the "real" theater of the self). The instrumentality of market exchange, political conflict, or social manners masked but did not negate an individual (emically construed) whose contours could not be reduced to the social role played. This at least was the premise of those social formations which we identify as modern. And, given the above attempt to define the individual in terms of some calculus of role identities, I would tend to think that it is a more or less apt description. The "difference" (between role commitments), the unique configuration that each social actor—as a vector of different role complexes—presented was tied to the noninstrumental nature of the "fit" between role and person.

Given this perspective, it is fitting to query the nature of more contemporary developments, developments characterized by endless backstages, by Riesman's other-oriented individual, by the extremely variable nature of role identities and the continual negotiation of roles and role complexes (at least in the United States). What is being queried is thus not only the reemergence of group identities in parts of the Third World in areas seen as not "sufficiently modernized," but also—and no less poignantly—the loss of that individual self which was taken as a necessary component of modern society in the North Atlantic and Western European communities.

Is it not possible that the very proliferation of "role-making" (that is of role negotiability) and the effectively infinite possibility of self-reflexive regression (through an endless array of curtains behind an endless series of stages) call into question the very idea of the individual whose self is deemed concomitant with a relatively fixed set of role complements? We may note here Robert Wuthnow's respondent in his research on contemporary spirituality, ". . . a 26-year old disabilities counselor, the daughter of a Methodist minister, who describes her religious preference as 'Methodist, Taoist, Native American, Quaker, Russian Orthodox, Buddhist, Jew.'"[33] As Wuthnow notes: "She appears to have so many religious identities that all or none are likely to matter little when the chips are down. Interesting as she might be, she raises doubts about how seriously religion can be taken when it becomes a mixture of everything, and she contrasts sharply with the unitary moral self on which most conceptions of democracy have been based."[34] This, what Wuthnow terms the "multispherical self," is a phenomenon with implications on more than the religious plane: it is an aspect of more and more of our role incumbencies. As such, it calls into question those of our more traditional and received ideas of the individual that we identify with the civilizational and civil component of bourgeois culture (MTV vs. the *Bildungsroman*, as it were).

Given this situation, we may thus query that if civility is the civilizational opposite of honor, marking the loss of the public and the triumph of the private and of the individual, are such phenomena as the extreme litigiousness of contemporary American life not a further step in the transformation of social identity, the loss of the private and of the individual in a pure calculus of interests and instrumental aggregation? Is the loss of self, of the individual, not precisely what is at the heart of the current blurring of all distinctions between public and private selves (and roles)? Are not the television talk shows dedicated to the most personal of issues (generally revolving around issues of sexual infidelity, incest, and so on) and the public regulation of each stage of sexual exploration among college students (at Antioch) essentially the same phenomenon, namely the loss of all individually constructed boundaries between roles (as well as any consensus regarding their contents, expectations, and modes of reciprocity) and their replacement with the type of public social regulation that characterized earlier periods?

The looser the fit between the person and the role, the more every aspect of role behavior and mutuality is negotiable. But as Durkheim taught us so long ago, there must be a limit to negotiation for society to exist. The limits of negotiation, the limits of contract, are of course the precontractual. And if the idea of the individual as moral agent (central here is the idea of intentionality which entered our moral lexicon with Abelard) no longer stands at the basis of the precontractual, something else must. It is in this context that I am suggesting we view the current return to group affiliations and identities predicated on what are often ascribed criteria of gender, ethnicity, or race (note too how much of the current discussion over sexual preference, especially by gay and lesbian advocates, posits such preferences as given, genetic, in some sense, essentially ascribed to people).

Not only must a Church be built on a rock, so must individual selves. At some point self-reflexivity must come home, at some point actors must remove their paint and find a face that cannot be changed, negotiated and twisted to any script, at some point one must settle on a name, hair color, gender, body dimension, percentage of fat and muscle tension that are not a function of a given job description but are in essence a self. If the idea of the individual can no longer provide this, this that exists behind the *persona*, behind the mask, something else will—and that something may well be renewed allegiance to group identities. We may then be left with the bourgeois political forms as modes of organizing social life but with forms devoid of their content. What this may mean for the organization of society is an open question.

Conclusion _____

IT WAS only in the mid-seventeenth century that the term probability began to achieve its current meaning.[1] Decision theory and probability reasoning, namely, modes of theorizing risk, developed in the decades following the 1640s and 1650s, and for the next two hundred years or so, models of rational decision-making and belief in conditions of uncertainty occupied the minds of some of Europe's greatest mathematicians. Interesting to note is that these concerns developed at roughly the same time that trust (as an aspect of promise-keeping) entered the lexicon of political philosophy. In this period, too, developing theories of "reasonableness" (and the idea of the "reasonable man") became influential among natural law philosophers and theologians—including, "reasonably" enough, Hugo Grotius.[2] To no small extent philosophies of risk became a staple concern of the emergent culture of modernity. Portentously, it was Pascal who "made the first application of probabilistic reasoning to problems other than games of chance."[3] He applied it to faith itself—at which point, of course, faith is longer faith, no longer confidence in the existence of God, but rather simply a component of a mathematical expression that can be summed into infinity.[4]

Pascal's wager can be seen as a crucial moment in the transformation of the terms of faith (which is really what secularization implies) and their (albeit gradual) replacement by a calculus of trust. Pascal's was not the only wager of the mid-seventeenth century. Both John Tillotson and Robert Boyle had developed similar arguments, as did Arnauld and Nicole in Port-Royal's *Logique*.[5] Turning the problem of faith into a problem of sufficient evidence (as did the English latitudinarians) added a calculable element of risk into Christian apologetics that brought them firmly into the early modern world. Mathematical, metaphysical, and (as we have claimed) societal risk all emerged at approximately the same period.[6] In the words of Lorraine Daston, in the late seventeenth and early eighteenth centuries, "Risk was apparently not only tolerated, but relished."[7]

Undoubtedly it would be useful at some point to explore the connections between these different forms of risk. Was it the emergence of mathematical probability that attuned thinkers to the increasing lability of their social arrangements? Or, was it the newly developing multiplicity of role relations and the consequent indeterminacy that began to characterize long-established standards of reciprocity that alerted thinkers to the more abstract and mathematical aspects of risk and probability? Or, contrariwise, was it the loss of faith that engendered both developments? Or, yet again, the social and more purely cognitive that brought in their wake a questioning of the metaphysical foundations of faith? These are all fascinating questions that cannot be answered here, though one can guess what the answers of the theologian, philosopher, and sociologist, respectively, would be. Interesting in this context, though, is the argument Daston makes on the important influence of legal and juridic writings on the developing mathematical consciousness of probability. Most especially the developing practice of contract law (especially of aleatory contracts which were very much in vogue in this period) and treatises attempting to specify the conditions of equity and rules for the exchange of goods had, she claims, "a strong influence on the calculation of probability at the level of definition and proofs as well as that of application."[8] It would seem then that the Durkheim-inspired sociologist who views the origins of all cognitive categories in the matrix of social relations could make as good a claim as any for the veracity of his approach. Whatever the causal relations between the awareness of the different forms of risk, taken together they all define the "project of modernity" or, *pace* MacIntyre, the Enlightenment more than we generally acknowledge. Risk, as an aspect of social relations (no less than metaphysical doubt or mathematical probability), has emerged as a constitutive aspect of life in modern society, and *trust* as a solution to this form of risk has similarly been a defining component of this life-world.

This connection of trust to the social conditions of risk has been the defining tenet of the present study. Risk, we have endeavored to argue, became inherent to role-expectations when, with the transformation of social roles and the development of role segmentation, there developed a built-in limit to systemically based expectations (what we have termed *confidence*) of role behavior. As role segmentation and complexity increased, so did the potential for those "Mertonian dissonances" between different aspects of ego's role behavior to become evident (necessitated by system differentiation). This ever so structural of dynamics was, we have argued, behind the development of both those new forms of risk and of trust as a solution to this risk that came to characterize modern forms of social relations. As such it stood behind, or as an important component of, such phenomena as the development of new forms of friendship, civility, the transformation of honor into conscience, and companionate marriage, as well as those more ideological or symbolic developments studied in the second part of this text: the developing ideas of the public and private as separate realms of life and as separate loci of value and virtue, and the idea of the moral and agentic individual as standing at the center of all modern ideas of private life.

As diverse as these social phenomena are, they are, in some respects, all of a set. They are all connected to the new terms of solidarity that have come to define the modern world and to the new sets of strong evaluations that define our terms of familiarity. Most especially, we have argued that the idea of trust as a condition of interaction between morally autonomous and economically agentic individuals became a central component of the principles of generalized exchange, or economic unconditionalities, that structure and mediate the workings of the market in contemporary societies. As such, trust stands as well at the center of current political and moral debates, specifically that between liberals and communitarians to which we have here attempted to give a rather novel interpretation.

To summarize in the most schematic of terms: we began our inquiry with an attempt to isolate, analytically, the phenomenon under investigation. We then progressed to a broader analysis of trust as an unconditional principle of generalized exchange unique to modern forms of social organization and ended with an analysis of trust as an aspect of the private realm (itself defined by the valuation of the individual who stood at its core). Uniting all these different aspects of the analysis was the continual emphasis on trust and agency as emerging at system limits, at the limits of role expectations, and on confidence in the reciprocity of behavior. Our attention to both the more micro- and macro-processes of trusting behavior was informed by this essentially structuralist argument.

We began with the more structural argument about the emergence of trust from the changing web of social relations and supplemented this more analytic approach with various micro and phenomenological insights into the meaning and implications of such ideas as trust, familiarity, confidence, the existence of system limits, and so on. These perspectives were then themselves supplemented by more generalized and generalizable macro-level analyses, painted with the broader brush of historical inquiry (whether in the emergent terms of society's unconditionalities under capitalism, different definitions of virtue, or the developing ideas of the individual, the private sphere, and the sources of virtue). Finally, in the last chapter we stepped back from these more historical and sometimes abstract perspectives to view, yet again, the changing terms of familiarity and of trust, not as they accompanied the emergence of modernity, but as they seem to be changing yet again, in our contemporary world. From the structural basis of micro-processes we thus sought a connection to, and an explanation of, more general analytic and historical developments rooted in the selfsame dynamic only to return with these insights to a new understanding of the manner in which the definitions and valuation of trust and familiarity seem to be changing yet again at the close of the twentieth century. In this latter endeavor we have again had recourse to a more pointillistic, or anecdotal approach, the analytic import of which we should perhaps address before concluding this inquiry.

For one of the questions that emerged from the final stages of our analysis was the very possibility that as Western societies are approaching the closing decade of the twentieth century, they are also, perhaps, increasingly losing their ability to establish trust as a mode of social inter-action. Trust then would seem to be a decidedly modern phenomenon, emerging from the changing terms of role behavior in the early modern period and, just possibly, declining with the changes that have accompa-nied the late- or post-modern world. Perhaps indeed, the idea of the indi-vidual as unconditionality or, *pace* Durkheim, as precontractual principle of social solidarity was too demanding a principle, one that carried too much baggage, to which, ultimately, there adhered too much risk to be maintained.

To put the matter somewhat differently: as role segmentation progresses exponentially and the limits on systemically based expectations increase at the same rate, it becomes less and less possible to assume shared strong evaluations with others and less and less possible (perhaps plausible) to constitute a moral community on the basis of the idea of the individual precisely because that familiarity upon which community and hence self must be based is increasingly eroded. To appreciate the essentially social aspect of individual selves—or of individualism itself as an ideology or principle of generalized exchange—recall here not only the social psychol-ogy of George Herbert Mead, but also the Smithian idea of the self as constituted by an internalized morality and our own argument on the struc-tural parallels between the development of individual identities and the changing nature of group involvement and solidarity. However, when that form of solidarity predicated on the shared strong evaluations of the indi-vidual can no longer maintain its sense of familiarity (due to purely struc-tural factors, i.e., increased system differentiation and role segmentation), the individual as basis of personal identity may disappear. In this disap-pearance the preconditions for trust do themselves disappear as well. And as people return more and more to group-based identities (often of an as-cribed or primordial nature), we may well ask if, in some cases—and in what is almost a case of historical reversal—risk is not giving way to dan-ger and the problems which were once encompassed by a calculus of trust and mistrust are not redefined by one of confidence or lack thereof? (Cer-tainly the inhabitants of major North American cities, as well as those of Latin America—where the expression the "feudalization of life" is increas-ingly being heard—would probably see the problems of their public spaces as those of danger rather than of risk.) Indeed, are relations between ethnic groups in North America and many parts of Western Europe (not to men-tion Eastern Europe) not being redefined in precisely these terms?

Without the individual as willful actor there can be no trust since there does not exist that peculiar type of risk to which trust is a solution. There is, in a sense, only danger—that danger inherent to all external systems (the physical system of a tornado, hurricane, forest fire, and so on). And we may or may not have confidence in the capabilities of our system to meet this danger (whether of our fire-fighting capacities or of our army—again in its struggle with a dangerous and external system). Risk, however, which (following Luhmann) is a framing of life's contingencies internally, rather than in terms of an external system, no longer comes into play. For, in terms of the foregoing analysis, we are no longer participants in the same (symbolic) system, no longer bound by a shared sense of familiarity based on shared strong evaluations. The resulting contingencies of alter's activity can thus no longer be framed internally (i.e., role negotiation within shared symbolic boundaries) but only externally, as dangerous threats. This is the difference between civil deference and carrying a can of mace in your purse, and if not mace, having to invoke at most every turn the skills of a lawyer, versed in the act of negotiating system boundaries rather than those of the self (though given the seemingly endless proliferation of technologies of self and their respective technocrats, we seem to need a good deal of help in this realm as well).[9]

Take a most insignificant yet quotidian example. Before the prohibition of smoking in public spaces I always asked people, in line at the bank or market or wherever, if my smoking bothered them and if it did I did not light up. However, when smoking began to be banned from public spaces and before it was banned from all places of work and sociability, I stopped asking the people around me if it bothered them. From my perspective the matter had been taken out of my hands: it was no longer something to be negotiated by the partners to the interaction but was now solely the function of legal and abstract dicta. Where I was legally prevented from smoking, I did not smoke, but where it was legally permissible I stopped thinking to ask people if it bothered them. If I could smoke, I did. I was no longer negotiating the boundaries of acceptable behavior. Freed from the burden of concern, indeed, of civility, the field of smoking was henceforth ruled by law, that is, by system, rather than by negotiation and by trust. Why trust? By voluntarily refraining from smoking and so circumscribing my will in favor of the interests of a stranger, I was establishing in however passing, fleeting, and inconsequential a manner, a social bond. I, in fact, both of us, were granting one another a measure (however infinitesimal) of symbolic credit to be redeemed at an unspecified time by a third unspecified party. Precisely this type of symbolic credit is what maintains that social capital that Fukuyama identified with trust. The point is that the increasing inability of people to engage in such negotiation and trust (itself the outcome of loss of familiarity, which in turn is rooted in greater role segmentation) leaves more and more realms of interaction defined solely by system constraints which are, in their very nature, inimicable to the development of trust.

More importantly, however, we seem to be losing our ability to trust to an extent proportional to our loss of the idea of the individual as principled locus of society's unconditionalities. Our increasing inability to negotiate the boundaries of interaction without involving hard and fast rules and regulations is but another manifestation of the replacement of the open-ended negotiation of trust with the rule-bound behavior of system confidence. The corollary of this with the aforenoted distinction of risk and danger is, I believe, made clear in the continual concern over "date rape," proper forms of speech, speech codes, and so on. All begin with assumptions as to the impossibility of trust, of negotiation. This assumption is, in turn, predicated on the idea that the interaction between the parties is best characterized as one of potential danger rather than risk. The parties to the interlocution or interaction are thus not seen as inhabiting an essentially shared symbolic, moral, or ethical space, especially in the case of relations between the genders (and thus, according to Luhmann, capable of framing the contingencies of their meeting in internal terms of risk). Rather the partners to myriad interactions are seen as inhabiting decidedly separate and potentially opposing, or hostile, symbolic universes (i.e., being external to one another, each actor is seen as an almost autonomous system) whose actions carry the threat of danger the one to the other.[10] And, if there is danger, there is the necessity to impose strict legal codes and regulations, to replace trust with strictly defined system boundaries. When every sentence, if not every word, that a university professor utters to colleagues or students has to be thought through twice to be sure that it conforms to current codes of racial, ethnic, or gender "sensitivity," it is clear that we are no longer defining interlocution in terms of risk and trust, but in terms of competing "systems" each potentially dangerous to the other—as we stand poised to call in those system experts who will analyze the speech for its potentially damaging (dangerous) components and impose the necessary sanctions.

Finally and as we have noted more than once, this devaluation of trust seems to be emerging with a revaluation of collective, often primordial group identities as defining the locus of self, if not of new terms of collective membership and participation. (The defeat of the referendum in October 1995 in Province Quebec over independence by less than 1% of the votes should disabuse any who feel that the political dimensions of this problem are only European in implications.) How such identities will reshape the politics of the next century is an open question, as is the continued existence of trust in either private or public realms (i.e., in its pristine or institutionalized forms) if this reorientation of society's principles of generalized exchange does indeed come to pass.

We have already noted, more than once, how the potential uncoupling of those traditional assumptions of liberal politics (on individual freedom, constitutional democracy, and market economics) may come to be and bring in its wake the dismantling of those institutional structures of generalized exchange upon which the public expressions of trust have rested.

Given the strong historical correlations between the emergence of these liberal assumptions and the development of new terms of substantive rationality in Western civilization, we may well query if the loss or transformation of trust as a mechanism of social interaction (public and private both) is not part of a broader transformation which will see a transformation of the very terms of rationality, perhaps in the direction of a *weiderbezauberte* world. Whether, as I suspect, an enchanted world is also a more brutal and Hobbesian one is an empirical question, the answer to which may not be long in coming.

Notes

Introduction

1. Ralf Dahrendorf, "A Precarious Balance: Economic Opportunity, Civil Society, and Political Liberty," *The Responsive Community* (Fall 1995): 13–39.
2. T. H. Marshall, *Class, Citizenship, and Social Development.* (Westport, Conn.: Greenwood Press, 1973).
3. Dahrendorf, "Precarious Balance." 37.
4. Daniel Bell, "American Exceptionalism Revisted: The Role of Civil Society," *The Public Interest* 95 (1989): 38–56; Edward Shils, "The Virtues of Civil Society," *Government and Opposition* 26, no. 2 (1991): 3–20; Vladimir Tismaneanu, *Reinventing Politics* (New York: Free Press, 1992); Amitai Etzioni, *The Spirit of Community: Rights and Responsibilities and the Communitarian Agenda* (New York: Crown, 1993).
5. A. I. Meldon, *Rights and Persons* (Berkeley: University of California Press, 1980), 9.
6. Niklas Luhmann, *Trust and Power* (New York: John Wiley, 1979); Diego Gambetta (ed.), *Trust: Making and Breaking of Cooperative Relations* (Oxford: Basil Blackwell, 1988).
7. Francis Fukyama, *Trust: Social Virtues and the Creation of Prosperity* (New York: Free Press, 1995); Robert Putnam, *Making Democracy Work: Civil Traditions in Modern Italy* (Princeton: Princeton University Press, 1993).
8. Niklas Luhmann: *Trust and Power.*

Chapter One
Trust, Role Segmentation, and Modernity

1. On these solutions to the problem of collective action see Mark Lichbach, *The Rebel's Dilemma* (Ann Arbor: University of Michigan Press, 1995); S. N. Eisenstadt, *Power, Trust, and Meaning* (Chicago: University of Chicago Press, 1995).
2. For some recent perspectives on social trust see S. N. Eisenstadt and L. Roniger, *Patrons, Clients, and Friends* (Cambridge: Cambridge University Press, 1984), especially 1–42; Anthony Giddens, *Consequences of Modernity* (Stanford: Stanford University Press, 1990); Niklas Luhmann, "Familiarity, Confidence, Trust: Problems and Perspectives," in *Trust: Making and Breaking of Cooperative Relations*, ed. Diego Gambetta (Oxford: Basil Blackwell, 1988), 94–107.
3. On these aspects of modernization see K. Deutsch, "Social Mobilization and Political Development," *American Political Science Review* 55 (1961): 493–513; S. N. Eisenstadt, *Modernization, Protest, and Change* (Englewood Cliffs: Prentice Hall, 1966); S. P. Huntington, *Political Order in Changing Societies* (New Haven: Yale University Press, 1968); A. Inkeles and D. H. Smith, *Becoming Modern: Individual Change in Six Developing Countries* (Cambridge: Harvard University Press, 1974).

4. One of the few studies of the concrete workings of this image of trust (and which throws important light on its limits) is that of Barber, *The Logic and Limits of Trust* (New Brunswick: Rutgers University Press, 1988).

5. On generalized exchange see Eisenstadt, *Power, Trust and Meaning*, 156, 211–15, 345–46.

6. On the role of promise-keeping in the modern natural law tradition, especially as it formed a basis for the development of contract law, see P. S. Atiyah, *The Rise and Fall of the Freedom of Contract* (Oxford: Clarendon Press, 1979), 140–43. This theme is also dealt with in P. S. Atiyah, *Promises, Morals, and Law* (Oxford: Clarendon Press, 1981), ch. 2, and in his *Essays on Contract* (Oxford: Clarendon Press, 1986), 32.

7. Meldon, *Rights and Persons.*

8. John Locke, *Two Treatises on Government*, ed. Peter Laslett (Cambridge: Cambridge University Press, 1960), 396; David Hume, *A Treatise of Human Nature*, bk. 3, pt. 1, ed. H. D. Aieken (New York: Macmillan, 1948), sec. 1: 185; Annette Baier, *Postures of the Mind: Essays on Mind and Morals* (Minneapolis: University of Minnesota Press, 1985), 181; John Dunn, "The Concept of Trust in the Politics of John Locke," in *Philosophy in History*, eds. Richard Rorty et al. (Cambridge: Cambridge University Press, 1984), 279–302.

9. En passant we should already note here the difference between Europe and the modernizing societies of the late twentieth century where such breakup of primordial and ethnic units has not accompanied the process of economic expansion. See Fukuyama, *Trust.*

10. Baier, *Postures of the Mind*, 174. On this aspect of promises as creating obligations see also Geoffrey Cupit, "How Requests and Promises Create Obligations," *Philosophical Quarterly* 44, no. 177 (1994): 439–55.

11. Emile Durkheim, "Individualism and the Intellectuals," in *Emile Durkheim on Morality and Society*, ed. Robert Bellah (Chicago: University of Chicago Press, 1973), 52.

12. See Talcott Parsons, *The Social System* (New York: Free Press, 1951).

13. Reference here is to Karl Polanyi's *The Great Transformation* (Boston: Beacon Press, 1957).

14. On this use of trust as more or less interchangeable with confidence see such works as S. M. Lipset and W. Schneider, "The Decline of Confidence in American Institutions," *Political Science Quarterly* 98, no. 3 (Fall 1983): 379–402; Robert Lane, "The Politics of Consensus in the Age of Affluence," *American Political Science Review* 59 (1965): 874–95.

15. The version attributed to V. I. Lenin (and still used by East Berlin border guards in the 1970s) ran: "*Vertrauen ist gut, Kontrol noch besser.*"

16. Richard Holton, "Deciding to Trust, Coming to Believe," *Australasian Journal of Philosophy* 72, no. 1 (March 1994): 63–76; Annette Baier, *Postures of the Mind*; idem, "Trust and Anti-Trust," *Ethics* 96 (1986): 231–60.

17. David Lewis and Andrew J. Weigert, "Trust as Social Reality," *Social Forces* 63, no. 4 (June 1985): 976.

18. See also Lewis and Weigert, "Social Atomism, Holism, and Trust," *The Sociological Quarterly* 26, no. 4 (1985): 455–71, which gives an excellent summary

of the sociological literature on trust. J. B. Rotter, "Generalized Expectancies for Interpersonal Trust," *American Psychologist* 26 (1971): 443–52.

19. Lars Hertzberg, "On the Attitude of Trust," *Inquiry* 31, no. 3 (September 1988): 307–22; T. Govier, "An Epistemology of Trust," *International Journal of Moral and Social Studies* 8, no. 2 (Summer 1993): 155–74; Holton, "Deciding to Trust"; Russell Hardin, "The Street-Level Epistemology of Trust," *Politics and Society* 21, no. 4 (December 1993): 505–29.

20. Giddens, *Consequences of Modernity*, 114.

21. Ibid., 119.

22. Ibid., 120.

23. In this context I can recall meeting a very eminent American sociologist and specialist on Durkheim at an international sociological conference in Europe; he told me how only recently, when hospitalized with a serious disease, did he fully understand the bonds of organic solidarity when visited daily at his hospital bed by his university colleagues. What is this if not a modern form of institutionalized personal ties?

24. This insight belongs to Marx in the first chapter of volume 1 of *Capital* (New York: Vintage, 1977), ignorant though he was of the importance symbolic exchange—of knowledge—would acquire, coming almost to replace the more prevalent symbolic exchange of money. General exchange, which is simply nonrestricted exchange, must be understood as referring to something very different than generalized exchange.

25. Luhmann has devoted a separate book to the study of "risk" within his systems frame of analysis. See his *Risk: A Sociological Theory* (New York: W. de Gruyter, 1993).

26. Luhmann, "Familiarity, Confidence, Trust," 102.

27. Luhmann, *Trust and Power*, 39.

28. Ibid., 48.

29. Ibid., 49.

30. Luhmann, *Trust and Power*; idem, "Familiarity, Confidence, Trust."

31. In Luhmann's footnote to the above quote he notes that "conscience serves as a control center for the reduction of the potential for action to the scale of individual personality. It could be said that trust is placed fundamentally in the functioning of conscience. This would explain the sense in which conscience at once individualizes and socializes." See Luhmann, *Trust and Power*, 46, n. 1. Given what Luhmann has to say about the socially visible aspects of personality, however, conscience could here only mean the degree to which ego identifies with role.

32. Eisenstadt and Roniger, *Patrons, Clients, and Friends*, 35.

33. Diego Gambetta, "Can We Trust Trust," in his *Trust*, 213–37; Eisenstadt and Roniger, *Patrons, Clients, and Friends*, 34.

34. Baier, "Trust and Anti-Trust."

35. Virginia Held, "On the Meaning of Trust," *Ethics* 78 (January 1968): 157.

36. Parsons, *Social System*, 58–67.

37. Ralph Turner, "The Role and the Person," *American Journal of Sociology* 84, no. 1 (1978): 1–23. idem, "Role Taking: Process versus Conformity," in *Human*

Behavior and Social Processes, ed. A. Rose (Boston: Houghton Mifflin, 1962), 20–40.

38. Turner, "Role Taking," 28, 36.

39. Ibid., 22.

40. Ralf Dahrendorf, "Homo Sociologicus," in his *Essays in the Theory of Society* (Stanford: Stanford University Press, 1968).

41. Ibid.

42. This point has in fact been recognized by Richard Hilbert, "Towards an Improved Understanding of Role," *Theory and Society* 10, no. 2 (1981): 207–26.

43. In Hilbert's article cited in the previous note he does discuss one such attempt to denote all aspects of role behavior (in the case of teachers involved in the CBTE experiment) and shows the total failure of such attempt. Every aspect of role could not, it turned out, be defined and calculated, nor could all contingencies be accounted for.

44. Dahrendorf, "Homo Sociologicus," 74–75.

45. On very different attitudes toward trust as belief see, for example: Judith Baker, "Trust and Rationality," *Pacific Philosophical Quarterly* 68 (1987): 1–13; and D. O. Thomas, "The Duty to Trust," *The Aristotelian Society* 79 (1978): 89–101. On accounts that interpret trust as a form of confidence see, for example: Annette Baier, "Trusting People in Philosophical Perspectives," *Ethics*, 102 (1992): 137–53; idem, "Trust and Anti-Trust," 231–60; Susan Shapiro, "The Social Control of Impersonal Trust," *American Journal of Sociology* 93, no. 3 (November 1987): 623–58. Hardin, "Street-Level Epistemology."

46. Baier, "Trust and Anti-Trust," 250.

47. Peter Blau, *Exchange and Power in Social Life* (New York: Wiley, 1964); Parsons, *Social System*; Barber, *Logic and Limits*.

48. Barber, *Logic and Limits*, 16–17.

49. Robert Axelrod, *Evolution of Cooperation* (New York: Basic Books, 1984); idem, "Effective Choice in the Prisoner's Dilemma," *Journal of Conflict Resolution* 24, no. 1 (March 1980): 3–25; Bernard Lahno, "Trust, Reputation, and Exit in Exchange Relationships," *Journal of Conflict Resolution* 39, no. 3 (September 1995): 495–510; P. Milgram and J. Roberts, *Economics, Organizations, and Managements* (Englewood Cliffs: Prentice Hall, 1992).

50. Partha Dasgupta, "Trust as a Commodity," in Gambetta, *Trust*, 59.

51. This understanding of trust as reliance or confidence in expectations is also the sense use by James Coleman in his *Foundations of Social Theory* (Cambridge: Harvard University Press, 1990), 91–118.

52. Keith Hart, "Kinship, Contract, and Trust: The Economic Organization of Migrants in an African City Slum," in Gambetta, *Trust*, 178.

53. Ibid., 188.

54. Ibid., 191.

55. Eric Voegelin, *Order and History*, vol. 1, *Israel and Revelation* (Baton Rouge: Louisiana State University Press, 1956).

56. Montgomery Watt, *Muhammad at Mecca* (London: Oxford University Press, 1960); idem, "The Place of Economic and Social Factors," *Islam and the Integration of Society* (London: North West University Press, 1961), 4–43. See also

Irfan Shahid, "Pre-Islamic Arabia," in *The Cambridge History of Islam*, vol. 1, eds. P. M. Holt et al. (New York: Cambridge University Press), 1970, 3–29.

57. S. N. Eisenstadt, ed., *The Origins and Diversity of the Axial Age Civilizations* (Albany: State University of New York Press, 1986), 20.

58. Robert Merton, *Social Theory and Social Structure* (New York: Free Press, 1968), 425–30.

59. See, for example, Lloyd Fallers, *Bantu Bureaucracy—A Study of Integration and Conflict in the Political Institutions of an East African People* (Cambridge: W. Heiffer and Sons, n.d.).

60. Interesting to note is that a number of the most famous "boys' books" celebrating a life lived outside of roles were written when their authors were themselves in such "liminal" periods of transition between established social roles. Thus Booth Tarkington wrote *Penrod* when his own life was in shambles and Mark Twain wrote *Tom Sawyer* when he was courting his wife (and so between kinship roles). On these insights see Marcia Jacobson, *Being a Boy Again* (Tuscaloosa: University of Alabama Press, 1994).

61. We should note that definitions of these terms tend to be variable. Thus for Peter Johnson, "faith" is belief in the truths of transcendental religion while "confidence" is a sentiment firmly rooted in the world of man. See his *Frames of Deceit: A Study of the Loss and Recovery of Public and Private Trust* (Cambridge: Cambridge University Press, 1993).

62. Adam Ferguson, *An Essay on the History of Civil Society*, 5th ed. (London, 1782), 53.

63. Alan Silver, "Friendship and Trust as Moral Ideas: Historical Approach," *European Journal of Sociology* 30 (1989): 274–97.

64. Norbert Elias, *The Civilizing Process* (New York: Pantheon Books, 1982), 476.

65. Ferguson, *Essay on Civil Society*, 60.

66. Alan Silver, "Two Different Sorts of Commerce," in *Public and Private in Thought and Practice: Perspectives on a Grand Dichotomy*, eds. Jeff Weintraub and Krishan Kumar (Chicago: University of Chicago Press, 1997), 15.

67. Silver, "Friendship and Trust," 274.

68. Gabriel Herman, *Ritualised Friendship and the Greek City* (Cambridge: Cambridge University Press, 1987).

69. Ibid., 3.

70. S. N. Eisenstadt, "Ritualized Personal Relations," *Man* 56 (1956): 90–95.

71. Eisenstadt's article "Ritualized Personal Relations" was part of a long polemic on the functionalist analysis of particularistic societies and as such was contextualized in Robert Paine's "Anthropological Approaches to Friendship," *Humanitas* 6, no. 2 (1970): 139–60. These debates, however, are not our concern, though they do tend to reinforce the point made above: that modern friendship in universalistically based societies (to use the functionalist language of the time) is predicated on very different sets of assumptions—those of trust—and is of a very different nature than friendship in other social formations.

72. Robert Paine, "Anthropological Approaches," 153. On the potential conflict between both types of "kinship" relations see E. E. Evans-Pritchard, "Zande Blood Brotherhood," *Africa* 6 (1933): 369–401.

73. Evans-Pritchard, "Zande Blood Brotherhood," 371.

74. Paine, "Anthropological Approaches," 153–54.

75. Eisenstadt, "Ritualized Personal Relations," 94.

76. It is impossible to extrapolate from archaic Greek society those codes of friendship that characterized Periclean Athens and the period of Greek democracy. In that period, the old aristocratic ideas of *hetaera* were transformed into the bonds of the city-state and later, with Aristotle, into a universalizing ideology of political justice. This, however, is very much the point. For friendship remained, even in later Greek society, a *public* and not a private ideal. It was seen as the bonds uniting its members into a community of will where "every citizen, every member of the demos, is as such a friend, and the *isonomia* of a *hetaera* belongs now to the people as a whole" (Horst Hutter, *Politics as Friendship: The Origins of Classical Notions of Politics in the Theory and Practice of Friendship* [Waterloo, Ont.: Wilfrid Laurier University Press, 1978], 45).

In Aristotle's philosophy friendship becomes coterminous with justice and reflective of the character attribute of *virtue* inscribed in true friends who were equal in the same. In some sense, friends were friends in virtue (their joint love of the good), just as, at a later date (and as will be discussed below), they would be friends in Christ.

Thus while we may note that in the *Nicomachean Ethics* Aristotle's understanding of friendship was quite different from those of archaic Greek society, it was still markedly different from our modern ideas of friendship. Moreover, of the five types of friendship posited by Aristotle (kinship, utility, pleasure, self-love, true friendship), only the last approaches our more modern understanding of friendship as an ideal. In Aristotle's usage such friendship is to be understood in terms of the shared moral virtues of the friends, which indeed presents the matrix for the interaction. See Judith Swanson, *The Public and the Private in Aristotle's Political Philosophy* (Ithaca: Cornell University Press, 1992), 165–92. On the idea of the friend as an other self in Aristotle see Paul Schollmeier, *Other Selves* (Albany: State University of New York Press, 1994). For a more general history of Greek ideas of friendship see, Hutter, *Politics as Friendship*.

77. A good example of this form of friendship as confidence is presented in Eric Wolfe, "Kinship, Friendship, and Patron-Client Relations in Complex Societies," in *Social Anthropology of Complex Societies*, ed. Michael Banton (New York: Praeger, 1963), 11–14.

78. Quotation marks have been used here to draw attention to the fact that all bonds of association and community are "fictive," are "imagined"—as indeed all communities are nothing but "imagined communities." Primordiality poses no firmer, essentialist ground for community than does, say, universal citizenship.

79. Note that this process is not always characterized by the formation of "fictive" kinship bonds. Sometimes a special category of "friendship" is formed to encompass relations of (importantly) contractual exchange that are unassimilable within the categories of kinship. On this see Robert Brain, *Friends and Lovers* (London: Hart Davis MacGibbon, 1979), 145–64.

80. Quoted in J. Fenter Van Vlissinger, "Friendship in History," in *Humanitas* 6, no. 2 (Fall 1970): 226–27.

81. On the continued existence of this type of trust in peasant societies see, for example, John Aguilar, "Trust and Exchange: Expressive and Instrumental Dimensions of Reciprocity in a Peasant Community," *Ethos* 12, no. 1 (Spring 1984): 3–29.

82. Just why that form of confidence seems to our eyes as more solidary than that occasioned by a system based on contract is another matter entirely and one that we cannot enter into here. That this is our perception of these societies does not make it necessarily correspond with reality, as the work by Edward Banfield has made clear (The Moral Basis of a Backward Society [New York: Free Press, 1958]).

83. Evans-Pritchard, "Zande Blood Brotherhood," 394.

84. In the following discussion of roles and status I follow the nomenclature of Merton in his *Social Theory and Social Structure* (New York: Free Press, 1968), which had become standard within sociological writing. These usages are also followed by Rose Laub Coser who, in her *In Defense of Modernity: Role Complexity and Individual Autonomy* (Stanford: Stanford University Press, 1991), develops arguments similar to those worked out below. There are other traditions that use these terms in different ways, especially within anthropological writings. Thus, for example, Ward Goodenough has developed a classificatory scheme where the term "identity relation" more or less replaces Merton's notion of "status" and "role" is used in a manner closely approximating Merton's definition of "status-set." See Ward Goodenough, "Rethinking 'Status' and 'Role': Towards a General Model of Cultural Organization of Social Relationships," in *Cognitive Anthropology*, ed. Stephen Tylor (New York: Holt, Rinehart and Winston, 1969), 311–30. For S. F. Nadel, in contrast, "role" is used in a manner quite similar to Merton's use of "status." See S. F. Nadel, *The Theory of Social Structure* (New York: Free Press, 1964). Other uses of these terms have been developed by other writers, but as Merton's definitions have become more or less standard within sociology we will abide with them.

85. A good discussion of this difference can be found in Burton Benedict, "Sociological Characteristics of Small Territories and the Implications for Economic Development," *The Social Anthropology of Complex Societies*, ed. Michael Banton (New York: Praeger, 1966), 23–35.

86. Ernest Gellner, *Plough, Sword, and Book: The Structure of Human History* (Chicago: University of Chicago Press, 1988), 44.

87. This dissonance is similar to what Goodenough has termed "ungrammatical" role reciprocity. Thus he notes: "If two people enter an interaction each assuming an identity that does not match the one assumed by the other, they fail to establish a relationship. The result is ungrammatical and there is social confusion." See Goodenough, "Rethinking Status and Role," 315. What I am claiming here is that one does not have to mistake the identity of role incumbents completely. Rather, for such confusion or dissonance to occur, it is enough to attribute certain expectations to a given role that are not matched by the incumbent.

88. Mary Douglas, *Natural Symbols* (New York: Vintage Press, 1976), 77–93.

89. An interesting modern corollary of this is to be found in the difference between middle-class and working-class friendship patterns as studied by Graham Allan. He found, not surprisingly, that middle-class folk, with more segmented role involvements, had more friends beyond their kin group than working-class

informants. Again, we see in this more micro, but empirically tested, example the correspondence between role diversification and segmentation and the ability to develop friendships that were "context free." See Graham Allan, *A Sociology of Friendship and Kinship* (London: George Allen and Unwin, 1979), 38–45, 46–92, passim.

90. Ferguson, *Essay on Civil Society*, 364.

91. The continuity of this ideal model of friendship as essentially predicated on the three characteristics of individual autonomy, unpredictability, and terminality (not open-ended) into our own contemporary idea of friendship is argued by Robert Paine, "In Search of Friendship: An Exploratory Analysis in 'Middle-Class' Culture," *Man* 4, no. 4 (December 1969): 505–24.

92. Hume, *Treatise on Human Nature*, sec. 3, 156.

Chapter Two
Agency, Civility, and the Paradox of Solidarity

1. On *fides* see Emile Benveniste, *Indo-European Language and Society* (London: Faber and Faber, 1973), 94–100.

2. Max Weber, *Economy and Society*, pt. 1, eds. Guenther Roth and Claus Wittich (Berkeley: University of California Press, 1978), 703.

3. On this theme see Stephen Darwall, *The British Moralists and the Internal "Ought," 1640–1740* (Cambridge: Cambridge University Press, 1995), 33–52.

4. Dunn, "The Concept of Trust," 288.

5. Ibid.

6. Ibid., 294.

7. Victor Turner, *The Ritual Process* (Chicago: Aldine, 1969), 94–202.

8. Ibid., 96, 128.

9. Ibid., 102–8.

10. G. van der Leeuw, *Religion in Essence and Manifestation* (Princeton: Princeton University Press, 1985); Emile Durkheim, *The Elementary Forms of Religious Life* (London: George Allen and Unwin, 1915); Rudolf Otto, *The Idea of the Holy* (London: Oxford University Press, 1950).

11. Durkheim, *Elementary Forms*, 37–38.

12. Otto, *Idea of the Holy*.

13. Leeuw, *Religion in Essence*, 24.

14. Ibid., 24.

15. Peter Berger, *The Sacred Canopy* (New York: Anchor Books, 1969), 88.

16. A. O. Lovejoy, *Reason, Understanding, and Time* (Baltimore: Johns Hopkins University Press, 1961), 110–11.

17. Benjamin Swartz, ed., *Wisdom, Revelation and Doubt: Perspectives on the First Millennium B.C., Daedelus* (Spring 1975).

18. S. N. Eisenstadt, "Transcendental Visions and the Rise of Clerics," *European Journal of Sociology* 23 (1982): 294–314.

19. Max Weber, *The Sociology of Religion* (Boston: Beacon Press, 1964).

20. Wolfgang Schluchter, "The Paradox of Rationalization: On the Relations of Ethics and the World," in *Max Weber's Vision of History: Ethics and Methods*, eds. Guenther Roth and Wolfgang Schluchter (Berkeley: University of California Press, 1979), 23.

21. Berger, *Sacred Canopy*, 113–18.

22. Benjamin Nelson, "Self Images and Systems of Spiritual Direction in the History of European Civilization," in *On the Roads to Modernity: Conscience, Science, and Civilizations*, ed. Toby Huff (Totowa, N.J.: Rowman and Littlefield, 1981), 43.

23. Ernst Troeltsch, *The Social Teachings of the Christian Churches*, vol. 1 (New York: Harper and Row, 1960), 55.

24. Marcell Mauss, "A Category of the Human Mind: The Notion of the Person, the Notion of the Self," in *The Category of the Person*, eds. Michael Carrithers, Steven Collins, and Steven Lukes (Cambridge: Cambridge University Press, 1985), 19–20.

25. Troeltsch, *Social Teachings*, 57.

26. Quoted in Hutter, *Politics as Friendship*, 176.

27. M. C. D'Arcy, *The Mind and Heart of Love, Lion, and Unicorn* (New York: H. Holt & Co., 1956).

28. A. Nygren, *Agape and Eros* (Chicago: University of Chicago Press, 1982).

29. On the different ideas of love in the Christian tradition see Irving Singer, *The Nature of Love*, vol. 1 (Chicago: University of Chicago Press, 1984).

30. Wolfgang Schluchter, *The Rise of Western Rationalism* (Berkeley: University of California Press, 1981), 171.

31. Wolfgang Schluchter, "Weber's Sociology of Rationalization and Topologies of Religious Rejection of the World," in *Max Weber, Rationality, and Modernity*, eds. Scott Lash and Sam Whimster (London: Allen and Unwin, 1987).

32. Ibid., 156–74.

33. E. Tuveson, *The Imagination as a Means of Grace: Locke and the Aesthetics of Romanticism* (Berkeley: University of California Press, 1964); J. Diggins, *The Lost Soul of American Politics* (New York: Basic Books, 1984); J. G. A. Pocock, *The Machiavellian Moment* (Princeton: Princeton University Press, 1975).

34. T. Todorov, *The Conquest of America* (New York: Harper and Row, 1984), 151–77.

35. Michel de Montaigne, *Essays of Montaigne*, vol. 1, trans. Charles Cotton, ed. W. C. Hazlett (London: Reeves and Turner, 1877).

36. Edmund Leach, *Social Anthropology* (New York: Oxford University Press, 1982), 55–85.

37. C. Kluckhohn, *Mirror for Man* (London: Harrap, 1950).

38. C. G. Jung, *The Archetypes of the Collective Unconscious* (London: Routledge and Kegan Paul, 1959), 43.

39. Michel Foucault, *The Order of Things: An Archeology of the Human Sciences* (New York: Vintage Books, 1973), 387.

40. O. Rank, *The Double: A Psychoanalytic Study* (Chapel Hill: University of North Carolina Press, 1971), 8–33.

41. Edgar Allan Poe, *The Works of Edgar Allan Poe: Tales* (London: Oxford University Press, 1927), 429.

42. Rank, *Double*, 69–86.

43. R. M. Adams, *Nil: Episodes in the Literary Conquests of Void during the Nineteenth Century* (New York: Oxford University Press, 1966).

44. Richard Wagner, *Werke*, band 1 (Zurich: Stauffacher Verlag, 1966), 257.

45. Adams, *Nil*, 244.

46. Paul Cantor, *Creature and Creator: Myth-Making and English Romanticism* (Cambridge: Cambridge University Press, 1984), 24.

47. T. Todorov, *Théories du symbole* (Paris: Seuil, 1977), 185.

48. Charles Taylor, "Language and Human Nature," in *Human Agency and Language: Philosophical Papers*, vol. 2 (Cambridge: Cambridge University Press, 1985), 230.

49. M. Masud and R. Kahn, "Montaigne, Rousseau, and Freud," in *The Privacy of the Self* (New York: International Universities Press, 1974), 100.

50. On notions of honor in Mediterranean and North African societies see: J. G. Peristiany, ed., *Honour and Shame: The Values of Mediterranean Society* (Chicago: University of Chicago Press, 1966); Julian Pitt-Rivers, *The Fate of Shechem: Essays in the Anthropology of the Mediterranean* (Cambridge: Cambridge University Press, 1977); Roy Mottahedeh, *Loyalty and Leadership in an Early Islamic Society* (Princeton: Princeton University Press, 1980); Peter Dodd, "Family Honor and the Forces of Change in Arab Society," *International Journal of Middle Eastern Studies* 4 (1973): 40–54. On European conceptions of honor and their comparison to other ideas of honor see Frank Henderson Stewart, *Honor* (Chicago: University of Chicago Press, 1994).

51. Stewart, *Honor*, 39–53.

52. Ibid., 40–41.

53. Ibid., 40.

54. It progressed as well with the rise of the ideal of domesticity in the aristocratic family and a more equalitarian notion of marriage. See R. Trumbach, *The Rise of the Equalitarian Family* (New York: Academy Press, 1978).

55. See Max Weber, *The Protestant Ethic and the Spirit of Capitalism* (New York: Scribner and Sons, 1958); Bernhard Groethuysen, *The Bourgeois: Catholicism vs. Capitalism in Eighteenth-Century France* (New York: Holt, Rinehart and Winston, 1968); Benjamin Nelson, *The Idea of Usury: From Tribal Brotherhood to Universal Otherhood* (Chicago: University of Chicago Press, 1969); Louis Dumont, *Essays on Individualism: Modern Ideology in Anthropological Perspective* (Chicago: University of Chicago Press, 1986).

56. This is an argument made by Mervyn James in his study of codes of honor and violence in early modern England. See his "English Politics and the Concept of Honour, 1485–1642," *Past and Present*, Supplement 3 (The Past and Present Society, 1978): 1–92, especially 43–54.

57. See discussion in chapter 5 below. See also Groethuysen, *Bourgeois: Catholicism vs. Capitalism*; Adam B. Seligman, *Innerworldly Individualism: Charismatic Community and Its Institutionalization* (New Brunswick: Transaction Press, 1994); Margaret Jacob, "The Enlightenment Redefined: The Formation of Modern Civil Society," *Social Research* 58 (1991): 475–95; eadem, "Private Beliefs in Public Temples: The New Religiosity of the 18th Century," *Social Research* 59 (1992): 59–84.

58. Benjamin Whichote, "The Uses of Reason in Matters of Religion," in *The Cambridge Platonists*, ed. C. A. Patrides (Cambridge: Cambridge University Press, 1969), 46.

59. Seligman, *The Idea of Civil Society*.

60. Some aspects of this development have been explored in the recent work of Margaret Jacob. See her "Private Beliefs in Public Temples," 59–84, and her "The Enlightenment Redefined," 475–95.

61. Mauss, "A Category of the Human Mind," 19, 21–22.

62. For an analysis of shame see Helen M. Lynd, *On Shame and the Search for Identity* (New York: Harcourt, 1958).

63. Peter Berger, "On the Obsolescence of the Concept of Honor," in *Revision: Changing Perspectives in Moral Philosophy*, eds. Stanley Hauerwas and Alasdair MacIntyre (Notre Dame: University of Notre Dame Press, 1983), 177.

64. On this see George Duby, *The Knight, the Lady and the Priest: The Making of Modern Marriage in Medieval France* (Chicago: University of Chicago Press, 1993), 23–56.

65. See, for example, R. M. Smith, "Marriage Processes in the English Past: Some Continuities," in *The World We Have Gained: Histories of Population and Social Structure*, eds. L. Bonfield, R. Smith, and K. Wrightson (Oxford: Basil Blackwell, 1986), 43–99.

66. Alan Macfarlane, *The Culture of Capitalism* (Oxford: Basil Blackwell, 1987), 123–143 gives a good summary of the debate between Macfarlane and other historians on the timing of these developments.

67. On the idea of love see Singer, *The Nature of Love*, vol. 2.

68. On these themes of agency in Greek thought see Bernard Williams, *Shame and Necessity* (Berkeley: University of California Press, 1993).

69. Berger, "Concept of Honor," 179.

70. The attempt to root the ethics of modernity solely on this aspect of human agency, on man's "self-determination," was perhaps most developed in Nicolai Hartmann's third volume of his *Ethics*, first published in Germany in 1926. It appears in English as "Moral Freedom," in *Ethics*, vol. 3, trans. Stanton Colt (New York: Macmillan, 1932).

71. Marvin B. Becker, *The Emergence of Civil Society in the Eighteenth Century* (Bloomington: Indiana University Press, 1994), 69, and passim.

72. Denis Diderot, "Refutation de l'ouvrage d'Helvétius intitulé de L'Homme," in *Oeuvres complètes* (Paris: 1975), 2: 382; quoted in Daniel Gordon, *Citizens without Sovereignty: Equality and Sociability in French Thought, 1670–1789* (Princeton: Princeton University Press, 1994).

73. Coser, *In Defense of Modernity*, 92–93.

74. Montaigne, *Essays*, vol. 3, 303–4.

75. Max Weber, "Science as a Vocation," in *From Max Weber: Essays on Sociology*, eds. G. H. Gerth and C. W. Mills (New York: Free Press, 1958).

76. Hannah Arendt, *The Human Condition* (Chicago: University of Chicago Press, 1958), 28–32.

77. On this reading of privateness see, for example: Martin Krygien, "Publicness, Privateness, and 'Primitive Law,'" 307–39; and Leslie Haviland and John B. Haviland, "Privacy in a Mexican Indian Village," 341–61, in *Public and Private in Social Life*, eds. S. I. Benn and G. F. Gauss (New York: St. Martin's Press 1983).

78. Ferguson, *Essay on Civil Society*, 57.

79. Adam Smith, *The Theory of Moral Sentiments* (Indianapolis: Liberty Classics, 1982), 50.

80. Albert Hirschman, *The Passions and the Interests* (Princeton: Princeton University Press, 1977), 109. See also Nicholas Phillipson, "Adam Smith as Civil Moralist," in *Wealth and Virtue: The Shaping of Political Economy in the Scottish Enlightenment*, eds. I. Hont and M. Ignatieff (Cambridge: Cambridge University Press, 1985), 179–202.

81. Smith, *Theory of Moral Sentiments*, 50.

82. Ferguson, *Essay on Civil Society*, 27.

83. Johnson, *Frames of Deceit*, 79.

84. Frederick Pollock and Frederic Maitland, *History of English Law before the Time of Edward I*, vol. 2 (Cambridge: Cambridge University Press, 1923), 228.

85. Arjun Appadurai, "Gratitude as a Social Mode in South India," *Ethos* 13, no. 1 (Spring 1985), 239.

86. The relation of this understanding of self to the broader terms of economic unconditionality in Western societies will be explicated in the following chapter.

87. Elias, *Civilizing Process*, 83–84.

88. Ibid., 35.

89. Harry Frankfurt, "Freedom of the Will and the Concept of the Person," *The Journal of Philosophy* 68, no. 1 (January 1971): 5–20.

90. Taylor, "What is Human Agency?" in his *Human Agency and Language*, 18–19.

91. Ibid., 23–24.

92. It is in this sense of familiarity, based on shared strong evaluations, that George Fletcher bases his use of the term "loyalty" in his *Loyalty: An Essay on the Morality of Relationships* (New York: Oxford University Press, 1993).

93. Daniel Kahneman, Paul Slovic, and Amos Tversky, eds., *Judgement under Uncertainty: Heuristics and Biases* (Cambridge: Cambridge University Press, 1982).

94. David Good, "Individuals, Interpersonal Relationships, and Trust," in Gambetta, *Trust*, 41.

95. Durkheim, "Individualism and the Intellectuals," 45.

96. Talcott Parsons, *The Structure of Social Action*, vol. 1 (New York: Free Press, 1968), 389.

97. Emile Durkheim, *Sociology and Philosophy* (New York: Free Press, 1968); Talcott Parsons, "Durkheim on Religion Revisited," in his *Action Theory and the Human Condition* (New York: Free Press, 1978), 213–32.

Chapter Three
Trust and Generalized Exchange

1. For a succinct summary of the relevant economic and sociological literature on social capital see Coleman, *Foundations of Social Theory* 300–321.

2. Kenneth Arrow, *The Limits of Organization* (New York: Norton, 1974), 23.

3. Fukuyama, *Trust*; Robert Putnam, *Making Democracy Work: Civic Traditions in Modern Italy* (Princeton: Princeton University Press, 1993).

4. Putnam, *Making Democracy Work*, 115.

5. Ibid.

6. Edward Banfield, *The Moral Basis of a Backward Society* (New York: Free Press, 1958), 83–90.

7. Ibid., 144–45.

8. Fukuyama, *Trust*, 26.

9. Ibid., 155–56.

10. Ibid., 153–54.

11. Ernest Gellner, "Trust, Cohesion, and the Social Order," in Gambetta, *Trust*, 152.

12. On the concept of self-reinforcing contracts see Geoffrey Hawthorn, "Three Ironies of Trust," in *Trust*, Gambetta, 115–26.

13. The attempt to argue this position in terms of the logic of economic action and the insufficiency of current profit-maximizing ideas thereof is well developed in Amitai Etzioni, *The Moral Dimension: Towards a New Economics* (New York: Free Press, 1988).

14. Bernard Harrison, "Moral Judgement, Action, and Emotion," *Philosophy* 59 (1984): 314.

15. Eisenstadt, *Power, Trust, and Meaning*, 345.

16. A good example of such credit may be that which exists between parents participating in rotating baby-sitting arrangements (whose currency is, usually, cork chits), which are common in the U.K. and less than common in the U.S.A. (for reasons to be discussed in the very last chapter of this work).

17. Eisenstadt, *Power, Trust, and Meaning*, 212.

18. Ibid.

19. On the interesting idea of how the very notion of the gift is self-contradictory see Jacques Derrida, *Given Time I: Counterfeit Money* (Chicago: University of Chicago Press, 1992), 34–70.

20. See Moses Maimonides, *Mishneh Torah* (*Code of Ethics*): *Seder Mishpatim, Hilchot Evel*, chapter 14, 1–7 (Warsaw, 1882).

21. Janet Tai Landa, *Trust, Ethnicity, and Identity: Beyond the New Institutional Economics of Ethnic Trading, Networks, Contract Law, and Gift Exchange* (Ann Arbor: University of Michigan Press, 1994); Avner Grief, "On the Political Foundations of the Late Medieval Commercial Revolution: Genoa during the Twelfth and Thirteenth Centuries," *The Journal of Economic History* 54, no. 2 (June 1994): 271–87; idem, "Historical Perspectives on the Economics of Trade: Institutions and International Trade: Lessons from the Commercial Revolution," *American Economic Review* 82, no. 1/2 (May 1992): 128–33; idem, "Reputation and Coalitions in Medieval Trade: Evidence on the Maghribi Traders," *The Journal of Economic History* 49, no. 4 (December 1989): 857–82; idem, "Contract Enforceability and Economic Institutions in Early Trade: The Maghribi Traders' Coalition," *American Economic Review* 83, no. 3 (June 1993), 525–48.

22. Coleman, *Foundations of Social Theory*, 91–115.

23. Eisenstadt, *Power, Trust, and Meaning*, 212–13.

24. Carlos G. Velez-Ibanez, *Bonds of Trust: The Cultural Systems of Rotating Credit Associations among Urban Mexicans and Chicanos* (New Brunswick: Rutgers University Press, 1983), 15.

25. Ibid., 28.

26. See Polanyi's *Great Transformation*. We may note here that the workings of unconditionalities and principles of generalized exchange are very different in economies of reciprocity and redistribution than in those of self-regulating markets. As its workings are more immediately visible in the former cases, those are where anthropologists and others have most often isolated its dynamics.

27. Henry Maine, *Ancient Law* (New York: Holt, 1888).

28. P. S. Atiyah, *Introduction to the Law of Contract* (Oxford: Oxford University Press, 1981), 2.

29. Weber, *Economy and Society*, vol. 2, 677, 698, 706.

30. Ibid., 668.

31. For this understanding of law see Eric Voegelin, *The Nature of Law and Other Writings*, vol. 27 (Baton Rouge: Louisiana State University Press, 1991).

32. Weber, *Economy and Society*, vol. 2, 669.

33. Atiyah, *Introduction to the Law of Contract*, 12.

34. George Simmel, *Philosophy of Money* (London: Routledge and Kegan Paul, 1978), 286.

35. Nelson, *The Idea of Usury*, 136.

36. Atiyah, *Promises, Morals, and Law*, chap. 3.

37. P. S. Atiyah, *Pragmatism and Theory in English Law* (London: Stevens and Sons, 1987), 18–27.

38. Atiyah, "The Liberal Theory of Contract," in his *Essays on Contract*, chap. 6, 122ff.

39. David Campbell, "The Relational Constitution of Discrete Contract" (School of Financial Studies and Law, Sheffield Hallam University, 1995), unpublished manuscript, 5.

40. Atiyah, *Rise and Fall*, 464–79. See also W. S. Holdsworth, *A History of English Law*, vol. 8 (Boston: Little, Brown and Co., 1926), 68–69.

41. Macfarlane, *Origins,* 58.

42. Louis Dumont, *From Mandeville to Marx: The Genesis and Triumph of Economic Ideology* (Chicago: University of Chicago Press, 1977), 54.

43. Macfarlane, *Origins*, 163.

44. Ibid., 5.

45. Pollock and Maitland, *History of English Law*, 233.

46. Atiyah, *Rise and Fall*, 26–263.

47. Ibid., 402; see also 14–167.

48. Ibid., 408.

49. Dumont, *From Mandeville to Marx*, 61.

50. Ibid., 75.

51. Bernard Mandeville. *Fable of the Bees: Or Private Vices, Public Benefits* (Oxford: Clarendon Press, 1924), 18, 24.

52. Ibid., 343.

53. Ibid., 331.

54. Ibid., 327, 330.

55. Ibid., 178.

56. On these see Konrad Zweigert and Hein Kotz, *Introduction to Comparative Law* (Oxford: Clarendon, 1992), 353, 348–553.

57. Fukuyama, *Trust*, 62–63.

58. Hawthorn, "Three Ironies of Trust," 114.

59. Argument can be made that the distinction posited here between familiarity in its different meanings parallels that posited by Hume between "natural" and "artificial" virtues. On this point see Bernard Harrison, "Moral Judgement, Action, and Emotion," *Philosophy* 59 (1984): 295–321.

60. Emile Durkheim, *Professional Ethics and Civic Morals* (London: Routledge and Kegan Paul, 1957), 65.

61. Such a ritually expressive moment would exist in systems at all levels of differentiation. I know of a couple with two young children who periodically hire a baby-sitter just to spend the night alone in a hotel room a five-minute drive from their house in an attempt to reassert their original terms of unconditionality (romantic love in this case) in the face of the daily organization of productive roles (doing the laundry, paying the bills, fixing the car, etc.).

62. Seligman, *Innerworldly Individualism*.

63. Eisensadt, *Power, Trust, and Meaning*, 214.

64. Seyla Benhabib, *Critique: Norm and Utopia* (New York: Columbia University Press, 1986), 279.

65. The importance of these "weak ties" in the structuring of economic and exchange relations in modern societies has been central to Mark Granovetter's concept of "embeddedness." See his "The Strength of Weak Ties," *American Journal of Sociology* 78, no. 6 (May 1973): 1360–80; idem, "Economic Action and Social Structure: The Problem of Embeddedness," *American Journal of Sociology* 91, no. 3 (November 1985), 481–510. In both these articles it becomes quite clear how familiarity as a mechanism works to establish confidence in the system of role expectations among economic actors.

66. Edmund Burke, *Reflections on the Revolution in France*, ed. J. G. A. Pocock (Indianapolis: Hackett, 1987), 100.

67. Max Weber, *General Economic History* (New Brunswick: Transaction Press, 1981), 366.

68. Ibid., 57.

69. Nelson, *The Idea of Usury*, 136.

70. Anthony Pagden, "The Destruction of Trust and Its Economic Consequences in the Case of Eighteenth-Century Naples," in Gambetta, *Trust*, 139.

71. There is much debate over these aspects of 18th-century American politics, with modern day communitarians and liberals weighing in on one side or another in the interpretations of the Federalist and anti-Federalist positions. A good summary of this debate can be found in Issac Kramnick, *Republicanism and Bourgeois Radicalism: Political Ideology in Late Eighteenth-Century England and America* (Ithaca: Cornell University Press, 1990). Whatever the strength of the anti-Federalist position in the 18th-century, there can be little doubt that the "privileging of the individual, the moral legitimation of private interests and market society oriented commitments" was a fundamental aspect of 18th-century American political philosophy (see Kramnick, 262). It would moreover be interesting to view these two contrasting positions as an example of the awareness (if as yet unarticulated) of the growing disjunction between the terms of pristine trust (the classic republican legacy) and its role as a principle of generalized exchange (the Federalist position).

72. Atiyah, *Rise and Fall*, 353.

73. Ibid.: on marginal utility, 607–12: on transformation, 584ff.

Chapter Four
Public and Private in Political Thought: Rousseau, Smith, and
Some Contemporaries

1. For some aspects of this feminist critique see: Carole Pateman, "The Fraternal Social Contract," in *Civil Society and the State*, ed. J. Keane (London: Verso, 1988), 101–28; eadem, *The Sexual Contract* (Stanford: Stanford University Press, 1988); Mary Shanley and Carole Pateman, eds., *Feminist Interpretations and Political Theory* (University Park: Penn State University Press, 1991). On Quentin Skinner's position see his "The Idea of Negative Liberty," in *Philosophy in History: Essays on the Historiography of Philosophy*, eds. R. Rorty, J. B. Schneewind, and Q. Skinner (Cambridge: Cambridge University Press, 1984), 193–224. See also his "The Republican Idea of Political Liberty," in *Machiavelli and Republicanism*, eds. Gisela Bock, Quentin Skinner, and Maurizio Viroli (Cambridge: Cambridge University Press, 1990), 239–309.

2. Jane Schneider, "Of Vigilance and Virgins: Honor, Shame, and Access to Resources in Mediterranean Societies," *Ethnology* 10, no. 1 (1971): 1–24, Haviland and Haviland, "Privacy in a Mexican Indian Village," 341–61.

3. Norberto Bobbio, "Public and Private: The Great Dichotomy," in his *Democracy and Dictatorship* (Minneapolis: University of Minnesota Press, 1989).

4. Benjamin Constant, *Political Writings*, ed. B. Fontana (Cambridge: Cambridge University Press, 1988).

5. The importance of civic virtue in medieval Venice and Florence just exemplifies this point, in that it developed philosophically in autonomous cities, existing beyond feudal hierarchy. General perspectives on the development of civic humanist thought can be found in Quentin Skinner, *The Foundations of Modern Political Thought*, vol. 1 (Cambridge: Cambridge University Press, 1978).

6. This theme has been developed most dramatically by J. G. A. Pocock, *The Machiavellian Moment*. For a contrasting reading of political thought in this period see Issac Kramnick, *Republicanism and Bourgeois Radicalism*.

7. On this theme see Norberto Bobbio, *The Future of Democracy* (Minneapolis: University of Minnesota Press, 1987), 31.

8. Emile Durkheim, *The Division of Labor in Society* (New York: Free Press, 1933).

9. Arendt, *Human Condition*.

10. Here I am using the term *conscience collective* as Durkheim did in his earlier works—to describe the type of moral community constituted in societies characterized by mechanical solidarity. Some, notably Talcott Parsons, have argued that over time Durkheim changed his conception of the *conscience collective* to be an attribute of all societies, including modern ones in which the content of the *conscience collective* was radically different. On this idea see Parsons, *The Structure of Social Action*, vol. 1, 320. For a different view, which stresses the continuities between Rousseau and Durkheim and the parallels between the idea of the *volonté générale* and *conscience collective*, see Steven Lukes, *Emile Durkheim: His Life and Work* (Stanford: Stanford University Press, 1985), 283.

11. The importance of active participation of the citizenry for the pursuit of virtue is developed in Rousseau's *Social Contract*; see Jean-Jacques Rousseau, *The Social Contract and Discourses*, trans. and ed. G. D. H. Cole (London: Dent, 1973), 265.

12. Rousseau, "A Discourse on Political Economy," in his *Social Contract and Discourses*, 140.

13. Ibid., 139.

14. Rousseau, *Social Contract and Discourses*, 191.

15. Ibid.

16. Ibid., 203, 227.

17. See, for example, Charles Maier, ed., *Changing Boundaries of the Political* (Cambridge: Cambridge University Press, 1987).

18. A. Seligman, *The Idea of Civil Society* (New York: Free Press, 1992).

19. The case of John Locke is somewhat different since he posits a transcendent matrix to ethical behavior. On this see John Dunn, *The Political Theory of John Locke* (Cambridge: Harvard University Press, 1969). Hume, as is well known, fatally attacked this conception in what Alasdair MacIntyre has termed "the subversion of the Scottish Enlightenment from within." See A. MacIntyre, *Whose Justice? Which Rationality?* (Notre Dame: University of Notre Dame Press, 1988). Immanuel Kant's attempt to reply to Hume, which ended with the positing of a purely private morality, marked in effect the end of the idea of civil society as it was conceived in the 18th century and is, therefore, beyond the scope of our present inquiry. On these developments see Seligman, *The Idea of Civil Society*, 15–58.

20. Ferguson, *Essay on Civil Society*, 57–58.

21. See Anthony Shaftesbury, *Characteristics of Men, Manners, Opinions, Times*, vols. 1–3 (London: N.p., 1736), especially "An Inquiry Concerning Virtue and Merit," vol. 2, 117–21; Ferguson, *Essay on Civil Society*, 52–66.

22. Adam Smith, *Theory of Moral Sentiments*, 50.

23. It would be useful to compare this with Rousseau's idea of *volonté générale* to see just how much that latter conception rested on a "reasoned" set of decisions by the participants involved. See, for example, Rousseau, "The General Society of the Human Race," included in the "Geneva Manuscript" of *The Social Contract and Discourses*, 174.

24. In a manner not that distant from Rousseau's *volonté générale*, we may look at Emile Durkheim's following formulation: "The general will must be respected, not because it is stronger but because it is general. If there is to be justice among individuals, there must be something outside them, a being sui generis, which acts as arbiter and determines the law. This something is society, which owes its moral supremacy, not to its physical supremacy, but to its nature, which is superior to that of individuals" (Emile Durkheim, *Montesquieu and Rousseau* [Ann Arbor: University of Michigan Press, 1965], 103).

25. Ferguson, *Essay on Civil Society*, 52.

26. See Peter Brown, *The Body and Society: Men, Women, and Sexual Renunciation in Early Christianity* (New York: Columbia University Press, 1988), 6–32; Rousseau, *Social Contract and Discourses*, 192.

27. Rousseau, "A Discourse on the Moral Effects of Arts and Sciences," in his *Social Contract and Discourses*, 24.

28. John Dwyer, *Virtuous Discourse: Sensibility and Community in Late Eighteenth-Century Scotland* (Edinburgh: John Donald Publishers, 1987), 98.

29. Ibid., 10–38, 95–116.

30. Rousseau, *Social Contract and Discourses*, 192. Compare this with the passage of Durkheim quoted above on the role of society in inducing moral agency. What Durkheim posits as a teleological being, existing beyond individual conscience (or consciousness—as the distinction does not exist in the French), Smith posits as a psychological mechanism working within the individual.

31. Smith, *Theory of Moral Sentiments*, 110.

32. Ibid., 134.

33. Ibid., 135.

34. Knud Haakonssen, *The Science of a Legislator: The Natural Jurisprudence of David Hume and Adam Smith* (Cambridge: Cambridge University Press, 1981), 54–61.

35. On the sociological background to this move in Smith see Dwyer, *Virtuous Discourse*, 168–85.

36. Ibid., 173–80.

37. MacIntyre, *Whose Justice*, 218–325.

38. Smith, *Theory of Moral Sentiments*, 237–62.

39. Ferguson, *Essay on Civil Society*, 364, 454.

40. See, for example, Rousseau's "A Discourse on the Moral Effects of the Arts and Sciences," in his *Social Contract and Discourses*.

41. Leo Strauss, *Natural Right and History* (Chicago: University of Chicago Press, 1953), 130–35.

42. On the theme of corruption in 18th-century America see not only Pocock, *Machiavellian Moment*, but also Bernard Bailyn, *The Ideological Origins of the American Revolution* (Cambridge: Harvard University Press, 1967).

43. Pocock, *Machiavellian Moment*, 31–48.

44. Smith, *Theory of Moral Sentiments*, 61, 64.

45. Rousseau, "A Discourse on the Origins of Inequality," in his *Social Contract and Discourses*, 116.

46. Charles Taylor, "Cross Purposes: The Liberal-Communitarian Debate," in *Liberalism and the Moral Life*, ed. Nancy Rosenblum (Cambridge: Harvard University Press, 1989), 159–82. The "foundation text" of this view is John Rawls, *A Theory of Justice* (Cambridge: Harvard University Press, 1971). Description of its implications on citizenship can be found in M. Waters, "Citizenship and the Constitution of Structured Inequality," *International Journal of Comparative Sociology* 30 (1989): 159–80.

47. Michael Sandel, *Liberalism and the Limits of Justice* (Cambridge: Cambridge University Press, 1982); idem, "The Procedural Republic and the Unencumbered Self," *Political Theory* (1984): 81–96.

48. One of the interesting arenas where this conflict is being carried out is in the assessment of the interwar regimes within the different polities of Eastern and East Central Europe. The recent reinterment of the remains of the interwar regent of Hungary, Admiral Horthy, in early September of 1993 and the protest against the honor so accorded him by more democratic forces in society is just one of many contemporary examples of this continuing struggle. I will refrain from noting the

more violent and well-known conflicts currently being waged throughout the former Soviet empire and countries of East Central Europe. Some further perspectives on this can be found in Zora Butorova, "Two Years After November 17, 1989: The Hard Birth of Democracy in Slovakia," in *Zwischen den Zeiten*, eds. P. Gerlich and P. Glass (Vienna: VWGO, 1992); Zora and Martin Butorova, "Wariness Towards the Jews as an Expression of Post-Communist Panic," *Proceedings from the International Seminar on Anti-Semitism in Post-Totalitarian Europe* (Prague, 1992).

49. Yoav Peled, "Ethnic Democracy and the Legal Construction of Citizenship: Arab Citizens of the Jewish State," *American Political Science Review* 86, no. 2 (1992): 432–43.

50. Sandel, *Liberalism*, 179.

51. This was, as some have argued, *the* problem of Machiavelli—in his attempt to secure a love of patria as a foundation of virtue and civic duties—after the failure of Savonarola. See Pocock, *Machiavellian Moment*, 156–82. See also J. G. A. Pocock, "Custom and Grace, Form and Matter: An Approach to Machiavelli's Concept of Innovation," in *Machiavelli and the Nature of Political Thought*, ed. Martin Fleisher (New York: Atheneum, 1972), 153–74.

52. On different aspects of this theme see Pocock, *Machiavellian Moment*, 506–52; E. L. Tuveson, *Redeemer Nation: The Idea of America's Millennial Role* (Chicago: University of Chicago Press, 1968); N. O. Hatch, *The Sacred Cause of Liberty* (New Haven: Yale University Press, 1977); Ruth Block, *Visionary Republic: Millennial Themes in American Thought, 1765–1800* (Cambridge: Cambridge University Press, 1985).

53. On the sociological background to this development see Adam Seligman, *Innerworldly Individualism*.

54. Arendt, *Human Condition*, 248–325.

55. On the importance and dynamics of tradition see Edward Shils, *Tradition* (Chicago: University of Chicago Press, 1981).

56. On this dynamic see Linda Colley, *Britons: Forging the Nation, 1707–1837* (New Haven: Yale University Press, 1992), 101–28.

57. T. H. Marshall, *Class, Citizenship, and Social Development* (Westport: Greenwood Press, 1973).

58. Giddens, *Consequences of Modernity*. On this general theme see, Adam Seligman, "The Representation of Society and the Privatization of Charisma," *Praxis International* (1993): 68–84.

59. Eisenstadt, *Power, Trust, and Meaning*, 213.

60. Philip Selznick, *The Moral Commonwealth: Social Theory and the Promise of Community* (Berkeley: University of California Press, 1992).

Chapter Five
The Individual, the Rise of Conscience, and the Private Sphere:
A Historical Interpretation of Agency and Strong Evaluations

1. Roger Chartier, *The Cultural Origins of the French Revolution* (Durham: Duke University Press, 1991); Sarah Maza, *Private Lives and Public Affairs: The Causes Celebres of Pre-Revolutionary France* (Berkeley: University of California Press, 1993): Philippe Aries, *Centuries of Childhood* (New York: Vintage Press,

1962); Philippe Aries and George Duby, eds., *A History of Private Life*, vols. 1–5 (Cambridge: Belknap Press, 1987–1991).

2. Philippe Aries and George Duby, eds., *History of Private Life*, vol. 3, *Passions of the Renaissance* (Cambridge: Belknap Press, 1987), 9.

3. Jurgen Habermas, *The Structural Transformation of the Public Sphere* (Cambridge: Massachusetts Institute of Technology Press, 1989), 54.

4. Dennis Wrong, "The Oversocialized Conception of Man in Sociology," *American Sociological Review* 26, no. 2 (April 1961): 183–93.

5. Dwyer, *Virtuous Discourse*, 54–61.

6. Smith, *Theory of Moral Sentiments*, 134–35.

7. On these perspectives see Adam B. Seligman, "Animadversions upon Civil Society and Civic Virtue in the Last Decade of the Twentieth Century," in *Civil Society: Theory, Politics, Comparison*, ed. J. Hall (Oxford: Polity Press, 1995), 200–223.

8. P. F. Strawson, *Individuals: An Essay in Descriptive Metaphysics* (London: Methuen, 1959), 10.

9. Weber, *Protestant Ethic*; Mauss, "Category of the Human Mind," 1–25; Charles Taylor, *Sources of the Self: The Making of the Modern Identity* (Cambridge: Harvard University Press, 1989); Dumont, *Essays on Individualism*.

10. Dumont, *Essays on Individualism*, 31.

11. Troeltsch, *Social Teachings*, 39–89.

12. Brown, *Body and Society*.

13. On these perspectives see Peter Brown, *The Making of Late Antiquity* (Cambridge: Harvard University Press, 1978); Sheldon Wolin, *Politics and Vision* (Boston: Little, Brown and Company, 1960).

14. See Louis Dumont, *Essays on Individualism*, on the relativization of ontologically constituted role expectations.

15. On the Christian conception of time and history see: Robert Cushman, "The Greek and Christian Views of Time," *Journal of Religion* 33 (1953): 254–65; Lynn White, "The Christian Myth and Christian History," *Journal of the History of Ideas*" 3 (1942): 145–58; Anton Chroust," The Metaphysics of Time and History in Early Christian Thought," *New Scholasticum* 19 (1945): 322–52; Oscar Cullmann, *Early Christian Worship* (London: SCM Press, 1953). A comparative, if somewhat unmethodical, perspective is provided by S. G. F. Brandon, *History, Time, and the Deity: A Historical and Comparative Study of the Conception of Time in Religious Thought and Practice* (Manchester: University of Manchester Press, 1965).

16. See: Wolin, *Politics and Vision*, 95–140; Charles Cochrane, *Christianity and Classical Culture* (New York: Oxford University Press, 1957); Brown, *Making of Late Antiquity*, 56–77.

17. Galatians 4:28.

18. On communitas see Victor Turner, *Dramas, Fields, and Metaphors* (Ithaca: Cornell University Press, 1974), 131–65. On the community of grace as a form of social organization see Troeltsch, *Social Teachings*, 39–89. On Weber's claim to the universality of the charismatic experience as opposed to its specificity in Christian culture, see Weber, *Economy and Society*, 1112.

19. 1 Corinthians 12:12–13.

20. Wolin, *Politics and Vision*, 101.

21. Schluchter, *Rise of Western Rationalism*, 152.

22. Walter Ullmann, *The Individual and Society in the Middle Ages* (Baltimore: Johns Hopkins University Press, 1966), 9.

23. This process, which witnessed the development of "authority" at the expense of "community," was already well underway by the 2nd century, as illustrated in the writings of St. Cyprian:

> The episcopate is one; the individual members have each a part, and the parts make up the whole. The Church is a unity . . . the Church is made up of the people united to the priest as the flock that cleaves to the shepherd. Hence you should know that the bishop is in the Church and the Church in the bishop, and that if any one be not with the bishop he is not in the Church . . . the Church is one and may not be rent or sundered, but should assuredly be bound together and united by the glue of the priests who are in harmony one with another (*De Catholicae Ecclesiae Unitate*, 5; Epistle 66, 7, quoted in Wolin, *Politics and Vision*, 108).

24. The following précis is based on: R. W. Southern, *The Making of the Middle Ages* (London: Hutchinson, 1953); Caroline Bynum, "Did the Twelfth Century Discover the Individual?" *Journal of Ecclesiastical History* 31 (1980): 1–17; eadem, *Jesus as Mother: Studies in the Spirituality of the High Middle Ages* (Berkeley: University of California Press, 1982); Ullmann, *The Individual and Society*; Harold Berman, *Law and Revolution: The Formation of the Western Legal Tradition* (Cambridge: Harvard University Press, 1983); Marie-Dominique Chenu, *Nature, Man, and Society in the Twelfth Century* (Chicago: University of Chicago Press, 1968).

25. Bynum, "Did the Twelfth Century Discover the Individual?"

26. Peter Brown, *Society and the Holy in Late Antiquity* (Berkeley: University of California Press, 1982), 302–32.

27. Berman, *Law and Revolution*, 103, 145, 149–51.

28. Benjamin Nelson, "Self Images and Systems of Spiritual Direction" in *On the Roads to Modernity: Conscience, Science, and Civilizations*, ed. Toby Huff (Totowa, N.J.: Rowman and Littlefield, 1981), 43.

29. Colin Morris, *The Discovery of the Individual, 1050–1200* (London: S.P.C.K., 1972), 75.

30. Nelson, "Self Images and System of Spiritual Direction," 45. See also Odon D. Lottin, "Synderese et conscience au XIIe et XIIIe Siècles," premiere partie, *Psychologie et morale aux XIIe et XIIIe Siècles* (Louvain: Abbaye du mont César, 1948), 104–350.

31. On these developments see also John F. Benton, "Consciousness of Self and Perceptions of Individuality," in *Renaissance and Renewal in the Twelfth Century*, eds. R. Benson and G. Constable (Cambridge, Harvard University Press, 1982), 263–95.

32. Quoted in Morris, *Discovery of the Individual*, 88.

33. Ibid., 118.

34. Bynum, *Jesus as Mother*, 11.

35. Ibid., 15.

36. Southern, *Making of the Middle Ages*, 221.

37. Ibid.

38. Bynum, *Jesus as Mother*, 89.

39. Ibid., 95.

40. On some of these developments see Marvin Becker, *Civility and Society in Western Europe, 1300–1600* (Bloomington: Indiana University Press, 1988), 21, 32–33, 88, 94–96.

41. Benjamin Nelson, "Conscience and the Making of Early Modern Culture: The Protestant Ethic beyond Max Weber," *Social Research* 36 (1969): 4–21.

42. Adam B. Seligman, "Innerworldly Individualism and the Institutionalization of Puritanism in Late 17th-Century New England," *British Journal of Sociology* 41, no. 4 (December 1990): 537–58; idem, *Innerworldy Individualism.*

43. William Hunt, *The Puritan Moment: The Coming of Revolution in an English Country* (Cambridge: Harvard University Press, 1983); David Little, *Religion, Order, and Law: A Study of Pre-Revolutionary England* (New York: Harper and Row, 1969); Patrick Collinson, *The Puritan Character: Polemics and Polarities in Early Seventeenth-Century Culture* (Los Angeles: William Andrews Clark Memorial Library, 1989); William Haller, *The Rise of Puritanism* (Philadelphia: University of Pennsylvania Press, 1972); Avihu Zakai, *Exile and Kingdom* (Cambridge: Cambridge University Press, 1992).

44. Herman S. Schmalenbach, "The Sociological Category of Communion," in *Theories of Society*, eds. Talcott Parsons et al. (New York: Free Press, 1961), 331–47.

45. Talcott Parsons, "Christianity and Modern Industrial Society," in *Sociological Theory, Values, and Socio-Cultural Change*, ed. E. Tiryakian (New York: Harper and Row, 1967), 51.

46. Nelson, *The Idea of Usury*, 241. More recent perspectives on Weber's fundamental insight are followed in Miriam Eliav-Feldon, *Realistic Utopias: The Ideal Imaginary Societies of the Renaissance, 1516–1630* (Oxford: Clarendon Press, 1982).

47. Nelson, "Self Images and Systems of Spiritual Direction," 51.

48. The development of a sense of moral responsibility at this time was not restricted to Puritan or even Protestant societies. A similar development characterized the Jansenist religious elites in France. On these see Groethuysen, *The Bourgeois: Catholicism vs. Capitalism*; Nigel Abercrombie, *The Origins of Jansenism in France* (Oxford: Oxford University Press, 1936); and in comparison to the Puritans of England see Robin Briggs, "The Catholic Puritans: Jansenists and Rigorists in France," in *Puritans and Revolutionaries: Essays in Seventeenth-Century History Presented to Christopher Hill*, eds. D. Pennington and K. Thomas (Oxford: Clarendon Press, 1978), 333–57.

49. On these aspects of Calvinism see Harro Hopfl, *The Christian Polity of John Calvin* (Cambridge: Cambridge University Press, 1982); Sheldon Wolin, "Calvin and Reformation: The Political Education of Protestantism," *American Political Science Review* 51 (1957): 425–54; Troeltsch, *Social Teachings*, vol. 2, 576–690; David Little, "Max Weber Revisited: The Protestant Ethic and the Puritan Experience of Order," *Harvard Theological Review* 59 (1966): 415–28; idem, *Religion, Order, and Law*; Michael Waltzer, *The Revolution of the Saints* (Cambridge: Har-

vard University Press, 1965). For an opposing view to those of David Little and Michael Waltzer see John McNeill, "Natural Law and the Teachings of the Reformers," *Journal of Religion* 26 (1946): 168–82. On the place of Calvinism in the history of Western European political thought see Skinner, *Foundations of Modern Political Thought*, 189–348. On some of its social implications see Steven Ozment, *The Reformation in the Cities* (New Haven: Yale University Press, 1975); Norman Birnbaum, "The Zwinglian Reformation in Zurich," *Archive Sociologie de Religion* 4 (1959): 15–30; J. E. Ellemers, "The Revolt of the Netherlands: The Part Played by Religion in the Process of Nation Building," *Social Compass* 14 (1967): 93–103.

50. Troeltsch, *Social Teachings*, vol. 2, 590–92.

51. Ibid., 596–97. In Calvin's thought the freedom within which the true body of believers lived must be differentiated from the state of existing, political society and from the unregenerate, among whom the command of God had to be enforced by coercion until the coming of the Kingdom of God. At its coming, according to Calvin, the separation between those "in Christ" participating in the world of freedom and those still subject to coercion would be dissolved.

52. Little, *Religion, Order, and Law*, 71.

53. John Calvin, *Institutes of the Christian Religion*, ed. John McNeill (Philadelphia: Westminster Press, 1960), 4: 3,15.

54. Thus, for example, Archbishop Thomas Cranmer, in arguing against the Catholic conception of a priest's sacramental duties, stated that

> Christ made no such difference between the priest and the layman, that the priest should make oblation and sacrifice the Christ for the layman, and eat the Lord's supper from him all alone, and distribute and apply it as him liketh. Christ made no such difference; but the difference that is between the priest and the layman in this matter is only in the ministration: that the priest, as a common minister of the Church, doth minister and distribute the Lord's supper unto other, and other receive it at his hands" (quoted in Francis Clark, *Eucharist, Sacrifice, and the Reformation* [London: Darton, Longmans and Todd, 1960], 131.)

55. Donald Kelly, *The Beginnings of Ideology* (London: Cambridge University Press, 1981), 80.

56. Troeltsch, *Social Teachings*, vol. 2, 595. For a recent study of Puritan religious practice in a comparative perspective see Mary Fulbrook, *Piety and Politics: Religion and the Rise of Absolutism in England, Württemberg, and Prussia* (Cambridge: Cambridge University Press, 1983).

57. Much has been written on the institutional implications of Puritan religiosity. For some of the more relevant analyses see Michael Waltzer, "Puritanism as a Revolutionary Ideology," *History and Theory* 3 (1963): 59–90; George Mosse, "Puritanism and Reasons of State in Old and New England," *William and Mary Quarterly* 9 (1952): 67–80; idem, "Puritan Political Thought and the Case of Conscience," *Church History* 23 (1954): 109–25; idem, *The Holy Pretence: A Study in Christianity and Reasons of State from William Perkins to John Winthrop* (Oxford: Basil Blackwell, 1957); C. George and K. George, "Puritanism as History and Historiography," *Past and Present* 41 (1968): 77–104; C. H. George, "Protestantism and Capitalism in Pre-Revolutionary England," *Church History* 27 (1958): 351–446; W. Lamont, "Puritanism, History, and Historiography," *Past and Present* 44

(1969): 133–46; Jerald Brauer, "The Nature of English Puritanism: Three Interpretations," *Church History* 23 (1954): 99–108; Gordon Marshall, *Presbyteries and Profits: Calvinism and the Development of Capitalism in Scotland, 1560–1707* (Oxford: Clarendon Press, 1980).

58. On the centrality of the covenant in the lives of the Puritans see Patrick Collinson, "Towards a Broader Understanding of the Dissenting Tradition," in *The Dissenting Tradition*, eds. C. Cole and M. Moody (Athens: Ohio University Press, 1975), 3–38. On the relation of covenant theology to Calvinist doctrine see Everett Emerson, "Calvin and Covenant Theology," *Church History* 25 (1956): 136–44; Perry Miller, *Errand into the Wilderness* (New York: Harper and Row, 1964), 48–98; J. Moller, "The Beginnings of Puritan Covenant Theology," *The Journal of Ecclesiastical History* 14 (1963): 46–67. Further theological issues are explored in: Klaus Baltzer, *The Covenant Formulary* (Philadelphia: Fortress Press, 1971); C. Burrage, *The Church Covenant Idea: Its Origins and Development* (Philadelphia: American Baptist Publication Society, 1904). Different political aspects of the covenant are developed by: S. A. Burell, "The Covenant Idea as a Revolutionary Symbolic: Scotland, 1596–1635," *Church History* 27 (1958): 13–58; David Zaret, *The Heavenly Contract: Ideology and Organization in Pre-Revolutionary Puritanism* (Chicago: University of Chicago Press, 1984).

59. The extent to which the covenants regulated the lives of those who entered into them, especially in maintaining the symbolic and physical boundaries of the new community, is evinced in the 1642 Independent Covenant presented by John Bastwick and reproduced by Michael Tolmie, *The Triumph of the Saints: The Separate Churches of London, 1616–1649* (Cambridge: Cambridge University Press, 1977), 196. See also Michael Watts, *The Dissenters* (Oxford: Oxford University Press, 1978), 30–31, 41–42, 55–56.

60. Haller, *Rise of Puritanism*. In addition to the above-noted references see Michael Knappen, *Tudor Puritanism: A Chapter in the History of Idealism* (Chicago, University of Chicago Press, 1939).

61. For these aspects of Puritanism see Geoffrey Nuttle, *The Holy Spirit in Puritan Faith and Experience* (Oxford: Basil Blackwell, 1946); Norman Pettit, *The Heart Prepared: Grace and Conversion in Puritan Spiritual Life* (New Haven: Yale University Press, 1966). For a less theological and more historical view see Hunt, *The Puritan Moment*, 94. For the importance of this form of religious expression among the separatists see Watts, *The Dissenters*, 26. For a general history of Christian enthusiasm see Ronald Knox, *Enthusiasm: A Chapter in the History of Religion with Special Reference to the XVII and XVIII Centuries* (Oxford: Oxford University Press, 1950). For a discussion of its changing temper in the seventeenth century see Michael Heyd, "The Reaction to Enthusiasm in the Seventeenth Century," *Journal of Modern History* 53 (1981): 258–80. From a sociological standpoint these expressions of a noninstitutional grace were manifestations of a genuinely charismatic dimension whose importance in the process of social restructuring will be taken up in the following chapters.

62. Just how drastic this "dichotomizing" of society was, is a matter of some historical debate, though there is a relative consensus among historians that by the early decades of the 17th century it was radically more evident than in the Elizabethan period. By the later period the desire to make the community of the godly "real

and visible" led to palpable tensions between the community of the gathered Church and the rest of the "Christian nation." Recent discussion of this problem can be found in Collinson, *The Puritan Character.*

63. A slightly different view is offered by Patrick Collinson in his *The Elizabethan Puritan Movement* (Berkeley: University of California Press, 1967); see especially the idea of *ecclesiola in ecclesia,* 375.

64. Avihu Zakai, "The Gospel of Reformation, the Origins of the Great Puritan Migration," *Journal of Ecclesiastical History* 37 (1986): 14. Impressive discussions of this process whereby new loci of community were formed within the overall Puritan movement and its separatist tradition can be found in: Collinson, "A Broader Understanding," 3–38; Watts, *The Dissenters,* 14–26; Tolmie, *Triumph of the Saints*; Haller, *Rise of Puritanism.* The tension formed within society by the growth of Puritanism is amply attested in such satires as "Zeal-of-the-land-Busy" in Ben Jonson's *Bartholomew Faire* (London, 1964), or in the 1633 *Declaration of Sports,* which explicitly ordered the Puritans "to conform themselves or to leave the country" if they would not abide "our good people's law for recreation," for which the king's pleasure decreed "that after the end of divine service our good people be not disturbed, letted or discouraged from any lawful recreation, such as dancing, either men or women; archery for men, leaping, vaulting, or any other such harmless recreation, nor from having of May-games, Whitsunales, and Morris-dances; and the setting up of May-poles and other sports therewith used . . ."(S. R. Gardiner, ed., *The Constitutional Documents of the Puritan Revolution, 1625–1660* [Oxford: Clarendon Press, 1906], 101). A good understanding of the social importance of the local games, rites, and feasts (with which the Puritans broke) can be found in V. A. Kolve, *A Play Called Corpus Christi* (Stanford: Stanford University Press, 1966); James Mervyn, "Ritual Drama and Social Body in the Late Medieval English Town," *Past and Present* 98 (1983): 3–29; Peter Laslett, *The World We Have Lost* (London: Methuen and Co., 1965). Other aspects of the Puritan break with established authority can be found in J. F. New, *Anglican and Puritan: The Basis of their Opposition, 1558–1640* (Stanford: Stanford University Press, 1966). Comparative perspectives on ritual among Protestants and Catholics on the continent can be gained from Natalie Davis, "The Sacred and the Body Social in Sixteenth-Century Lyon," *Past and Present* 90 (1981): 40–70. Further perspectives on the Puritan aversion to the *Declaration of Sports* can be found in W. DeLoss, *The Fast and Thanksgiving Days of New England* (Boston: Houghton Mifflin Co., 1895), 1–27.

65. This fact is also stressed in Theodore Bozeman, *To Live Ancient Lives* (Chapel Hill: University of North Carolina Press, 1988).

66. On the importance of sacred space in the ritual of the Eucharist and elsewhere see Edmund Leach, *Culture and Communication: The Logic by which Symbols Are Connected* (Cambridge: Cambridge University Press, 1976), 81–93. On the conflict between the Puritans and Archbishop Laud on the nature of the sacramental rite see Watts, *The Dissenters,* 65. See: A. Morton, *The World of the Ranters* (London: Lawrence and Wishart, 1970), 11, on the destructuring of sacred space. On the provisory and profane nature of the communion table among Puritans in New England see Elizabeth Winslow, *Meetinghouse Hill, 1630–1783* (New York: Norton, 1972), 52, 56. Explicit injunctions on the profane nature of the communion table can be found in Nicholas Ridley's *Reasons Why the Lord's Board Should*

rather be after the Form of a Table than of an Altar, where he states: "The form of a Table shall more move the simple from the superstitious opinions of the popish Mass, unto the right use of the Lord's Supper. For the use of an altar is to make sacrifice upon it: the use of a table is to serve men to eat upon" (quoted in Clark, *Eucharist, Sacrifice, and the Reformation*, 132).

67. For the relation of the sacred to the collective see Durkheim, *Elementary Forms of Religious Life*, 23–47. Explications of Durkheim's theory may be found in Anthony Giddens, *Capitalism and Modern Social Theory* (Cambridge: Cambridge University Press, 1971), 105–18. The importance of moral authority and moral community as aspects of this connection in Durkheim's thought can be found in Parsons, "Durkheim on Religion Revisited: Another Look at The Elementary Forms of Religious Life," in his *Action Theory and the Human Condition*, 213–32. See also Parsons, *Social Action*, 378–90.

68. Richard Rogers, *Seven Treatises Called the Practice of Christianity*, 2nd ed. (London, 1605), 497–98.

69. See, for example, Keith Thomas, "Cases of Conscience in Seventeenth-Century England," 29–56, and John Ferris, "Official Members in the Commons, 1660–1690: A Study in Multiple Loyalties," 278–304, in *Public Duty and Private Conscience in Seventeenth-Century England*, eds. John Morrill, Paul Slack, and Daniel Woolf (Oxford: Clarendon Press, 1993).

70. Herman Schmalenbach, "The Sociological Category of Communion," *Theories of Society*, eds. Talcott Parsons et al. (New York: Free Press, 1961), 331–47.

71. Andrew Fix, *Prophecy and Reason: The Dutch Collegiants in the Early Enlightenment* (Princeton: Princeton University Press, 1991), 118.

72. Ibid., 119.

73. Margaret Jacob, "Private Beliefs in Public Temples: The New Religiosity of the Eighteenth Century," *Social Research* 59 (1991), 64.

74. Seligman, *Innerworldly Individualism*.

75. Roger Caillois, *Man and the Sacred* (New York: Free Press, 1959), 132.

76. Ibid., 192.

77. Paul Lucas, *Valley of Discord: Church and Society along the Connecticut River, 1636–1725* (Middletown: Wesleyan University Press, 1968), 242.

78. Ibid., 126.

79. Jacob, "Private Beliefs," 65.

80. Darwall, *British Moralists*, 17.

81. This is not the place to enter into a comparative history of Western and Eastern European developments (not to mention those of other civilizational complexes). Yet in highly schematic terms we may follow the organizational topology of S. N. Eisenstadt in stressing the great degree of structural differentiation that characterized Western developments. These center on the organizational heterogeneity of Western European civilization, based on the multiplicity of socio-political centers, status hierarchies, and the changing boundaries of collectivities; and matched by a heterogeneity of symbolic orientations drawn from the cultural legacy of the Judeo-Christian religions and Greco-Roman civilization which, together with the Germanic tribal legacy, all contributed to the "very high degree of multiplicity and cross-cutting of cultural orientations and structural settings." In very brief terms, Eisenstadt's topology includes the following components as character-

istic of Western European civilization: *(a)* a multiplicity of social and political centers; *(b)* a high degree of permeation of the territorial peripheries by these centers, but also the impingement of the periphery on the centers; *(c)* a relatively small degree of overlapping of the boundaries of class, ethnic, religious, and political entities; *(d)* a relatively high degree of autonomy accorded the different groups and strata in terms of their access to the social center; *(e)* a multiplicity of different elite groups, each relatively autonomous of each other and of the social center; *(f)* the autonomy of the legal system, especially in respect to the political and religious systems; *(g)* the autonomy of the cities as centers of social and cultural life.

See S. N. Eisenstadt, L. Roniger, and Adam B. Seligman, *Center Formation, Protest Movements, and Class Structure in Europe and the United States* (New York: New York University Press, 1987), 11.

82. Becker, *Emergence of Civil Society,* 1994.

83. John Zomchick, *Family and the Law in Eighteenth-Century Fiction: The Public Conscience in the Private Sphere* (Cambridge: Cambridge University Press, 1993), 52.

Chapter Six
Spheres of Value and the Dilemma of Modernity

1. Seligman, *Idea of Civil Society.*

2. John Rundell, *Origins of Modernity* (Madison: University of Wisconsin Press, 1987); Seligman, *Idea of Civil Society,* chap. 1.

3. See S. M. Lipset, "Radicalism and Reformism: The Sources of Working Class Politics," *The American Political Science Review* 77 (1983): 1–18; also John Laslett and S. M. Lipset, eds., *Failure of a Dream: Essays in the History of American Socialism* (Berkeley: University of California Press, 1984).

4. Donald Levine, *The Flight from Ambiguity* (Chicago: University of Chicago Press, 1985), 20–43.

5. See Rahel Wasserfall, "Gender Encounters in America: An Outsider's View of Continuity and Ambivalence," in *Distant Mirrors: America as a Foreign Culture,* eds. Philip DeVita and James Armstrong (Belmont, Cal.; Wadsworth, 1993), 103–11.

6. Ibid., 106.

7. Seligman, "Representation of Society," 68–84.

8. See, for example, James Davidson Hunter, *Before the Shooting Begins: Searching for Democracy in America's Culture War* (New York: Free Press, 1994).

9. Niklas Luhmann, "The Representation of Society within Society," *Current Sociology* 35 no. 2 (1987): 101–6.

10. Mary Ann Glendon, *The Transformation of Family Law: State, Law, and Family in the United States and Western Europe* (Chicago: University of Chicago Press, 1989), 102.

11. Ibid., 103, 297.

12. Arendt, *Human Condition,* 38–49.

13. Robert Brustein, "Culture by Coercion," *New York Times,* 29 November 1994, p. A21.

14. V. Wright, "Fragmentation and Cohesion in the Nation State: France, 1870–1871," paper presented at the European Science Foundation Seminar on the Construction and Reconstruction of Center-Periphery Relations in Europe (Jerusalem, May/June, 1984). See also Sudhir Hazareesingh, *Political Traditions in Modern France* (Oxford: Oxford University Press, 1994), 85–89.

15. Barry Barnes, *The Elements of Social Theory* (Princeton: Princeton University Press, 1995), 112–18.

16. See, for example, Robert Rector of the Heritage Foundation on the issue of welfare reform: *New York Times*, 28 June 1995, p. A8.

17. Daniel Bell, "The Disunited States of America: Middle Class Fears Turn Class Wars into Culture Wars," *Times Literary Supplement*, 9 June 1995, 16–17. There is some debate about current marriage trends and indications that remarriage rates are in fact beginning to decrease. For discussions of these issues see Andrew Cherlin and Frank Furstenberg Jr., "Stepfamilies in the United States: A Reconsideration," *Annual Review of Sociology* 20 (1994): 359–81; Frank Furstenberg Jr., "Divorce and the American Family," *Annual Review of Sociology* 16 (1990): 379–403; U.S. Bureau of the Census, "Marriage, Divorce, and Remarriage in the 1990's," in *Current Population Reports*, Washington D.C., 1992, 1–13.

18. Ronald Ingelhart, *Culture Shift in Advanced Industrial Society* (Princeton: Princeton University Press, 1990), 167. Ingelhart presents this thesis as an explanation of the role of an informant's father's SES rather than his or her own in determining if an informant privileges postmaterialist or materialist values. The analytic point of the role of early experiences on the establishment of value orientations, however, is our concern here.

19. Bell, "The Disunited States of America," 16.

20. See Christopher Lasch, *The Revolt of the Elites* (New York: Norton, 1995), 25–80. Interestingly, Simmel notes the awareness of this correlation between the embedment of elites in local contexts and the development of Public Goods, as early as the seventeenth century. See his *Philosophy of Money*, 342–43.

21. David Harvey, *Condition of Postmodernity* (Cambridge: Basil Blackwell, 1989), 151–52.

22. Ibid., 152.

23. These developments are discussed in Harvey, *Condition of Postmodernity*, and in Scott Lash and John Urry, *The End of Organized Capitalism* (Cambridge: Polity Press, 1987). Some indications of the implications of these developments for role behavior are explored in Jerald Hage and Charles Powers, *Post-Industrial Lives: Roles and Relationships in the 21st Century* (California: Sage, 1992).

24. Harvey, *Condition of Postmodernity*, 54.

25. A good feel for this aspect of the sport can be found in the writings of Roger Angell, *Late Innings* (New York: Simon and Schuster, 1982); idem, *The Summer Game* (New York: Popular Library, 1978).

26. Good, "Individuals, Interpersonal Relationships, and Trust," 37.

27. Deirdre Boden and Harvey Molotch, "The Compulsion of Proximity," in *NowHere: Space, Time, and Modernity*, eds. Roger Friedland and Deirdre Boden (Berkeley: University of California Press, 1994), 266.

28. Foucault, *The Order of Things*, 386–87.

29. Ralph Turner, "The Role and the Person," *American Journal of Sociology* 84, no. 1. (1978): 1–23.

30. Erving Goffman, *Presentation of Self in Everyday Life* (New York: Doubleday, 1959); David Riesman, *The Lonely Crowd* (New Haven: Yale University Press, 1961).

31. On the "generalized other" see George Herbert Mead, *Mind, Self, and Society* (Chicago: University of Chicago Press, 1934), 154–63.

32. Some of these themes have been explored in: Leo Lowenthal, *Literature and the Image of Man* (Boston: Beacon Press, 1957); Ian Watt, *The Rise of the Novel: Studies in Defoe, Richardson, and Fielding* (Berkeley, University of California Press, 1967); Lionel Trilling, *Sincerity and Authenticity* (Cambridge: Harvard University Press, 1972).

33. Robert Wuthnow, "A Reasonable Role for Religion? Moral Practices, Civic Participation, and Market Behavior," paper presented at the Institute for the Study of Economic Culture Conference (Boston, Mass., October 1995), 2.

34. Ibid.

Conclusion

1. Ian Hacking, *The Emergence of Probability* (Cambridge: Cambridge University Press, 1975).

2. Lorraine Daston, *Classical Probability in the Enlightenment* (Princeton: Princeton University Press, 1988), 58–67.

3. Hacking, *Emergence of Probability*, 11.

4. Pascal, *Pensées* (Harmondsworth: Penguin Books, 1966), 149–52.

5. Daston, *Classical Probability*, 61–67.

6. Agreeing here with Luhmann's distinction of risk from danger.

7. Daston, *Classical Probability*, 168.

8. Ibid., 19.

9. Niklas Rose, *Governing the Soul: The Shaping of the Private Self* (London: Routledge Press, 1989).

10. The parallels of these assumptions to the "methodological individualism" of rational-choice theory are, I believe, striking.

Bibliography

Abercrombie, Nigel. *The Origins of Jansenism in France*. Oxford: Oxford University Press, 1936.

Adams, R. M. *Nil: Episodes in the Literary Conquests of Void during the Nineteenth Century*. New York: Oxford University Press, 1966.

Aguilar, John. "Trust and Exchange: Expressive and Instrumental Dimensions of Reciprocity in a Peasant Community." *Ethos* 12, no. 1 (Spring 1984): 3–29.

Allan, Graham. *A Sociology of Friendship and Kinship*. London: George Allen and Unwin, 1979.

Angell, Roger. *The Summer Game*. New York: Popular Library, 1978.

———. *Late Innings*. New York: Simon and Schuster, 1982.

Appadurai, Arjun. "Gratitude as a Social Mode in South India." *Ethos* 13, no. 1 (Spring 1985): 236–45.

Arendt, Hannah. *The Human Condition*. Chicago: University of Chicago Press, 1958.

Aries, Philippe. *Centuries of Childhood*. New York: Vintage Press, 1962.

Aries, Philippe, and George Duby, eds. *A History of Private Life*. Vols. 1–5. Cambridge: Belknap Press, 1987–1991.

Arrow, Kenneth. *The Limits of Organization*. New York: Norton, 1974.

Atiyah, P. S. *The Rise and Fall of the Freedom of Contract*. Oxford: Clarendon Press, 1979.

———. *Introduction to the Law of Contract*. Oxford: Oxford University Press, 1981.

———. *Promises, Morals, and Law*. Oxford: Clarendon Press, 1981.

———. *Essays on Contract*. Oxford: Clarendon Press, 1986.

———. *Pragmatism and Theory in English Law*. London: Stevens and Sons, 1987.

Axelrod, Robert. "Effective Choice in the Prisoner's Dilemma." *Journal of Conflict Resolution* 24, no. 1 (March 1980): 3–25.

———. *Evolution of Cooperation*. New York: Basic Books, 1984.

Baier, Annette. *Postures of the Mind: Essays on Mind and Morals*. Minneapolis: University of Minnesota Press, 1985.

———. "Trust and Anti-Trust." *Ethics* 96 (1986): 231–60.

———. "Trusting People in Philosophical Perspectives." *Ethics* 102 (1992): 137–53.

Bailyn, Bernard. *The Ideological Origins of the American Revolution*. Cambridge: Harvard University Press, 1967.

Baker, Judith. "Trust and Rationality." *Pacific Philosophical Quarterly* 68 (1987): 1–13.

Baltzer, Klaus. *The Covenant Formulary*. Philadelphia: Fortress Press, 1971.

Banfield, Edward. *The Moral Basis of a Backward Society*. New York: Free Press, 1958.

Banton, Michael, ed. *The Social Anthropology of Complex Societies*. New York: Praeger, 1966.

Barber, Bernard. *The Logic and Limits of Trust*. New Brunswick: Rutgers University Press, 1988.

Barnes, Barry. *The Elements of Social Theory*. Princeton: Princeton University Press, 1995.

Becker, Marvin, *Civility and Society in Western Europe, 1300–1600*. Bloomington: Indiana University Press, 1988.

———. *The Emergence of Civil Society in the Eighteenth Century*. Bloomington: Indiana University Press, 1994.

Bell, Daniel. "American Exceptionalism Revisited: The Role of Civil Society." *The Public Interest* 95 (1989): 38–56.

———. "The Disunited States of America: Middle Class Fears Turn Class Wars into Culture Wars." *Times Literary Supplement*, 9 June 1995, 16–17.

Bellah, Robert, ed. *Emile Durkheim on Morality and Society*. Chicago: University of Chicago Press, 1973.

Benedict, Burton. "Sociological Characteristics of Small Territories and Implications for Economic Development." In *Social Anthropology of Complex Societies*, ed. Michael Banton. New York: Praeger, 1966.

Benhabib, Seyla. *Critique: Norm and Utopia*. New York: Columbia University Press, 1986.

Benn S. I., and G. F. Gauss, eds. *Public and Private in Social Life*. New York: St. Martin's Press, 1983.

Benson, R., and G. Constable, eds. *Renaissance and Renewal in the Twelfth Century*. Cambridge: Harvard University Press, 1982.

Benton, John F. "Consciousness of Self and Perceptions of Individuality." In *Renaissance and Renewal in the Twelfth Century*, eds. R. Benson and G. Constable. Cambridge: Harvard University Press, 1982.

Benveniste, Emile. *Indo-European Language and Society*. London: Faber and Faber, 1973.

Berger, Peter. *The Sacred Canopy*. New York: Anchor Books, 1969.

———. "On the Obsolescence of the Concept of Honor." In *Revision: Changing Perspectives in Moral Philosophy*, eds. Stanley Hauerwas and Alasdair MacIntyre. Notre Dame: University of Notre Dame Press, 1983.

Berman, Harold. *Law and Revolution: The Formation of the Western Legal Tradition*. Cambridge: Harvard University Press, 1983.

Birnbaum, Norman. "The Zwinglian Reformation in Zurich." *Archive Sociologie de Religion* 4 (1959): 15–30.

Blau, Peter. *Exchange and Power in Social Life*. New York: Wiley, 1964.

Block, Ruth. *Visionary Republic: Millennial Themes in American Thought, 1765–1800*. Cambridge: Cambridge University Press, 1985.

Bobbio, Norberto. *The Future of Democracy*. Minneapolis: University of Minnesota Press, 1987.

———. "Public and Private: The Great Dichotomy." In his *Democracy and Dictatorship*. Minneapolis: University of Minnesota Press, 1989.

Bock, Gisela, Quentin Skinner, and Maurizio Viroli, eds. *Machiavelli and Republicanism*. Cambridge: Cambridge University Press, 1990.

Boden, Deirdre, and Harvey Molotch. "The Compulsion of Proximity." In *NowHere: Space, Time, and Modernity*, eds. Roger Friedland and Deirdre Boden. Berkeley: University of California Press, 1994.

Bonfield, L., R. Smith, and K. Wrightson, eds. *The World We Have Gained: Histories of Population and Social Structure*. Oxford: Basil Blackwell, 1986.

Bozeman, Theodore. *To Live Ancient Lives*. Chapel Hill: University of North Carolina Press, 1988.

Brain, Robert. *Friends and Lovers*. London: Hart Davis MacGibbon, 1976.

Brandon, S. G. F. *History, Time, and the Deity: A Historical and Comparative Study of the Conception of Time in Religious Thought and Practice*. Manchester: University of Manchester Press, 1965.

Brauer, Jerald. "The Nature of English Puritanism: Three Interpretations." *Church History* 23 (1954): 99–108.

Briggs, Robin. "The Catholic Puritans: Jansenists and Rigorists in France." In *Puritans and Revolutionaries: Essays in Seventeenth-Century History Presented to Christopher Hill*, eds. D. Pennington and K. Thomas. Oxford: Clarendon Press, 1978.

Brown, Peter. *The Making of Late Antiquity*. Cambridge: Harvard University Press, 1978.

———. *Society and the Holy in Late Antiquity*. Berkeley: University of California Press, 1982.

———. *The Body and Society: Men, Women, and Sexual Renunciation in Early Christianity*. New York: Columbia University Press, 1988.

Brustein, Robert. "Culture by Coercion." *New York Times*, 29 November 1994, p. A21.

Burell, S. A. "The Covenant Idea as a Revolutionary Symbolic: Scotland, 1596–1635." *Church History* 27 (1958): 13–58.

Burke, Edmund. *Reflections on the Revolution in France*. Ed. J. G. A. Pocock. Indianapolis: Hackett, 1987.

Burrage, C. *The Church Covenant Idea: Its Origins and Development*. Philadelphia: American Baptist Publication Society, 1904.

Butorova, Zora. "Two Years after November 17, 1989: The Hard Birth of Democracy in Slovakia." In *Zwischen den Zeiten*, eds. P. Gerlich and P. Glass. Vienna: VWGO, 1992.

Butorova, Zora, and Martin Butorova. "Wariness Towards the Jews as an Expression of Post-Communist Panic." *Proceedings from the International Seminar on Anti-Semitism in Post-Totalitarian Europe*. Prague, 1992.

Bynum, Caroline. "Did the Twelfth Century Discover the Individual?" *Journal of Ecclesiastical History* 31 (1980): 1–17.

———. *Jesus as Mother: Studies in the Spirituality of the High Middle Ages*. Berkeley: University of California Press, 1982.

Caillois, Roger. *Man and the Sacred*. New York: Free Press, 1959.

Calvin, John. *Institutes of the Christian Religion*. Ed. John McNeill. Philadelphia: Westminster Press, 1960.

Campbell, David. "The Relational Constitution of Discrete Contract." School of Financial Studies and Law, Sheffield Hallam University. Unpublished paper, 1995.

Cantor, Paul. *Creature and Creator: Myth-Making and English Romanticism*. Cambridge: Cambridge University Press, 1984.

Carrithers, Michael, Steven Collins, and Steven Lukes, eds. *The Category of the Person*. Cambridge: Cambridge University Press, 1985.

Chartier, Roger. *The Cultural Origins of the French Revolution*. Durham: Duke University Press, 1991.

Chenu, Marie-Dominique. *Nature, Man, and Society in the Twelfth Century*. Chicago: University of Chicago Press, 1968.

Cherlin, Andrew, and Frank Furstenberg Jr. "Stepfamilies in the United States: A Reconsideration." *Annual Review of Sociology* 20 (1994): 359–81.

Chroust, Anton. "The Metaphysics of Time and History in Early Christian Thought." *New Scholasticum* 19 (1945): 322–52.

Clark, Francis. *Eucharist, Sacrifice, and the Reformation*. London: Darton, Longmans and Todd, 1960.

Cochrane, Charles. *Christianity and Classical Culture*. New York: Oxford University Press, 1957.

Cole, C., and M. Moody, eds. *The Dissenting Tradition*. Athens: Ohio University Press, 1975.

Coleman, James. *Foundations of Social Theory*. Cambridge: Harvard University Press, 1990.

Colley, Linda. *Britons: Forging the Nation, 1707–1837*. New Haven: Yale University Press, 1992.

Collinson, Patrick. *The Elizabethan Puritan Movement*. Berkeley: University of California Press, 1967.

———. "Towards a Broader Understanding of the Dissenting Tradition." In *The Dissenting Tradition*, eds. C. Cole and M. Moody. Athens: Ohio University Press, 1975.

———. *The Puritan Character: Polemics and Polarities in Early Seventeenth-Century Culture*. Los Angeles: William Andrews Clark Memorial Library, 1989.

Constant, Benjamin. *Political Writings*. Ed. B. Fontana. Cambridge: Cambridge University Press, 1988.

Coser, Rose Laub. *In Defense of Modernity: Role Complexity and Individual Autonomy*. Stanford: Stanford University Press, 1991.

Cullmann, Oscar. *Early Christian Worship*. London: SCM Press, 1953.

Cupit, Geoffrey. "How Requests and Promises Create Obligations." *Philosophical Quarterly* 44, no. 177 (1994): 439–55.

Cushman, Robert. "The Greek and Christian Views of Time." *Journal of Religion* 33 (1953): 254–65.

Dahrendorf, Ralf. "Homo Sociologicus." In his *Essays in the Theory of Society*. Stanford: Stanford University Press, 1968.

———. "A Precarious Balance: Economic Opportunity, Civil Society, and Political Liberty." *The Responsive Community* 5, no. 3 (Fall 1995): 13–39.

D'Arcy, M. C. *The Mind and Heart of Love, Lion, and Unicorn*. New York: H. Holt & Co., 1956.

Darwall, Stephen. *The British Moralists and the Internal "Ought," 1640–1740*. Cambridge: Cambridge University Press, 1995.

Dasgupta, Partha. "Trust as a Commodity." In *Trust: Making and Breaking of Cooperative Relations*, ed. Diego Gambetta. Oxford: Basil Blackwell, 1988.

Daston, Lorraine. *Classical Probability in the Enlightenment*. Princeton: Princeton University Press, 1988.

Davis, Natalie. "The Sacred and the Body Social in Sixteenth-Century Lyon." *Past and Present* 90 (1981): 40–70.

DeLoss, W. *The Fast and Thanksgiving Days of New England.* Boston: Houghton Mifflin Co., 1895.

Derrida, Jacques. *Given Time I: Counterfeit Money.* Chicago: University of Chicago Press, 1992.

Deutsch, K. "Social Mobilization and Political Development." *American Political Science Review* 55 (1961): 493–513.

DeVita, Philip, and James Armstrong, eds. *Distant Mirrors: America as a Foreign Culture.* Belmont, Cal.: Wadsworth, 1993.

Diderot, Denis. "Refutation de l'ouvrage d'Helvétius intitulé *De l'Homme.*" In *Oeuvres Complètes.* Paris: N.p., 1975.

Diggins, J. *The Lost Soul of American Politics.* New York: Basic Books, 1984.

Dodd, Peter. "Family Honor and the Forces of Change in Arab Society." *International Journal of Middle Eastern Studies* 4 (1973): 40–54.

Douglas, Mary. *Natural Symbols.* New York: Vintage Press, 1976.

Duby, George. *The Knight, the Lady, and the Priest: The Making of Modern Marriage in Medieval France.* Chicago: University of Chicago Press, 1993.

Dumont, Louis. *From Mandeville to Marx: The Genesis and Triumph of Economic Ideology.* Chicago: University of Chicago Press, 1977.

———. *Essays on Individualism: Modern Ideology in Anthropological Perspective.* Chicago: University of Chicago Press, 1986.

Dunn, John. *The Political Theory of John Locke.* Cambridge: Harvard University Press, 1969.

———. "The Concept of Trust in the Politics of John Locke." In *Philosophy in History*, eds. Richard Rorty et al. Cambridge: Cambridge University Press, 1984.

Durkheim, Emile. *The Elementary Forms of Religious Life.* London: George Allen and Unwin, 1915.

———. *The Division of Labor in Society.* New York: Free Press, 1933.

———. *Professional Ethics and Civic Morals.* London: Routledge and Kegan Paul, 1957.

———. *Montesquieu and Rousseau.* Ann Arbor: University of Michigan Press, 1965.

———. *Sociology and Philosophy.* New York: Free Press, 1968.

———. "Individualism and the Intellectuals." In *Emile Durkheim on Morality and Society*, ed. Robert Bellah. Chicago: University of Chicago Press, 1973.

Dwyer, John. *Virtuous Discourse: Sensibility and Community in Late Eighteenth-Century Scotland.* Edinburgh: John Donald Publishers, 1987.

Eisenstadt, S. N. "Ritualized Personal Relations." *Man* 56 (1956): 90–95.

———. *Modernization, Protest, and Change.* Englewood Cliffs: Prentice Hall, 1966.

———. "Transcendental Visions and the Rise of Clerics." *European Journal of Sociology* 23 (1982): 294–314.

———. *Power, Trust, and Meaning.* Chicago: University of Chicago Press, 1995.

———, ed. *The Origins and Diversity of the Axial Age Civilizations.* Albany: State University of New York Press, 1986.

Eisenstadt, S. N., and L. Roniger. *Patrons, Clients, and Friends*. Cambridge: Cambridge University Press, 1984.

Eisenstadt, S. N., L. Roniger, and Adam B. Seligman. *Center Formation, Protest Movements, and Class Structure in Europe and the United States*. New York: New York University Press, 1984.

Elias, Norbert. *The Civilizing Process*. New York: Pantheon Books, 1982.

Eliav-Feldon, Miriam. *Realistic Utopias: The Ideal Imaginary Societies of the Renaissance, 1516–1630*. Oxford: Clarendon Press, 1982.

Ellemers, J. E. "The Revolt of the Netherlands: The Part Played by Religion in the Process of Nation Building." *Social Compass* 14 (1967): 93–103.

Emerson, Everett. "Calvin and Covenant Theology." *Church History* 25 (1956): 136–44.

Etzioni, Amitai. *The Moral Dimension: Towards a New Economics*. New York: Free Press, 1988.

———. *The Spirit of Community: Rights and Responsibilities and the Communitarian Agenda*. New York: Crown, 1993.

Evans-Pritchard, E. E. "Zande Blood Brotherhood." *Africa* 6 (1933): 369–401.

Fallers, Lloyd. *Bantu Bureaucracy—A Study of Integration and Conflict in the Political Institutions of an East African People*. Cambridge: W. Heiffer and Sons, n.d.

Ferguson, Adam. *An Essay on the History of Civil Society*. 5th ed. London: T. Cadell, 1782.

Ferris, John. "Official Members in the Commons, 1660–1690: A Study in Multiple Loyalties." In *Public Duty and Private Conscience in Seventeenth-Century England*, eds. John Morrill, Paul Slack, and Daniel Woolf. Oxford: Clarendon Press, 1993.

Fix, Andrew. *Prophecy and Reason: The Dutch Collegiants in the Early Enlightenment*. Princeton: Princeton University Press, 1991.

Fleisher, Martin. *Machiavelli and the Nature of Political Thought*. New York: Atheneum, 1972.

Fletcher, George. *Loyalty: An Essay on the Morality of Relationships*. New York: Oxford University Press, 1993.

Foucault, Michel. *The Order of Things: An Archeology of the Human Sciences*. New York: Vintage Books, 1973.

Frankfurt, Harry. "Freedom of the Will and the Concept of the Person." *The Journal of Philosophy* 68, no. 1 (January 1971): 5–20.

Friedland, Roger, and Deirdre Boden, eds. *NowHere: Space, Time, and Modernity*. Berkeley: University of California Press, 1994.

Fukuyama, Francis. *Trust: Social Virtues and the Creation of Prosperity*. New York: Free Press, 1995.

Fulbrook, Mary. *Piety and Politics: Religion and the Rise of Absolutism in England, Württemberg, and Prussia*. Cambridge: Cambridge University Press, 1983.

Furstenberg, Frank, Jr. "Divorce and the American Family." *Annual Review of Sociology* 16 (1990): 379–403.

Gambetta, Diego, ed. *Trust: Making and Breaking of Cooperative Relations*. Oxford: Basil Blackwell, 1988.

———. "Can We Trust Trust?" In *Trust: Making and Breaking of Cooperative Relations*, ed. Diego Gambetta. Oxford: Basil Blackwell, 1988.

Gardiner, S. R., ed. *The Constitutional Documents of the Puritan Revolution, 1625–1660*. Oxford: Clarendon Press, 1906.

Gellner, Ernest. *Plough, Sword, and Book: The Structure of Human History*. Chicago: University of Chicago Press, 1988.

———. "Trust, Cohesion, and the Social Order." In *Trust: The Making and Breaking of Cooperative Relations*, ed. Diego Gambetta. Oxford: Basil Blackwell, 1988.

George, C. H. "Protestantism and Capitalism in Pre-Revolutionary England." *Church History* 27 (1958): 351–446.

George, C. H., and K. George. "Puritanism as History and Historiography." *Past and Present* 41 (1968): 77–104.

Gerlich, P., and P. Glass, eds. *Zwischen den Zeiten*. Vienna: VWGO, 1992.

Gerth, G. H., and C. W. Mills. *From Max Weber*. New York: Free Press, 1958.

Giddens, Anthony. *Capitalism and Modern Social Theory*. Cambridge: Cambridge University Press, 1971.

———. *The Consequences of Modernity*. Stanford: Stanford University Press, 1990.

Glendon, Mary Ann. *The Transformation of Family Law: State, Law, and Family in the United States and Western Europe*. Chicago: University of Chicago Press, 1989.

Goffman, Erving. *Presentation of Self in Everyday Life*. New York: Doubleday, 1959.

Good, David. "Individuals, Interpersonal Relationships, and Trust." In *Trust: Making and Breaking of Cooperative Relations*, ed. Diego Gambetta. Oxford: Basil Blackwell, 1988.

Goodenough, Ward. "Rethinking Status and Role: Towards a General Model of Social Relationships." In *Cognitive Anthropology*, ed. Stephen Tylor. New York: Holt, Rinehart and Winston, 1969.

Gordon, Daniel. *Citizens without Sovereignty: Equality and Sociability in French Thought, 1670–1789*. Princeton: Princeton University Press, 1994.

Govier, T. "An Epistemology of Trust." *International Journal of Moral and Social Studies* 8, no. 2 (Summer 1993): 155–74.

Granovetter, Mark. "The Strength of Weak Ties." *American Journal of Sociology* 78, no. 6 (May 1973): 1360–80.

———. "Economic Action and Social Structure: The Problem of Embeddedness." *American Journal of Sociology* 91, no. 3 (November 1985): 481–510.

Grief, Avner. "Reputations and Coalitions in Medieval Trade: Evidence on the Maghribi Traders." *The Journal of Economic History* 49, no. 4 (December 1989): 857–82.

———. "Historical Perspectives on the Economics of Trade: Institutions and International Trade: Lessons from the Commercial Revolution." *American Economic Review* 82, no. 1/2 (May 1992): 128–33.

———. "Contract Enforceability and Economic Institutions in Early Trade: The Maghribi Traders' Coalition." *American Economic Review* 83, no. 3 (June 1993): 525–48.

Grief, Avner. On the Political Foundations of the Late Medieval Commercial Revolution: Genoa during the Twelfth and Thirteenth Centuries." *The Journal of Economic History* 54, no. 2 (June 1994): 271–87.

Groethuysen, Bernhard. *The Bourgeois: Catholicism vs. Capitalism in Eighteenth-Century France.* New York: Holt, Rinehart and Winston, 1968.

Haakonssen, Knud. *The Science of a Legislator: The Natural Jurisprudence of David Hume and Adam Smith.* Cambridge: Cambridge University Press, 1981.

Habermas, Jurgen. *The Structural Transformation of the Public Sphere.* Cambridge: Massachusetts Institute of Technology Press, 1989.

Hacking, Ian. *The Emergence of Probability.* Cambridge: Cambridge University Press, 1975.

Hage, Jerald, and Charles Powers. *Post-Industrial Lives: Roles and Relationships in the 21st Century.* Newbury Park, Cal.: Sage, 1992.

Hall, John, ed. *Civil Society: Theory, History, Comparison.* Oxford: Polity Press, 1995.

Haller, William. *The Rise of Puritanism.* Philadelphia: University of Pennsylvania Press, 1972.

Hardin, Russell. "The Street-Level Epistemology of Trust." *Politics and Society* 21, no. 4 (December 1993): 505–29.

Harrison, Bernard. "Moral Judgement, Action, and Emotion." *Philosophy* 59 (1984): 295–321.

Hart, Keith. "Kinship, Contract, and Trust: The Economic Organization of Migrants in an African City Slum." In *Trust: Making and Breaking of Cooperative Relations*, ed. Diego Gambetta. Oxford: Basil Blackwell, 1988.

Hartmann, Nicolai. *Ethics.* Vol. 3. Trans. Stanton Colt. New York: Macmillan, 1932.

Harvey, David. *Condition of Postmodernity.* Cambridge: Basil Blackwell, 1989.

Hatch, N. O. *The Sacred Cause of Liberty.* New Haven: Yale University Press, 1977.

Hauerwas, Stanley, and Alasdair MacIntyre, eds. *Revision: Changing Perspectives in Moral Philosophy.* Notre Dame: University of Notre Dame Press, 1983.

Haviland, Leslie, and John B. Haviland. "Privacy in a Mexican Indian Village." In *Public and Private in Social Life*, eds. S. I. Benn and G. F. Gauss. New York: St. Martin's Press, 1983.

Hawthorn, Geoffrey. "Three Ironies of Trust." In *Trust: Making and Breaking of Cooperative Relations*, ed. Diego Gambetta. Oxford: Basil Blackwell, 1988.

Hazareesingh, Sudhir. *Political Traditions in Modern France.* Oxford: Oxford University Press, 1994.

Held, Virginia. "On the Meaning of Trust." *Ethics* 78 (January 1968): 156–59.

Herman, Gabriel. *Ritualised Friendship and the Greek City.* Cambridge: Cambridge University Press, 1987.

Hertzberg, Lars. "On the Attitude of Trust." *Inquiry* 31, no. 3 (September 1988): 307–22.

Heyd, Michael. "The Reaction to Enthusiasm in the Seventeenth Century." *Journal of Modern History* 53 (1981): 258–80.

Hilbert, Richard. "Towards an Improved Understanding of Role." *Theory and Society* 10, no. 2 (1981): 207–26.

Hirschman, Albert. *The Passions and the Interests*. Princeton: Princeton University Press, 1977.

Holdsworth, W. S. *A History of English Law*. Vol. 8. Boston: Little, Brown and Company, 1926.

Holt, P. M., et al., eds. *The Cambridge History of Islam*. New York: Cambridge University Press, 1991.

Holton, Richard. "Deciding to Trust, Coming to Believe." *Australasian Journal of Philosophy* 72, no. 1 (March 1994): 63–76.

Hont, I., and M. Ignatieff, eds. *Wealth and Virtue: The Shaping of Political Economy in the Scottish Enlightenment*. Cambridge: Cambridge University Press, 1983.

Hopfl, Harro. *The Christian Polity of John Calvin*. Cambridge: Cambridge University Press, 1982.

Hume, David. *Treatise on Human Nature*. Ed. H. D. Aieken. New York: Macmillan, 1948.

Hunt, William. *The Puritan Moment: The Coming of Revolution in an English Country*. Cambridge: Harvard University Press, 1983.

Hunter, James Davidson. *Before the Shooting Begins: Searching for Democracy in America's Culture War*. New York: Free Press, 1994.

Huntington, S. P. *Political Order in Changing Societies*. New Haven: Yale University Press, 1968.

Hutter, Horst. *Politics as Friendship: The Origins of Classical Notions of Politics in Theory and Practice of Friendship*. Waterloo, Ont.: Wilfrid Laurier University Press, 1978.

Ingelhart, Ronald. *Culture Shift in Advanced Industrial Society*. Princeton: Princeton University Press, 1990.

Inkeles, A., and D. H. Smith. *Becoming Modern: Individual Change in Six Developing Countries*. Cambridge: Harvard University Press, 1974.

Jacob, Margaret. "Private Beliefs in Public Temples: The New Religiosity of the 18th Century." *Social Research* 58 (1991): 59–84.

———. "The Enlightenment Redefined: The Formation of Modern Civil Society." *Social Research* 59 (1992): 475–95.

Jacob, Margaret, and Wijnand Mijnhardt, eds. *The Dutch Republic in the Eighteenth Century*. Ithaca: Cornell University Press, 1992.

Jacobson, Marcia. *Being a Boy Again*. Tuscaloosa: University of Alabama Press, 1994.

James, Mervyn. "English Politics and the Concept of Honour, 1485–1642." *Past and Present*. Supplement 3. The Past and Present Society, 1978.

Johnson, Peter. *Frames of Deceit: A Study of the Loss and Recovery of Public and Private Trust*. Cambridge: Cambridge University Press, 1993.

Jonson, Ben. *Bartholomew Faire*. London, 1964.

Jung, C. G. *The Archetypes of the Collective Unconscious*. London: Routledge and Kegan Paul, 1959.

Kahneman, Daniel, Paul Slovic, and Amos Tversky, eds. *Judgement under Uncertainty: Heuristics and Biases*. Cambridge: Cambridge University Press, 1982.

Kapur, Neera Badhwar. "Why It Is Wrong to be Always Guided by the Best: Consequentialism and Friendship." *Ethics* 101 (April 1992): 483–504.

Keane, J., ed. *Civil Society and the State*. London: Verso, 1988.

Kelly, Donald. *The Beginnings of Ideology*. London: Cambridge University Press, 1981.

Kluckhohn, C. *Mirror for Man*. London: Harrap, 1950.

Knappen, Michael. *Tudor Puritanism: A Chapter in the History of Idealism*. Chicago: University of Chicago Press, 1939.

Knox, Ronald. *Enthusiasm: A Chapter in the History of Religion with Special Reference to the XVII and XVIII Centuries*. Oxford: Oxford University Press, 1950.

Kolve, V. A. *A Play Called Corpus Christi*. Stanford: Stanford University Press, 1966.

Kopstein, Jeff. "Chipping Away at the State." *World Politics* 48, no. 3 (April 1996): 391–423.

Kramnick, Isaac. *Republicanism and Bourgeois Radicalism: Political Ideology in Late Eighteenth-Century England and America*. Ithaca: Cornell University Press, 1990.

Krygien, Martin. "Publicness, Privateness, and 'Primitive Law.'" In *Public and Private in Social Life*, eds. S. I. Benn and G. F. Gauss. New York: St. Martin's Press, 1983.

Lahno, Bernard. "Trust, Reputation, and Exit in Exchange Relationships." *Journal of Conflict Resolution* 39, no. 3 (September 1995): 495–510.

Lamont, William. "Puritanism, History, and Historiography." *Past and Present* 44 (1969): 133–46.

Landa, Janet Tai. *Trust, Ethnicity, and Identity: Beyond the New Institutional Economics of Ethnic Trading, Networks, Contract Law, and Gift Exchange*. Ann Arbor: University of Michigan Press, 1994.

Lane, Robert. "The Politics of Consensus in the Age of Affluence." *American Political Science Review* 59 (1965): 874–95.

Lasch, Christopher. *The Revolt of the Elites*. New York: Norton, 1995.

Lash, Scott, and John Urry. *The End of Organized Capitalism*. Cambridge: Polity Press, 1987.

Lash, Scott, and Sam Whimster, eds. *Max Weber, Rationality, and Modernity*. London: Allen and Unwin, 1987.

Laslett, Peter. *The World We Have Lost*. London: Methuen and Company, 1965.

Laslett, John, and S. M. Lipset, eds. *Failure of a Dream: Essays in the History of American Socialism*. Berkeley: University of California Press, 1984.

Leach, Edmund. *Culture and Communication: The Logic by which Symbols Are Connected*. Cambridge: Cambridge University Press, 1976.

———. *Social Anthropology*. New York: Oxford University Press, 1982.

Leeuw, G. van der. *Religion in Essence and Manifestation*. Princeton: Princeton University Press, 1985.

Levine, Donald. *The Flight from Ambiguity*. Chicago: University of Chicago Press, 1985.

Lewis, David, and Andrew J. Weigert. "Trust as Social Reality." *Social Forces* 63, no. 4 (June 1985): 967–85.

———. "Social Atomism, Holism, and Trust." *The Sociological Quarterly* 26, no. 4 (1985): 455–71.

Lichbach, Mark. *The Rebel's Dilemma*. Ann Arbor: University of Michigan Press, 1995.

Lipset, S. M. "Radicalism and Reformism: The Sources of Working Class Politics." *The American Political Science Review* 77 (1983): 1–18.

Lipset, S. M., and W. Schneider. "The Decline of Confidence in American Institutions." *Political Science Quarterly* 98, no. 3 (Fall 1983): 379–402.

Little, David. "Max Weber Revisited: The Protestant Ethic and the Puritan Experience of Order." *Harvard Theological Review* 59 (1966): 415–28.

———. *Religion, Order, and Law: A Study of Pre-Revolutionary England*. New York: Harper and Row, 1969.

Locke, John. *Two Treatises on Government*. Part 2. Ed. Peter Laslett. Cambridge: Cambridge University Press, 1960.

Lottin, Odon D. *Psychologie et morale aux XIIᵉ et XIIIᵉ Siècles*. Louvain: Abbaye du Mont César, 1948.

Lovejoy, A. O. *Reason, Understanding, and Time*. Baltimore: Johns Hopkins Press, 1961.

Lowenthal, Leo. *Literature and the Image of Man: Sociological Studies of European Drama and Novel, 1600–1900*. Boston: Beacon Press, 1957.

Lucas, Paul. *Valley of Discord: Church and Society along the Connecticut River, 1636–1725*. Middletown: Wesleyan University Press, 1968.

Luhmann, Niklas. *Trust and Power*. New York: John Wiley and Sons, 1979.

———. "The Representation of Society within Society." *Current Sociology* 35, no. 2 (1987): 101–6.

———. "Familiarity, Confidence, Trust: Problems and Perspectives." In *Trust: Making and Breaking of Cooperative Relations*, ed. Diego Gambetta. Oxford: Basil Blackwell, 1988.

———. *Risk: A Sociological Theory*. New York: W. de Gruyter, 1993.

Lukes, Steven. *Emile Durkheim: His Life and Work*. Stanford: Stanford University Press, 1985.

Lynd, Helen M. *On Shame and the Search for Identity*. New York: Harcourt, 1958.

Macfarlane, Alan. *The Origins of English Individualism: The Family, Property, and Social Transition*. New York: Cambridge University Press, 1979.

———. *The Culture of Capitalism*. Oxford: Basil Blackwell, 1987.

MacIntyre, A. *Whose Justice? Which Rationality?* Notre Dame: University of Notre Dame Press, 1988.

Maier, Charles, ed. *Changing Boundaries of the Political*. Cambridge: Cambridge University Press, 1987.

Maimonides, Moses. *Mishneh Torah*. (In Hebrew.) Warsaw, 1882.

Maine, Henry. *Ancient Law*. New York: Holt, 1888.

Mandeville, Bernard. *Fable of the Bees: Or Private Vices, Public Benefits*. Oxford: Clarendon Press, 1924.

Marshall, Gordon. *Presbyteries and Profits: Calvinism and the Development of Capitalism in Scotland, 1560–1707*. Oxford: Clarendon Press, 1980.

Marshall, T. H. *Class, Citizenship, and Social Development*. Westport, Conn.: Greenwood Press, 1973.

Marx, Karl. *Capital.* Vol. 1., New York: Vintage, 1977.

Masud M., and R. Khan. "Montaigne, Rousseau, and Freud." In *The Privacy of the Self.* New York: International Universities Press, 1974.

Mauss, Marcell. "A Category of the Human Mind: The Notion of the Person, the Notion of the Self." In *The Category of the Person,* eds. Michael Carrithers, Steven Collins, and Steven Lukes. Cambridge: Cambridge University Press, 1985.

Maza, Sarah. *Private Lives and Public Affairs: The Causes Celebres of Pre-Revolutionary France.* Berkeley: University of California Press, 1993.

McNeill, John. "Natural Law and the Teachings of the Reformers." *Journal of Religion* 26 (1946): 168–82.

Mead, George Herbert. *Mind, Self, and Society.* Chicago: University of Chicago Press, 1934.

Meldon, A. I. *Rights and Persons.* Berkeley: University of California Press, 1980.

Merton, Robert. *Social Theory and Social Structure.* New York: Free Press, 1968.

Mervyn, James. "Ritual Drama and Social Body in the Late Medieval English Town." *Past and Present* 98 (1983): 3–29.

Milgram, P., and J. Roberts. *Economics, Organizations, and Managements.* Englewood Cliffs: Prentice Hall, 1992.

Miller, Perry. *Errand into the Wilderness.* New York: Harper and Row, 1964.

Moller, J. "The Beginnings of Puritan Covenant Theology." *The Journal of Ecclesiastical History* 14 (1963): 46–67.

Montaigne, Michel de. In *Essays of Montaigne.* Trans. Charles Cotton. Ed. W. C. Hazlitt. Vols. 1 and 3. London: Reeves and Turner, 1877.

Morrill, John, Paul Slack, and Daniel Woolf, eds. *Public Duty and Private Conscience in Seventeenth-Century England.* Oxford: Clarendon Press, 1993.

Morris, Colin. *The Discovery of the Individual, 1050–1200.* London: S.P.C.K. for the Church Historical Society, 1972.

Morton, A. *The World of the Ranters.* London: Lawrence and Wishart, 1970.

Mosse, George. "Puritanism and Reasons of State in Old and New England." *William and Mary Quarterly* 9 (1952): 67–80.

———. "Puritan Political Thought and the Case of Conscience." *Church History* 23 (1954): 109–25.

———. *The Holy Pretence: A Study in Christianity and Reasons of State from William Perkins to John Winthrop.* Oxford: Basil Blackwell, 1957.

Mottahedeh, Roy. *Loyalty and Leadership in an Early Islamic Society.* Princeton: Princeton University Press, 1980.

Nadel, S. F. *The Theory of Social Structure.* New York: Free Press, 1964.

Nelson, Benjamin. "Conscience and the Making of Early Modern Culture: The Protestant Ethic beyond Max Weber." *Social Research* 36 (1969): 4–21.

———. *The Idea of Usury: From Tribal Brotherhood to Universal Otherhood.* Chicago: University of Chicago Press, 1969.

———. "Self Images and Systems of Spiritual Direction." In *On the Roads to Modernity: Conscience, Science, and Civilizations, Selected Writings by Benjamin Nelson,* ed. Toby Huff. Totowa, N. J.: Rowman and Littlefield, 1981.

New, J. F. *Anglican and Puritan: The Basis of Their Opposition, 1558–1640.* Stanford: Stanford University Press, 1966.

Nuttle, Geoffrey. *The Holy Spirit in Puritan Faith and Experience.* Oxford: Basil Blackwell, 1946.

Nygren, A. *Agape and Eros.* Chicago: University of Chicago Press, 1982.

Otto, Rudolf. *The Idea of the Holy.* London: Oxford University Press, 1950.

Ozment, Steven. *The Reformation in the Cities.* New Haven: Yale University Press, 1975.

Pagden, Anthony. "The Destruction of Trust and Its Economic Consequences in the Case of Eighteenth-Century Naples." In *Trust: Making and Breaking of Cooperative Relations,* ed. Diego Gambetta. Oxford: Basil Blackwell, 1988.

Paine, Robert. "In Search of Friendship: An Exploratory Analysis in 'Middle-Class' Culture." *Man* 4, no. 4 (December 1969): 505–24.

———. "Anthropological Approaches to Friendship." *Humanitas* 6, no. 2 (1970): 139–60.

Parsons, Talcott. *The Social System.* New York: Free Press, 1951.

———. "Christianity and Modern Industrial Society." In *Sociological Theory, Values, and Socio-Cultural Change,* ed. E. Tiryakian. New York: Harper and Row, 1967.

———. *The Structure of Social Action.* Vol. 1. New York: Free Press, 1968.

———. "Durkheim on Religion Revisted." In his *Action Theory and the Human Condition.* New York: Free Press, 1978.

Parsons, Talcott, et al., eds. *Theories of Society.* New York: Free Press, 1961.

Pascal, Blaise. *Pensées.* Trans. J. Krailsheimer. Harmondsworth: Penguin Books, 1966.

Pateman, Carole. *The Sexual Contract.* Stanford: Stanford University Press, 1988.

———. "The Fraternal Social Contract." In *Civil Society and the State,* ed. J. Keane. London: Verso, 1988.

Patrides, C. A. *The Cambridge Platonists.* Cambridge: Harvard University Press, 1969.

Peled, Yoav. "Ethnic Democracy and the Legal Construction of Citizenship: Arab Citizens of the Jewish State." *American Political Science Review* 86, no. 2 (1992): 432–43.

Pennington, D., and K. Thomas, eds. *Puritans and Revolutionaries: Essay in Seventeenth-Century History Presented to Christopher Hill.* Oxford: Clarendon Press, 1978.

Peristiany, J. G., ed. *Honour and Shame: The Values of Mediterranean Society.* Chicago: University of Chicago Press, 1966.

Pettit, Norman. *The Heart Prepared: Grace and Conversion in Puritan Spiritual Life.* New Haven: Yale University Press, 1966.

Phillipson, Nicholas. "Adam Smith as Civil Moralist." In *Wealth and Virtue: The Shaping of Political Economy in the Scottish Enlightenment,* eds. I. Hont and M. Ignatieff. Cambridge: Cambridge University Press, 1985.

Pitt-Rivers, Julian. *The Fate of Shechem: Essays in the Anthropology of the Mediterranean.* Cambridge: Cambridge University Press, 1977.

Pocock, J. G. A. "Custom and Grace, Form and Matter: An Approach to Machiavelli's Concept of Innovation." In *Machiavelli and the Nature of Political Thought,* ed. Martin Fleisher. New York: Atheneum, 1972.

Pocock, J. G. A. *The Machiavellian Moment*. Princeton: Princeton University Press, 1975.

Poe, Edgar Allan. *The Works of Edgar Allan Poe: Tales*. London: Oxford University Press, 1927.

Polanyi, Karl. *The Great Transformation*. Boston: Beacon Press, 1957.

Pollock, Frederick, and Frederic Maitland. *History of English Law before the Time of Edward I*. Vol. 2. Cambridge: Cambridge University Press, 1923.

Putnam, Robert. *Making Democracy Work: Civic Traditions in Modern Italy*. Princeton: Princeton University Press, 1993.

Rank, Otto. *The Double: A Psychoanalytic Study*. Chapel Hill: University of North Carolina Press, 1971.

Rawls, John. *A Theory of Justice*. Cambridge: Harvard University Press, 1971.

Rector, Robert. "On the Issue of Welfare Reform." *New York Times*, 28 June 1995, p. A8.

Riesman, David. *The Lonely Crowd*. New Haven: Yale University Press, 1961.

Rogers, Richard. *Seven Treatises Called the Practice of Christianity*. 2nd ed. London, 1605.

Rorty, R., J. B. Schneewind, and Q. Skinner, eds. *Philosophy in History: Essays on the Historiography of Philosophy*. Cambridge: Cambridge University Press, 1984.

Rose, A., ed. *Human Behavior and Social Processes*. Boston: Houghton Mifflin, 1962.

Rose, Niklas. *Governing the Soul: The Shaping of the Private Self*. London: Routledge Press, 1989.

Rosenblum, Nancy, ed. *Liberalism and the Moral Life*. Cambridge: Harvard University Press, 1989.

Roth, Guenther, and Wolfgang Schluchter, eds. *Max Weber's Vision of History: Ethics and Methods*. Berkeley: University of California Press, 1979.

Rotter, J. B. "Generalized Expectancies for Interpersonal Trust." *American Psychologist* 26 (1971): 443–52.

Rousseau, Jean-Jacques. *The Social Contract and Discourses*. Trans. and ed. G. D. H. Cole. London: Dent, 1973.

Rundell, John. *Origins of Modernity*. Madison: University of Wisconsin Press, 1987.

Sandel, Michael. *Liberalism and the Limits of Justice*. Cambridge: Cambridge University Press, 1982.

———. "The Procedural Republic and the Unencumbered Self." *Political Theory* (1984): 81–96.

Schluchter, Wolfgang. "The Paradox of Rationalization: On the Relations of Ethics and the World." In *Max Weber's Vision of History: Ethics and Methods*, eds. Guenther Roth and Wolfgang Schluchter. Berkeley: University of California Press, 1979.

———. *The Rise of Western Rationalism*. Berkeley: University of California Press, 1981.

———. "Weber's Sociology of Rationalization and Topologies of Religious Rejections of the World." In *Max Weber, Rationality, and Modernity*, eds. Scott Lash and Sam Whimster. London: Allen and Unwin, 1987.

Schmalenbach, Herman S. "The Sociological Category of Communion." In *Theories of Society*, eds. Talcott Parsons et al. New York: Free Press, 1961.

Schneider, Jane. "Of Vigilance and Virgins: Honor, Shame, and Access to Resources in Mediterranean Societies." *Ethnology* 10, no. 1 (1971): 1–24.

Schollmeier, Paul. *Other Selves*. Albany: State University of New York Press, 1994.

Seligman, Adam B. "Innerworldly Individualism and the Institutionalization of Puritanism in Late 17th-Century New England." *British Journal of Sociology* 41, no. 4 (December 1990): 537–58.

———. *The Idea of Civil Society*. New York: Free Press, 1992.

———. "The Representation of Society and the Privatization of Charisma." *Praxis International* (1993): 68–84.

———. *Innerworldly Individualism: Charismatic Community and Its Institutionalization*. New Brunswick: Transaction Press, 1994.

———. "Animadversions upon Civil Society and Civic Virtue in the Last Decade of the Twentieth Century." In *Civil Society: Theory, History, Comparison*, ed. John Hall. Oxford: Polity Press, 1995.

Selznick, Philip. *The Moral Commonwealth: Social Theory and the Promise of Community*. Berkeley: University of California Press, 1992.

Sennett, Richard. *The Fall of Public Man*. New York: Knopf, 1976.

Shaftesbury, Anthony. *Characteristics of Men, Manners, Opinions, Times*. Vols. 1–3. London: N.p., 1736.

Shahid, Irfan. "Pre-Islamic Arabia." In *The Cambridge History of Islam*, eds. P. M. Holt et al. Vol 1. New York: Cambridge University Press, 1970.

Shanley, Mary, and Carole Pateman, eds. *Feminist Interpretations and Political Theory*. University Park: Penn State University Press, 1991.

Shapiro, Susan. "The Social Control of Impersonal Trust." *American Journal of Sociology* 93, no. 3 (November 1987): 623–58.

Shils, Edward. *Tradition*. Chicago: University of Chicago Press, 1981.

———. "The Virtues of Civil Society." *Government and Opposition* 26, no. 2 (Winter 1991): 3–20.

Silver, Alan. "Friendship and Trust as Moral Ideas: Historical Approach." *European Journal of Sociology* 30 (1989): 274–97.

———. "Two Different Sorts of Commerce." In *Public and Private in Thought and Practice: Perspectives on a Grand Dichotomy*, eds. Jeff Weintraub and Krishan Kumar. Chicago: University of Chicago Press, 1997.

Simmel, George. *Philosophy of Money*. London: Routledge and Kegan Paul, 1978.

Singer, Irving. *The Nature of Love*. Vols. 1 and 2. Chicago: University of Chicago Press, 1984.

Skinner, Quentin. *The Foundations of Modern Political Thought*. Vol. 1. Cambridge: Cambridge University Press, 1978.

———. "The Idea of Negative Liberty." In *Philosophy in History: Essays on the Historiography of Philosophy*, eds. R. Rorty, J. B. Schneewind, and Q. Skinner. Cambridge: Cambridge University Press, 1984.

———. "The Republican Ideal of Political Liberty." In *Machiavelli and Republicanism*, eds. Gisela Bock, Quentin Skinner, and Maurizio Viroli. Cambridge: Cambridge University Press, 1990.

Smith, Adam. *The Theory of Moral Sentiments*. Indianapolis: Liberty Classics, 1982.

Smith, R. M. "Marriage Processes in the English Past: Some Continuities." In *The World We Have Gained: Histories of Population and Social Structure*, eds. L. Bonfield, R. Smith, and K. Wrightson. Oxford: Basil Blackwell, 1986.

Southern, R. W. *The Making of the Middle Ages*. London: Hutchinson, 1953.

Stewart, Frank Henderson. *Honor*. Chicago: University of Chicago Press, 1994.

Strauss, Leo. *Natural Right and History*. Chicago: University of Chicago Press, 1953.

Strawson, P. F. *Individuals: An Essay in Descriptive Metaphysics*. London: Methuen, 1959.

Swanson, Judith. *The Public and the Private in Aristotle's Political Philosophy*. Ithaca: Cornell University Press, 1992.

Swartz, Benjamin, ed. *Wisdom, Revelation, and Doubt: Perspectives on the First Millennium B.C. Daedelus* (Spring 1975).

Taylor, Charles. *Human Agency and Language: Philosophical Papers*. Vol 1. Cambridge: Cambridge University Press, 1985.

———. *Sources of the Self: The Making of the Modern Identity*. Cambridge: Harvard University Press, 1989.

———. "Cross Purposes: The Liberal-Communitarian Debate." In *Liberalism and the Moral Life*, ed. Nancy Rosenblum. Cambridge: Harvard University Press, 1989.

Thomas, D. O. "The Duty to Trust." *The Aristotelian Society* 79 (1978): 89–101.

Thomas, Keith. "Cases of Conscience in Seventeenth-Century England." In *Public Duty and Private Conscience in Seventeenth-Century England*, eds. John Morrill, Paul Slack, and Daniel Woolf. Oxford: Clarendon Press, 1993.

Tiryakian, E., ed. *Sociological Theory, Values, and Socio-Cultural Change*. New York: Harper and Row, 1967.

Tismaneanu, Vladimir. *Reinventing Politics*. New York: Free Press, 1992.

Todorov, T. *Théories du symbole*. Paris: Seuil, 1977.

———. *The Conquest of America*. New York: Harper and Row, 1984.

Tolmie, Michael. *The Triumph of the Saints: The Separate Churches of London, 1616–1649*. Cambridge: Cambridge University Press, 1977.

Trilling, Lionel. *Sincerity and Authenticity*. Cambridge: Harvard University Press, 1972.

Troeltsch, Ernst. *The Social Teachings of the Christian Churches*. Vol. 1., New York: Harper and Row, 1960.

Trumbach, R. *The Rise of the Equalitarian Family*. New York: Academy Press, 1978.

Turner, Ralph. "Role Taking: Process Versus Conformity." In *Human Behavior and Social Processes*, ed. A. Rose. Boston: Houghton Mifflin, 1962.

———. "The Role and the Person." *American Journal of Sociology* 84, no. 1 (1978): 1–23.

Turner, Victor. *The Ritual Process*. Chicago: Aldine, 1969.

———. *Dramas, Fields, and Metaphors*. Ithaca: Cornell University Press, 1974.

Tuveson, E. L. *The Imagination as a Means of Grace: Locke and the Aesthetics of Romanticism*. Berkeley: University of California Press, 1964.

———. *Redeemer Nation: The Idea of America's Millennial Role*. Chicago: University of Chicago Press, 1968.

Tyler, Stephen, ed. *Cognitive Anthropology*. New York: Holt, Rinehart and Winston, 1969.

Ullmann, Walter. *The Individual and Society in the Middle Ages*. Baltimore: Johns Hopkins University Press, 1966.

U.S. Bureau of the Census. "Marriage, Divorce, and Remarriage in the 1990s." In *Current Population Reports*. Washington, D.C., 1992.

Van Vlissinger, J. Fenter. "Friendship in History." *Humanitas* 6, no. 2 (Fall 1970): 226–27.

Velez-Ibanez, Carlos G. *Bonds of Mutual Trust: The Cultural Systems of Rotating Credit Associations among Urban Mexicans and Chicanos*. New Brunswick: Rutgers University Press, 1983.

Voegelin, Eric. *Order and History*. Vol. 1, *Israel and Revelation*. Baton Rouge: Louisiana State University Press, 1956.

———. *The Nature of Law and Other Writings*. Vol. 27. Baton Rouge: Louisiana State University Press, 1991.

Wagner, Richard. *Werke*. Band 1. Zurich: Stauffacher Verlag, 1966.

Waltzer, Michael. "Puritanism as a Revolutionary Ideology." *History and Theory* 3 (1963): 59–90.

———. *The Revolution of Saints*. Cambridge: Harvard University Press, 1965.

Wasserfall, Rahel. "Gender Encounters in America: An Outsider's View of Continuity and Ambivalence." In *Distant Mirrors: America as a Foreign Culture*, eds. Philip DeVita and James Armstrong. Belmont: Wadsworth, 1993.

Waters, M. "Citizenship and the Constitution of Structured Inequality." *International Journal of Comparative Sociology* 30 (1989): 159–80.

Watt, Ian. *The Rise of the Novel: Studies in Defoe, Richardson, and Fielding*. Berkeley: University of California Press, 1967.

Watt, Montgomery. *Muhammad at Mecca*. London: Oxford University Press, 1960.

———. *Islam and the Integration of Society*. London: North West University Press, 1961.

Watts, Michael. *The Dissenters*. Oxford: Oxford University Press, 1978.

Weber, Max. *The Protestant Ethic and the Spirit of Capitalism*. New York: Scribner and Sons, 1958.

———. "Science as a Vocation." In *From Max Weber: Essays on Sociology*, ed. G. H. Gerth and C. W. Mills. New York: Free Press, 1958.

———. *The Sociology of Religion*. Boston: Beacon Press, 1964.

———. *Economy and Society*. Eds. Guenther Roth and Claus Wittich. Berkeley: University of California Press, 1978.

———. *General Economic History*. New Brunswick: Transaction Press, 1981.

Weintraub, Jeff, and Krishan Kumar, eds. *Public and Private in Thought and Practice: Perspectives on a Grand Dichotomy*. Chicago: University of Chicago Press, 1997.

Whichote, Benjamin. "The Uses of Reason in Matters of Religion." In *The Cambridge Platonists*, ed. C. A. Patrides. Cambridge: Harvard University Press, 1969.

White, Lynn. "The Christian Myth and Christian History." *Journal of the History of Ideas*. 3 (1942): 145–58.

Williams, Bernard. *Shame and Necessity*. Berkeley: University of California Press, 1993.

Winslow, Elizabeth. *Meetinghouse Hill, 1630–1783*. New York: Norton, 1972.

Wolfe, Eric. "Kinship, Friendship, and Patron-Client Relations in Complex Societies." In *Social Anthropology of Complex Societies*, ed. Michael Banton. New York: Praeger, 1963.

Wolin, Sheldon. "Calvin and Reformation: The Political Education of Protestantism." *American Political Science Review* 51 (1957): 425–54.

––––––. *Politics and Vision*. Boston: Little, Brown and Company, 1960.

Wright, V. "Fragmentation and Cohesion in the Nation State: France, 1870–1871." Paper presented at the European Science Foundation Seminar on the Construction and Reconstruction of Center-Periphery Relations in Europe, Jerusalem, May/June 1984.

Wrong, Dennis. "The Oversocialized Conception of Man in Sociology." *American Sociological Review* 26, no. 2 (April 1961): 183–93.

Wuthnow, Robert. "A Reasonable Role for Religion? Moral Practices, Civic Participation, and Market Behavior." Paper presented at the Institute for the Study of Economic Culture Conference, Boston University, Boston, Mass., October 1995.

Zakai, Avihu. "The Gospel of Reformation, the Origins of the Great Puritan Migration." *Journal of Ecclesiastical History* 37 (1986): 584–602.

––––––. *Exile and Kingdom*. Cambridge: Cambridge University Press, 1992.

Zaret, David. *The Heavenly Contract: Ideology and Organization in Pre-Revolutionary Puritanism*. Chicago: University of Chicago Press, 1984.

Zomchick, John. *Family and the Law in Eighteenth-Century Fiction: The Public Conscience in the Private Sphere*. Cambridge: Cambridge University Press, 1993.

Zweigert, Konrad, and Hein Kotz. *Introduction to Comparative Law*. Oxford: Clarendon Press, 1992.

Index